CW00449177

Political & Military History of Tibet

Vol-I

Gyaltse Namgyal Wangdue
(Ex - Dapon)

Translated by
Yeshi Dhondup

LIBRARY OF TIBETAN WORKS AND ARCHIVES

Copyright © 2012: Library of Tibetan Works & Archives

ALL RIGHTS RESERVED

No part of this publication may be reproduced, stored in a
retrieval system, or transmitted in any form or by any means, electronic,
mechanical, photo-copying, recording or otherwise, without the prior permission of the publisher.

ISBN: 978-93-80359-62-5

Published by the Library of Tibetan Works and Archives, Dharamsala, H.P.
176215, and printed at Indraprastha Press (CBT), Nehru House, New
Delhi-110002

Contents

THE DALAI LAMA

༄༅། །བོད་གཞུང་དགའ་ལྡན་ཕོ་བྲང་པའི་དམག་ཁབས་སྲིང་པ་རྒྱ་གར་འཕགས་

ཡུལ་དུ་བཅན་ཕྱིལ་འབྱོར་པ་རྣམས་ལ་བོད་དམག་གི་ལོ་རྒྱུས་བྱུང་རབས་འབྲི་དགོས་

འདི་ནས་བཀོད་མངགས་ལྟར། དང་སྐྱོབ་མདའ་རུ། སྤྱི་འཐུས་རྒྱལ་ཚེ་རྣམ་རྒྱལ་

དབང་འདུས་ཀྱིས་(བོད་རྒྱལ་ཁབ་ཀྱི་ཆབ་སྲིད་དང་འབྲེལ་བའི་དམག་དོན་ལོ་རྒྱུས་)

ཞེས་པ། གངས་ཅན་བོད་ཀྱི་རྒྱལ་རབས་དང་འབྲེལ་བའི་གདོང་མོའི་རྒྱལ་སྲུང་དམག་

དཔུང་སྐྱིག་འདྲོགས་བྱུང་བ་ནས་བཟུང་རིམ་བཞིན་གནས་དུས་ཀྱི་ཆྱལ་ལུགས་དེ་ལྟར་

འཕེལ་འགྱུར་དང་། དེའི་ཆེ་དེའི་དུས་དགྲ་འཐབ་གཡུལ་འགྱེད་བྱུང་རབས་ཀྱི་ཡིག་

ཆ་ཕྱོགས་སྐྱིག་བཀྱིས་པའི་དགའ་ཉི་མ་རབས་གསར་པ་རྣམས་ལ་ལོ་རྒྱུས་བྱུང་བ་བཟོང་

པའི་སྐྱེས་སུ་གྱུར།

ཆོས་ལྡན་རྒྱལ་སྲུང་གི་ཉི་ཤུ་བ་དང་དམ་འགྱུར་མེད་ནད་ནད་པོ་རྣམས་ནས་སྒྲོག་

བཟློས་ཀྱི་ཁབས་འདེགས་ཆུར་བསྐྱེད་ཞུས་པར་འཕུལ་ཡུན་དགེ་བའི་སྐྱབས་སྐྱོན་དང་།

རྗེས་ཕྱལ་རྒྱུད་བཅས་རྣམས་ནས་ཀྱང་རང་དོན་ཆུང་དུར་མ་ཞིན་པར་ཕ་མེས་ཀྱི་བྱས་

རྗེས་བཟང་པོའི་རྗེས་སུ་བསྒྲགས་ཏེ་ཆོས་ལྡན་མི་རིགས་ཀྱི་ཡ་རབས་བཟང་པོའི་སྤྱོད་

རྒྱལ་མ་འདོར་བར་བསྐུན་སྲིད་ལ་ཁབས་འདེགས་སྐྱབ་པའི་སྐྱག་བསམ་ཞེ་བཙུན་བསྐྱེད་

ཤོས་བཅས། དུ་འདི་བླ་མས། རབ་བྱུང་བཅུ་བདུན་པའི་རྒྱ་ད་ཟླ་ ༡༠ ཆེས་ ༡༥

ཕྱི་ལོ་ ༢༠༠༡ ཟླ་ ༡༡ ཆེས་ ༢༢ ལ།

Foreword

Like all countries, small or large, Tibet had its own military to protect itself against foreign invasion and harassment, until it lost its independence in 1959. Unfortunately, even though the Tibetan army played very important roles in the preservation of Tibet's independent status and the protection of its people against enemies throughout the country's history, appropriate due attention has not been paid to its historiography. The result is that there is hardly any literature available about the Tibetan army.

It is therefore a great pleasure for us that Mr. Namgyal Wangdu, a retired army officer in the Special Frontier Force (SFF), who also served in the traditional Tibetan army before he arrived in India, has composed a Tibetan military history. The volume illustrates in detail how the Tibetan army evolved throughout history and the various wars it fought against foreign forces up until 1959.

This volume may not be technically a scholarly work, but as the first comprehensive history of the Tibetan army, it will definitely serve as an important source of reference for the study of Tibetan history and its political status pre 1959 in general, and about Tibetan military history in particular. The Library of Tibetan Works and Archives is very happy to make this volume available in the complete English translation, as a part of the library's extensive activities for the preservation and promotion of Tibetan culture and history.

This book on the Tibetan Army unfortunately also contains stories of killing between the Chinese and the Tibetan army. You will be able to clearly see the helplessness of the Tibetans in the face of the massive Chinese invasion of our country first of all, and secondly that repeated efforts to find a peaceful solution had no effect on the Chinese leaders. This book also makes it clear that the relations between Tibet, at least since the communist takeover of China has been a relationship of continuous deception, lies and cold-blooded distortion of facts from the Chinese side versus a sustained attitude of trust and hope from the Tibetan side. The Chinese side had a determined strategy that they should invade Tibet through deceptive means in the 'sweet name' of liberation and so forth, for their own gain.

The book also tells the story of how Tibetans are treated by their two big neighbors, one which so generously provided a home and healing for the Tibetan refugees in their country and the another which ruthlessly invaded, looted and murdered Tibetans and in many cases forced them out from their own country.

This book also gives the message that if the world, and humanity, and especially the leaders of the world support only those bigger countries that have the allure of money and business, and completely turn a blind eye and shut off their conscience to truth, justice and the long term well-being of this planet, the whole of humanity will suffer, and suffer terribly, whether by conflict, recession, environmental degradation or increasing shortage of natural resources like water.

It also illustrates the pertinent truth to Tibetans and others in a similar situation that unless you take care of yourself no one can really take care of you, in the true ultimate sense of the term.

The translator, Yeshi Dhondup, is on the staff of the Research and Translation Department of LTWA. His enthusiasm and hard work has made this translation possible, despite the many challenges that were presented by such an endeavor. I would like to thank him for this great job. I also would like to thank Mr. Dawa Tsering, a Tibetan veteran, who had personally experienced the conflicts with the Chinese army as detailed in this book. It is mainly his initiative and insistence that helped us translate and publish this English version. I also like to thank Mr. Matt Gruninger, the former Head of the Tibet Relief Committee, for looking after the expenses incurred in translating and publishing this two volume book on the *Political and Military History of Tibet.*

We dedicate this publication to all the Tibetan soldiers who laid down their precious lives for the sake of the Dharma, polity and people of Tibet.

Geshe Lhakdor
Director
Library of Tibetan Works and Archives

Author's Preface

—✦—

Our past scholars, adepts and translators have bequeathed to us a large volume of literature, the fruit of their hard work. These literary works are a source of inspiration and pride to us, and they are like a mirror that reflects the real history of our country, Tibet. We should therefore feel very grateful to their creators. Sadly, there is not a single literary work dedicated to Tibetan military history. Some Tibetan annals contain accounts of historical military events in Tibet, but they are quite meager. Therefore, it has been necessary to compile an extensive Tibetan military history, which is devoid of fabrication and exaggeration, by combining all the fragments of Tibetan military history found in various sources, so as to prove that Tibet has been an independent nation throughout its history.

THE INSPIRATION BEHIND THIS BOOK

His Holiness the Fourteenth Dalai Lama has suggested on many occasions that those Tibetans who have done something for the benefit of their country should write their memoirs and experiences, so that other people will know their real stories, and that this would be particularly important for the next generation, so they would know what we have done for the country. On 8 March 1989, during the long-life prayers for His Holiness at the Tsuglakhang Temple in Dharamsala, organized by the Tibetan ex-Army Association, His Holiness advised the former soldiers of Tibet, "You, former Tibetan soldiers, should write about your past experiences before you leave this world. Those of you who live in a free country should write your memoirs, describing what you have done for the common cause of Tibet, or your personal life stories. I have made this request before and I am making it again here today. This is very important. You may think that your story is not worth writing about, but the fact is that our generation has experienced various types of misery and hardship, and we have become an example to others. It is therefore very important to record in writing everything that befell our generation. If we do not do this, in the future only distorted versions of our real stories, published by other people, will remain, and our real stories will disappear along with us when we leave this world. Therefore, I request once again that all Tibetans living in various free countries should write their own life stories. If you do not know how to write, you can record your story on a tape-recorder."

This advice greatly inspired me to initiate this book. However, due to a lack of the necessary reference sources, among other things, I had to leave the work uncompleted for several years. Some old Tibetan soldiers residing in Dharamsala, such as Sonam Tashi, Gyapon Kaldam of the Khadang Regiment and the veteran Drakjun Dawa Tsering urged me several times to complete the book. To help me finish the book on time, they also requested the Department of Security of the Central Tibetan Administration to extend their cooperation and assistance to me whenever I needed to access documents related to the Tibetan army which are preserved at the office. Greatly encouraged by their request and their enthusiasm for my work, I agreed to their request joyfully, since doing such a task is tantamount to performing a service for the country.

THE AIM AND OBJECTIVE OF THIS BOOK

Every nation, big or small, has recorded histories of their government, military, society, economy, culture, science, chronology, etc., in their own or foreign languages. However, a country's military history is the most important evidence of the historical status of the country. In the past Tibet also used to have an army. It is therefore very important to have a comprehensive Tibetan military history for our own benefit, both at the present time and in the future.

REFERENCE SOURCES

I based this work on the reference sources mentioned below, oral accounts of some former Tibetan soldiers, and documents related to the Tibetan army preserved at the Department of Security of the Central Tibetan Administration, Dharamsala. Since military activities and political affairs are interconnected, the military history of Tibet should be told in tandem with Tibet's political activities. Therefore, I have entitled this volume the *Political and Military History of Tibet*.

In this book, I have used simple and lucid language, devoid of hyperbole and exaggeration. Kungo Jamtsul-la went through the entire manuscript of this volume and made some necessary corrections. Mr. Drakten-la, a retired CTA official, also read the whole draft and did a few corrections. I would like to express my sincere thanks to both of them for their kind help.

Some publications from Tibet that I have used as reference sources for this book contain Chinese government propaganda, with the aim of concealing the historical independence of Tibet. These works were written under the duress and censorship of the Chinese government.

Because of my very limited knowledge and due to the lack of necessary reference sources, I feel that I have failed to make this book satisfactory even to me, let alone to scholars and learned readers. I apologize sincerely for the mistakes and shortcomings found in this work.

HOW THIS BOOK WAS ORGANIZED

This volume has two parts. The first part has eight chapters, all of which are about the Tibetan military institution and its system. The second part, which has 16 chapters, narrates various wars fought by the Tibetan army for the protection of the country.

Aspiration Prayer

The veterans of the great nation of Tibet
Served the country in their lifetime with great dedication
With a sense of gratitude to the government;
This military history of Tibet is the result of their service.

By the power of the truth in this book
May the darkness of evil be dispelled and
Happiness and freedom prevail in Tibet.

Translator's Note

❖

Bod rgyal khab kyi chab srid dang 'brel ba'i dmag don lo rgyus (Political and Military History of Tibet) tells the military story of Tibet in tandem with the political history of the country, from the period of King Songtsen Gampo until 1959 when Tibet lost its independence. This is the first Tibetan work which is fully dedicated to the military history of Tibet, and it can serve as a good source of knowledge about the military conditions and political status of Tibet in the pre-independence period.

It was a gigantic task and a big challenge for me to translate this voluminous work within the short time limit given to me by the project owner, considering the limitations of my knowledge and professional expertise. However, on the other hand, it was a great joy for me to undertake the task—a task which is tantamount to paying a tribute to the military heroes of Tibet.

The book contains innumerable names of people and places. For the benefit of general readers, I have used throughout this translation the phonetic pronunciation of all the Tibetan proper names. Their correct spelling in Wylie style is given at the end of the book. The Tibetan army ranks were patterned on the British system. Therefore, I have equated the Tibetan army ranks with the Indian army ranks, in consultation with the author of this book, as below: Chupon (Section Leader), Dingpon (Lieutenant), Gyapon (Captain), Rupon (Colonel), Dapon (Brigadier) and Magchi (Commander-in-Chief). In the case of difficult Tibetan terms and phrases, the translations are followed by Tibetan in transliteration put in parentheses. As for military and official titles such as *khendrung* and *rupon*, if they are with names, they are capitalized and treated as part of the name, for examples, Tsedron Jampa Tenzin and Dapon Karnawa. Tibetan terms that have no equivalent in English are separately annotated in the endnotes.

I have tried my best to make the translation faithful to the spirit of the original, but I have surely made mistakes and oversights, and I apologize to readers for any errors. I welcome criticism and suggestions from learned readers for the further improvement of the translation for the next edition.

In conclusion, I would like to acknowledge the help of a number of people who made this translation and publication possible. The Venerable Geshe Lhakdor-la,

Director of the LTWA, entrusted the project to me and gave me an inspirational prod from time to time, without which I would not have been able to finish this work in due time. Geshe-la also read the whole manuscript of this translation and pointed out some important errors in the translation. Mr. Wangdu Tsering, Head of the Oral History Department of the LTWA, shared with me his extensive knowledge of modern Tibetan history. Mr. Jules Pearson (American), Ms. Kerry Wright (Australian) and Ms. Gill Winter (New Zealander) checked the English and made necessary corrections. Most of the images in the first volume of this book were supplied by Mr. Sonam Tsering, in charge of the Photo Archive Section of the LTWA. Mr. Dawa Tsering, a member of the Tibetan Ex-Army Association, prodded me from time to time to accelerate my work. Mr. Matt Gruninger, former Head of the Tibet Relief Committee, funded the project. I want to thank all the above people from the depth of my heart, as without them this book would not have seen the light of day.

Last, but not least, I should also thank Mr. Tsering Namgyal and Ms. Chemi Wangmo of our Publication Department for putting extra efforts in order to expedite the publication process of this book to meet the deadline at our request.

In the snowy mountain paradise
You are the source of good and happiness.
Powerful Tenzin Gyatso, Chenrezig,
May you stay until samsara ends!

Part I

Chapter One

Tibetan Military System during the Period of the Tibetan Buddhist Kings

❖

Military service system

According to the *Chronicles about Minister*[1], from around the time of Songtsen Gampo, Tibet had six military divisions: U-ru (*dbu ru*), Yeru (*g.yas ru*), Yoru (*g.yo ru*), Rulag (*ru lag*), Shangshung (*zhang zhung*) and Sumpa (*sum pa*). These divisions were composed of regiments called "*rgod kyi tongde*", each consisting of 1,000 soldiers. There were altogether 61 *tongde* regiments in Tibet - 10 each in U-ru, Yeru, Yoru, Rulag and Shangshung and 11 in Sumpa. In Gendun Choephel's *White Annals*, it is stated that in those days the Tibetan army had the strength of about 200,000 soldiers.

The term *rgod* means "brave" or "aggressive". Each *tongde*, a contingent of 1,000 soldiers, had one chief leader called *Tongpon*. Under each Tongpon, there was a commander-in-chief (*dmag dpon*), a deputy commander-in-chief (*dmag spyi gzhon pa*), colonels (*ru dpon*), rearguard, vanguard, and soldiers. Every regiment had their own horses, regimental flags, military equipment such as armours, helmets, bows, arrows, swords and lances, and insignias of ranks, military emblems and so forth.

In ancient times, it was customary in Tibet for young men to join the army. We are able to understand from the genuine history of Tibet, as narrated below, that Tibet's political status had a direct connection with the rise and fall of its military power.

Ancient Tibetan art of warfare

Songtsen Gampo made great efforts for the progress of the country through his political and military activities. Military forces were indispensible for the protection of the country. The "Precious General" and the "Precious Horse" among the "seven

---

1 The Chronicles on Ministers is one of the *Five Chronicles,* the other four being the Chronicles about king, queen, translators and scholars, and gods and demons.

royal emblems"[2] have military connotations. Similarly, the treatises on royal laws (*rgyal khrims bstan bcos*) codified by the Tibetan Buddhist kings contain a section on the art of warfare. For example, the "three achievements" (*mdzad pa gsum*), "three kinds of glory" (*bstod pa gsum*) and "three kinds of humiliation" (*smad pa gsum*) mentioned in the section "Fifteen Codes of Royal Law" from the *Six Great Royal Codes of Law* are all related to warfare. According to the royal laws, war heroes were honoured by having tiger skins put on them while cowards were humiliated by tying foxtails on them. There were obviously many other ways of complimenting war heroes and disgracing cowards. The first code of the "Fifteen Codes of Royal Law" is, "Destroy the enemy for the protection of the Country" and it is very clear from its title that various kinds of military tactics are discussed within it. The royal laws further state that it is better to die in a battle rather than to die a natural death.

Every regiment used to hold a large annual gathering at its own district headquarters which all members attended. On the occasion, all the members would take a great oath; with the sun, the moon and the stars as witnesses, pledging that they would sacrifice their lives for the sake of the country. They would erect new fortifications at strategic and populated areas to keep the enemies at bay. It is said that the remnants of those ancient structures are still found in various areas of Tibet.

Tibet in those times was very powerful militarily, not simply because she had a large army, good military supplies and geographical advantages. Tibet also had patriotic and brave people who were ready to sacrifice their lives for the sake of the country, in addition to good military law, strategies and tactics.

Ancient Tibetan military strategies and tactics

When a war broke out, the military leader would lead his troops to the battlefield. The weapons included swords, lances, darts, etcetera. All kinds of physical manoeuvres were employed when fighting, depending on the condition of the enemy's troops. As for military tactics, they would make an offensive on the enemy, advance or capture strategic locations in accordance with the situation. Tactics such as "making ambush", "defending the garrison", "retreating and reorganising the troops", "conducting surprise raids on the enemy's camps", and "fighting guerrilla warfare", were also practised. There were other military tactics used also, such as deceiving the enemy, gaining support from the people living near the battle sites, conducting political campaigns, etcetera. Besides using military tactics, Tibet also deployed sentry troops at borders and sent reconnaissance missions to gather secret

---

2   The seven royal emblems: the precious wheel (*'khor lo rin po che*), the precious jewel (*nor bu rin po che*), precious queen (*btsun mo rin po che*), precious minister (*blon po rin po che*), precious elephant (*glang po rin po che*), precious horse (*rta mchog rin po che*) and precious general (*dmag dpon rin po che*).

information about the enemy's military situation. I will not discuss these in detail here to avoid too much detail. To cite an example, the *New Tang Annals* and other Chinese sources mention that Minister Gar Tongsten of Tibet was an intelligent, dignified and expert military leader. Besides Minister Gar and his sons, Tibet had many other talented military leaders in early times, including Lhotang Yangje, Ngothang Yangje, Mon Tore Pungtsen and Nyangpoje Shanang, as we know from various Tibetan war accounts and inscriptions on the stone pillar installed in Lhasa. Tibetan army leaders of those times were said to be extremely brave, physically powerful and experts in the art of warfare, martial arts and horse riding, and as a result the neighbouring kingdoms of Tibet feared them.

Procurement of military supplies and the intelligence system of Tibet

It seems that the Tibetan army used to collect their military requirements such as uniforms, flags, food, horses and weapons from the soldiers' own recruiting sources. In times of large battles, every regiment had to take with them a band party, big drums and different types of bugles. The band parties had to practise and rehearse their songs before they set off for the battlefield. The weapons, food, horses and any other goods seized from the enemy during wars were also used. In short, all the army regiments of Tibet had to procure their own military supplies, as they did not receive them from the government. However, the government sometimes used to arrange a grand feast and gave rewards to the soldiers after they returned from a mission. We can understand from this that the evolution of Tibetan civilisation and the Tibetan army was similar to that of others in the world, and that Tibet's military was at its zenith during the Tibetan imperial period. For example, modern mechanical means of transportation that can travel through space, water and land have developed from ancient means of transportation such as horses and boats. From ancient war weapons, modern automatic weapons and bombs have developed. Different types of modern fortifications and armoured vehicles are improvements over ancient armours, helmets and shields. Historically, no country in the world possessed the sophisticated military equipment compared to modern days. When Buddhist kings ruled Tibet, no other countries could rival it in military strength and military science, and other nations including China, always had to remain cautious. Tibet had such a marvellous military history and one should study it.

In those days (during the period of Tibetan Dharma kings), Tibet used spies, royal envoys and matrimonial relations, in accordance with the situation, as a means to obtain secret information about the political and military conditions of enemies. The Tibetan army would first try to know the situation of the enemy and then prepare, before declaring war. King Drigum Tsenpo, for example, sent a woman to spy on his contender, Longam. Namri Songtsen bribed Singpoje's own ministers, Nyang Tsegu and Non Dronpo, and with their help, he defeated Singpoje. Likewise, Songtsen Gampo gave his sister, Sema Karshang, as a bride to the king of Shangshung, and through her, he managed to gather secret information about the Shangshung kingdom. Tibetan kings sent their royal envoys to the Tang court of China to beg Chinese princesses, Wencheng Kungjo and Jincheng Kungjo, to become their queens. King Songtsen also sent an envoy to Nepal to ask for Princess Brikuti's hand in marriage. The Tibetans must often have certain political and military purposes behind their marriage proposals. China and Tibet exchanged emissaries many times, and the emissaries were entrusted with the secret task of gathering political and military information about each other's country. In 757, Tibetan forces captured Kaotig, Patig, Mintig, Hiyonchun and Maominchun. Tibet sent delegates to China several times and solved the disputes through peaceful reconciliation. The old and new *Tang Annals* say that the Chinese Emperor later came to know that the Tibetans had deceived him. According to the inscription on a wooden plate (*shing khram*) discovered from Khotan (*Liyul*), a Tibetan spy named Shang Khyuchung arrived in Nyergum. According to Deu's *History of Buddhism*[3], during the time of King Trisong, Tibet sent Tropan and Mang Ar to Chan'gian, the capital of the Tang. The purpose was to observe the military situation of China, on the pretext of delivering gifts to the Emperor.

These have been cited as simple examples. Nowadays, as in ancient days, large nations employ spies to acquire confidential information about other nations. Moreover, every country sends news reporters, diplomats, delegates and so forth to foreign countries, with the secret mission to collect confidential information about foreign countries.

Camping and expedition style of Tibetan army

Whenever necessary, the Tibetan government would send a posting order to a particular regiment through its leader. Upon receiving the order, the regiment concerned would leave immediately for the posting destination. Regarding their style of travelling, the regiment's cavalry and infantry troops would march separately, led by their leaders. Every regiment had its own regimental colours and flags attached to the spears and helmets of the soldiers. The flying of the flags in the wind would create an amazing sight. As for the manner of camping on their journey, they used to pitch tents in sets of columns and rows. The spears were set

---

3   It is a commentary written by Mkhas pa lde'u in 1261 on the versified text said to be authored by Mkhas pa jo bum (1123-1175).

upright with their points up in front of their respective tents. According to the *White Annals*, the Tibetan prayer flags or *lungdar* (*rlung dar*) that we use nowadays have originated from ancient Tibetan military flags. Nomads are called *rupa* (*ru pa*) and weapons are called *rutson* (*ru mtshon*), derived from the military term "*ru*", meaning "military division,"

The upper and lower U-ru had a red flag with multicoloured flaps (*dar lce*)[4] and a red heroic banner or *padar* (*dpa' dar*). When the soldiers marched, it looked as if it was snowing. The upper and lower Yoru had a white flag, with an image of a black-chested lion at the centre. When they marched, it appeared similar to rains falling on a lake. The upper and lower Yeru had a black flag with a white-chest *garuda* bird as its emblem. Their *padar* flag was gray and had colourful borders. When their soldiers marched, it looked as if grassland has caught fire.

According to old Tibetan records, the flag of the upper and lower Rulag had a leaping snow lion as the emblem. They had a black *padar*-flag. When they marched, they resembled a snow lion climbing a snowy mountain.

Regarding the style of their expedition journey and camping on the way, Yeru, Yoru, U-ru and Rulag all followed the same style. The soldiers would move or stop in accordance with the signal given by their leaders that would be the sounding of a bugle or waving of a flag. When they setup camp, the leader would blow a bugle and all the soldiers would immediately gather at the centre tent. They would stand in line in accordance with their ranks. They were assigned different tasks, such as preparing mattresses, cooking food, etcetera, and the distribution of the tasks was done by means of a lottery method. They had code-languages and code-signals to communicate amongst themselves.

Bugles and flags were used as signal instruments not only during expedition journeys, but also during battles to give a signal of dangers or to command the troops on battlefields. The Tibetan army also used to send reconnaissance missions to strategic areas such as valleys and rivers to observe the areas before they advanced further.

Geographical size of the five military divisions of Tibet

1. U-ru: It stretched from Shugpa Pundun in Olka (nowadays in Olka county of Lhoka) in the east to Shu Nyomo in the west, Drakyi Langma Gurphu in the north to Mala Mountain in the south (between the Tsangpo and the Kyichu rivers), (nowadays Nyemo County in Shu).

2. Yoru: It comprised Kongyul Drena (nowadays Nyingtri county of Kongpo) in the east, Shayuk Tago (Shayuk village in Tsona district) in the south, Kharag Gangtse

---

4 *Dar lce* are pieces of cloth attached at the side of a flag horizontally.

(Kharag region in Nakartse district) in the west and Mala Rang in the north, also touching Yarlung Traduk in Central Tibet (Tradug in Nedong district).

3. Yeru: It extended from Dragkyi Langma Gurphub in the east to the border of Yagpo in Nyanang in the south (Nyanang district), Jema Lagu (Ngamring district) in the west and Mitri Chunag in the north (Mitri in Lhari county) with Shongpa Tsal in Shang in U (Namling Shongshong) as the central limit.

4. Rulag: Its border touched Jamnata in the east, Balpo Langna in the south (Tibet-Nepal border), Kemyak Mig in the west and Jema Langon in the north, with its central border at Durpana in Sad in Central Tibet (Sakya County).

5. Sumpa: It included all the areas between Nye Bumnag in the east, Mitri Chunag in the south, Yelshab Dingpoche in the west and Nagsho Sitring in the north. In short, Tibet had five military divisions: 1) Yeru, 2) Rulag 3) U-ru, 4) Yoru and 5) Sumpa. Also, the country was divided into 18 administrative regions, as below:

Region's name	Ruler's clan name
1. U-ru Shochen	Tsenpo
2. Phodrang Nechen	Jebang
3. Yarlung Sogkha	Khunyag
4. Yamdrok Gangkyim	Kuring Denga
5. Chinga Chingyul	Go and Nub
6. Jayuk Satsig	Drangje Phanga
7. Dredang Shongpa	Nanam
8. Drakrum Tome	Tsepong
9. Tsangto Tangme	Dro and Khyung
10. Lungsho Nampo	Dru and Khyungtsam
11. Phanyul Tongde	Dro and Ma
12. Nyangra Domapa	Dro and Che
13. Shang Lechi	Ri and Le
14. Yungwache and Yungwachung	Drenka
15. Sha, Ge and De	Pe
16. Namra Changong	Dring and Chag
17. Damshong Karmocha	Chad and Ra
18. Dokham Dochen	Gotong Derge.

In those days, there were six great divisions, including Shangshung. Each military division had 10 *tongde* regiments except for Sumpa, which had 11. In total, there were 61 *tongde* regiments, as shown below:

Ten *tongde* regiments of U-ru

U-ru To
1. Dor
3. Detsam
5. Chompa
7. Dritsam
9. Yelrab Tongbuchung

U-ru Me
2. Chugtsam
4. Drangtsam
6. Kyito
8. Kyime
10. Kusung Sharchokpa.

Ten *tongde* regiments of Yoru

Yoru To
1. Yarlung
3. Chinglung
5. Dakpo
7. Nyagyi
9. Loro Tongbuchung

Yoru Me
2. Nyal
4. Lhodrag
6. Yartsam
8. Yubang
10. Kusung Jangchokpa.

Ten *tongde* regiments of Yeru

Yeru To
1. Tongchen
3. Shangchen
5. Langmi
7. Phokar
9. Shang Tongbuchung

Yeru Me
2. Nyenkar
4. Drangtsam
6. Porab
8. Songde
10. Kusung Nubchokpa

Ten *tongde* regiments of Rulag

Rulag To
1. Mangkar
3. Tripom
5. Drampa
7. Lhatse
9. Tsongo Tongbuchung

Rulag Me
2. Nyangro
4. Trithang
6. Khangsar
8. Gangtrom
10. Kusung Lhochog

Ten *tongde* regiments of Shangshung

Shangshung To
1. Ocho
2. Mangma
3. Nema
4. Tsamo
5. Baga Tongbuchung

Shangshung Me
1. Guge
2. Chogla
3. Chitsang
4. Yartsang
5. Chidey Tongbuchung

Eleven *tongde* regiments of Sumpa

1. Tsethon
3. Gotsangto
5. Jongto
7. Reto
9. Kharo
11. Nagsho Tongbuchung

2. Phothon
4. Gotsangme
6. Jongme
8. Reme
10. Khasang

Old Tibetan annals say that each of the above 61 *tongde* regiments had one leader known as *tongpon*. However, the territorial demarcation of *rudey* and *tongde* and the names of their military units did not remain consistent, but kept changing throughout the time so it is very difficult to identify their exact locations. Therefore, I request all concerned scholars to do research and confirm their locations.

Chapter Two

The Situation of Tibetan Military during the Rules of Sakya, Phagdru, Rinpung and Tsangpa

❖

With the disintegration of the Tibetan empire, the political status of Tibet declined and the institution of the Tibetan national army disappeared. Many independent regions emerged in different parts of Tibet, and the regional leaders maintained their own armies to protect their own dominions. However, the army system remained the same as that which was created during the period of the Buddhist kings of Tibet.

During the successive regimes of Sakya (1236-1354), Phagdru (1354-1434), Rinpung (1434-1563) and Tsangpa (1563-1641), there were many independent regions in the country and no one was able to establish a central rule over the whole of Tibet. These regions often engaged in armed conflicts amongst themselves, causing great destruction and many casualties, as discussed in the latter part of this book.[1] Phagdru Desi Jangchup Gyaltsen (1302-1364), who was born into a Lhasig Lang family of the *dbra* clan—one of the lineages of the Six Little Men of Tibet *(mi'u gdung drug)*[2] — codified a law called *15-Code Law,* based mainly on the laws of the Three Buddhist Kings of Tibet, in accordance with the social condition of that time. One of the fifteen codes was titled, "Code of Tiger". In *Deb ther rdzogs ldan shon nu'i dga' ston*[3], it states, "In order to accomplish his plan, Tai Situ composed a book on the art of warfare and how to defend garrisons." Thereafter, Tsangpa Desi Karma Tenkyong Wangpo (1606-1642)[4] created the *16-Code Law* based on the laws codified by the Three Buddhist Kings of Tibet. It also had a

---

1   (Author's note: I have not found any sources that describe the military system and art of warfare of those times.)

2   It is spelled *gdung drug* or *gdong drug*. The six original clans of Tibetans were *se, rmu, ldong, stong, dbra* and *'dru,* and they were said to be descendants of monkey parents.

3   Full title: *gangs can yul gyi sa la spyod pa'i mtho ris kyi rgyal blon gtso bor brjod pa'i debt ther rdzogs ldan gzhon nu'i dga' ston spyid kyi rgyal mo'i glu dbyangs//* Authored by the Great Fifth Dalai Lama, Ngawang Lobsang Gyatso, the book deals with the history of Tibet, with emphasis on the history of Tibet's political leaders.

4   Karma Tenkyong Wangpo was son of Tsangpa ruler Karma Phuntsok Namgyal, who died in 1620. His reign (1620-1642) was marked by the increasingly bitter struggle against the Gelugpa sect and its leader the Dalai Lama, who was backed by Mongols. The final outcome was the crushing of the Tsangpa regime by the Mongol forces and the establishment of the Ganden Phodrang Government headed by the Fifth Dalai Lama that endured until 1950.

code titled, "Code of Tiger." In both aforementioned laws, the "Code of Tiger" is mentioned first, and it deals with military tactics and strategies. In the Vinaya texts, the royal law says:

> Wise [leaders] achieve their conquest missions
> by means of peaceful negotiation,
> offering gifts, using deceptive methods, judging the enemy, or
> sending an armed force.[5]

The above verse mentions five important ancient military strategies to defeat an enemy: 1) peaceful negotiations (*gzhom par bya ba*), 2) giving bribes (*rab tub sbyin pa*), 3) using deceptive methods (*bslu bar byed pa*), 4) studying the enemy (*kun tu dpyad pa*) and 5) sending armed forces (*dpung gi don rnams 'grub pa byed*). These have been elaborated in the *16-Code Law*. As stated in its preface, the *16-Code Law* was composed by Palsar, who served as district officer of Dechen Dzong during the rule of Tsangpa King, and was based on ancient laws, classic literature and authentic folklores. In *Desi Sangye Gyatso's Answers to the Questions on Law of Sikkim King*[6], it states, "Making some changes and additions on the *15-Code Law* codified by Tai Situ Jangchup Gyaltsen, Tsangpa King composed the *16-Code Law*, with annotations by Palsar, district officer of Kyisho Dechen Dzong." The following are short notes on each of the five aforementioned military strategies:

1. To subdue an enemy by means of peaceful negotiation (*gzhom par bya*): This is a tactic to subjugate the opponents by means of peaceful negotiations. For example, a Tibetan king conquered Sumpa (a tribe living in northeastern Tibet) and Azha (Tuyuhun) through negotiations, without using military forces.

2. To subdue an enemy by giving bribes (*rab tu byin*): As for this strategy, the enemy can be made to conceded by being provided with gifts. Namri Songtsen, for example, granted lands as gifts to Nyang Tsegu, We Yitsab, Non Dronpo and Tse Songnag of Singpoje kingdom, and conquered the kingdom.

3. To defeat an enemy by using deceitful methods (*bslu bar byed*): For example, after Lang Darma died, two regional governors, Shang Pipi and Shang Phosher, became rival factions. Pipi secretly mobilized troops, made a surprise attack on Phosher and defeated him.

4. To subjugate an enemy after examining the enemy (*kun tu dpyad pa*): It is very important to send spies or a reconnaissance unit to study the military situation,

---

5 *mkhas pa rnams ni gzhom pa dang/ rab tu sbyin dang bslu ba dang/ kun tu dpyad dang lnga par ni/ dpung gi don rnams 'grub pa byed/*

6 Tibetan title: *sde srid sangs rgyas mtsho'i 'bras ljong. zhu lan*

strength, equipments and plan of the enemy. For example, during the imperial period of Tibet, it had confidential ministers, border police, garrisons, internal intelligence (*nang so*), and spies, etcetera, which were necessary for military purposes.

5. To subdue an enemy by sending an armed force (*dpung gis don grub*): In the event that war is inevitable, it is important to have a unified army, effective military organization, solid war plans, sufficient military supplies and continuous vigilance on the enemy before going to the battlefield. After developing war strategies, it is necessary to make preparations for battle. Once that is complete, all the troops should be ordered to be ready. This is just an example, and more details will be discussed in the chapters that follow.

Chapter Three

Tibetan Military System during the Reign of the Fifth Dalai Lama

—◆◆—

Simpa Regiment

During the hegemony of Sakya, Phagdru, Rinpung and Tsangpa in succession before the Ganden Phodrang Government was founded in 1642, all regional rulers maintained small armies for the purposes of personal security and for their own dominions. When the fifth Dalai Lama became the ruler of Tibet, the whole country was unified under his leadership, and he introduced many changes to the Tibetan government system. Whenever there was a war or emergency, the government mobilised from U-ru, Yoru, Yeru, Rulag, Ngari, Dokham and other military regions, established by the Tibetan Buddhist kings through regional leaders in accordance with the situation. In times of peace, the government would return all the troops to their homes as Tibet had no permanent army in those days. The army system in general including weaponry, organizational structure, training systems, and provisions in those times were the same as that used during the imperial period of Tibet.[1] Later, as a result of Tibet's close relations with Mongolia, Tibetan armies acquired some amount of Mongol influence. Tibetan army leaders were often called "*yasor,*" the Mongol term for army leader, and Tibetan troops used to wear Mongol dresses.

Desi Sangye Gyatso established a permanent army in Lhasa called *Simpa Chinang*, also known as, "Exterior and Interior Guards of the Dalai Lama's Palace." He created an army tax system and fixed a quota of men to be recruited by U and Tsang to the government's army, depending on the size of the area of the two provinces. The main duties of the troops were to serve as bodyguards of the Dalai Lama and to provide security at and around the Dalai Lama's Palaces, and to maintain law and order in Lhasa. During the Torma Throwing Ceremony *(gtor rgyag)* of the Monlam Festival, both infantry and cavalry of the Yeru and the Yonru Regiments, wearing historical Tibetan army uniforms and carrying traditional weapons such as locally made guns, bows and arrows, and spears, used to demonstrate ancient military parades and drills. They also used to perform *kha rbad*—dramatic heroic

---

1   Author's note: I have not found any records that mention about their changes.

acts and dialogues—and fire a Tibetan *dzamdrag*[2] gun after each break during their performance. Later, led by their leaders and while firing shots into the air, all the troops would follow the *torma* (carried to be burned). When the *torma* was put on the fire, the troops would circumambulate the fire and shout together and leave.

Regarding the program of the Monlam Festival, there was an archery contest on the 3rd day of the 1st Tibetan month. On the 26th and 27th days, there were sports events, followed by the Great Closing Ceremony at the end of the day on the picnic ground behind the Potala Palace. In the mornings and evenings of these two days, the members of the Simpa Army used to perform parade marches to honour the Dalai Lama or his regent. The Datsab *(mda' tshab)*, soldiers, the ceremony master called Tsogchen Umdze *(tshogs chen dbu mdzad)* and Dinpon *(lding dpon)*, all dressed in princely accoutrements *(rgya lu'i chas)*[3], would perform heroic dramas and shout boastfully while brandishing swords in the air. Customarily, the government would offer tea and *dresil*[4] (ceremonial rice mixed with butter and sugar) to all the members of the Simpa at the end of the ceremony. On that day, officials from different regions and expert archers from the Simpa Army would have an archery contest; each of them would shoot two arrows in the first round and one single arrow shot in the second round. The best archer and horse rider were granted prizes, and the awarding ceremony was accompanied by song and dance performances.

Whenever the government conducted a grand prayer ceremony on the Palha Hill, the sacred place of the protector deity Palden Lhamo, one unit of the Simpa Regiment had to be present. Whenever the Dalai Lama travelled out from his palace or returned from a journey, the Simpa troops and lieutenant officers, dressed in *gyalu* costume, had to stand in a line on the roadsides to greet him.

As a part of the *torgyag* ceremony of the Great Monlam Festival, the soldiers used to put a black cloth on a boulder on the slope of the Jagyag Karpo Hill, to the south of Lhasa. With this boulder as the target, they would fire two locally made cannons called *Sinmo Dreshon*, or the "Two Demon Sisters," one by one.

During a later period, the Simpa Army was dissolved and the Chadang Simchung Regiment was created in its place to be based permanently in Lhasa. However, the former members of the Simpa Army had to perform ancient Tibetan military styles of parade and drills during the Great Monlam Festival every year. Details about this have been discussed by Shodrung Nornang in his article, "History of Tibetan Military Headquarters and the Simpa Chinang Army," reproduced in Chapter 6 of this book.

---

2 '*dzam grags* is a Tibetan-made gun used at short range
3 It was a costume of *drungkor* officials in the traditional government worn during official ceremonies and functions.
4 Rice mixed with butter and sugar served during ceremonies, such as inauguration ceremony.

Chapter Four

Tibet's Military System during the Time of the Seventh Dalai Lama

Overview of Tibetan military

The evolution of the Tibetan army during the period of the Buddhist kings of Tibet has already been discussed in the previous chapters, and now we will discuss how the Tibetan army underwent modifications over time. Like the armies of other countries, the Tibetan army was instituted by its own country. It was an important institution of the Tibetan government and was indispensable for the protection of the country's borders, and for the maintenance of peace and law in the country. The Tibetan army was called Dharma Protecting Army *(bstan srung dmag)* or the God's Army of Tibet *(bod ljongs lha dmag)*. In various historical documents and edicts related to the Tibetan army, it is said, "It is the tradition of Buddhist kings not to offend the enemy; it is the tradition of worldly kings to defend against the enemy." Therefore, as is evident from many records, the Tibetan army was created not to protect the independent status of other countries, including China, or rights of any individual persons or organizations, or to oppress masses.

During the period of the Tibetan royal dynasty when Tibet was militarily very active, it annexed many areas of China and other neighboring countries. Tibet posed a great threat to many neighboring countries and has such an amazing history. When its military power gradually declined, it started experiencing invasions and military attacks by China at different times. Tibet's history has also such dark phases and the Tibetan army went through various phases of rise and fall. Its long history will not disappear nor can it be erased. Later, China took advantage of and manipulated the weak political and military situation of Tibet to integrate it into China. It continuously produced a large amount of publications, full of distorted facts, to achieve its goal. However, by doing so, the Chinese government merely demonstrates its ruthless and oppressive regime. Just as we cannot reverse the current of water, they cannot change the historical facts.

The organizational structure, weaponry and institutional system of the Tibetan army remained the same since the time of the Fifth Dalai Lama until the rule of the Seventh Dalai Lama. Later, due to Tibet's close relations with Gushri Khan and Dzungar Mongols, the Tibetan army absorbed some Mongolian characteristics. After that, in the name of the "priest-patron" relationship, the Ambans and troops sent by Manchu Emperor Kangxi arrived in Tibet for the first time in history, and they soon started meddling in the Tibetan government's affairs. Later when a civil war broke out between U and Tsang regions of Tibet, Pholawa brought a large number of Chinese troops in Tibet to help him. All of this led to the assimilation of Chinese characteristics into the Tibetan army.

Establishment of permanent Tibetan army

In 1747, Desi Pholawa died and his younger son, Gyurme Namgyal, succeeded to his father's post, which he held for four years. Unlike his father, who allied with the Manchus, Gyurme Namgyal tried hard to expel all the Manchus from Tibet, in accordance with the wishes of the Tibetan people. In order to strengthen his army, he created a compulsory service system in U-Tsang and collected 3,000 troops—1,056 from Drapchi, 1,052 from Shigatse, 526 from Dingri and 526 from Gyantse—in addition to the existing Simpa Army and the reserves in U, Tsang and Dokham. The army was initially instituted in the Mongolian style. The uniform consisted of a pale blue *chupa,* a Mongol hat (red *sog zhwa*) and black boots. Tradition has it that when the troops were in formation, the entire ground appeared completely red. They wore animals' skin hats *(pags zhwa)* in winter and felt hats *(ching zhwa)* in summer. They were allowed to wear anything inside *chupa.* The design and wearing style of the uniform were the same for all the army units throughout the country.

The uniforms of officers above the rank of lieutenant were brown *chupas,* and their insignias were worn on their shoulders. Their horses had ornament bells on their necks. The officers above the rank of captain wore *chagda (lcag mda')*[1] hats in summer and *wagir (wa sgir)* hats in winter. Their shoes were brown *ja chen ('ja' chen),*[2] traditional Tibetan boots. They had insignias made from turquoise and their horses had neck-ornaments. The uniform of the officers above the rank of brigadier *(mda' dpon)* consisted of yellow *chupa, jachen* boots, *chagda* hat in summer and *wagir* hat in winter. Their insignias were made from coral. Their horses had double neck-ornaments.

The weapons included bows and arrows, spears, swords, slings, and catapults, etcetera. Later, firearms, including explosives, were developed. Thereafter, Tibet made mortars called *uchen (dbu chen), sinmo dreshon (srin mo gres gzhon), seril (se*

---

1 A Tibetan hat similar to Panama hat, with pointed top, with equal length of many red strings dangling around the crest. This hat was worn by ministers of the traditional Tibetan government.

2 Tibetan manually made shoes worn by nobles and government officials. Brown *Jachen* boots were worn by lower officials.

ril) and wooden-wheeled field guns, all marked with the year of manufacture. The arms were issued to different regiments by their respective district headquarters. All the army equipment had been preserved in some large fortresses in U-Tsang and Kham before Tibet was invaded by the Communist Chinese.

Regarding the Tibetan army's salary system, when the troops were on border duty, they received salary directly from the government. When they were not on border duty and staying at their regimental cantonments, they did not get any salary from the government. Each soldier of the Shigatse, Gyantse and Dingri Regiments received ten *khal* measures of grain per annum as salary in the form of cash from Gashi, Rong Rampa and other private estates in Tsang. The soldiers of U used to receive their salary in the form of grains from the government's granary in Lhasa.

In times of peace, every regiment would organize a full gathering twice in a year, one in summer and one in winter. All the soldiers would gather at their respective regimental headquarters and do trainings, make new plans and so forth.

In 1751, the above-mentioned Manchu Ambans[3] in Lhasa murdered Desi Pholawa's son (Gyurme Namgyal) in the Tromsikhang building in a planned manner. After that, the Manchus started extending their powers in Tibet. They appointed Chinese instructors and introduced the Chinese style of military training to the Tibetan Dracphi Regiment. Resenting this, Tibetans nicknamed the regiment the "Chinese Trained Regiment *(rgya sbyong dmag sgar)*." After that, although its official name was still Drapchi Regiment, it was often known by this nickname.

This is a rise and fall history of the Tibetan army. The most important thing is that China and Tibet had been distinct countries, and the system and the objectives of the Tibetan Army had remained constant, as explained below.

Military strategies and tactics

As discussed above, the history of the Tibetan army traces back to the era of the Tibetan Buddhist kings. With changes in the political conditions of Tibet, the institution of the Tibetan military also underwent various phases of rise and fall. The Tibetan army was created by its own country, and it went through various changes and improvements. The Simpa Regiment was established by the Tibetan government to preserve the ancient Tibetan army system. In times of war or emergency, local rulers of U, Tsang and Kham used to mobilize troops from their own regions. Therefore, we see that the Tibetan military system was not backward.

All the activities of the Tibetan army were managed by the government. No soldier was allowed to carry out military actions, including making offensive actions

---

3   The Manchu Ambans were Fuqing and Labudun

on an enemy or retreating from a garrison, without consulting the government. However, they could sometimes resort to guerrilla warfare and ambush small detachments of the enemy. They were allowed to use the tactics of 'hit and run', frightening the enemy, besieging villages or towns or cutting off roads to the enemy, but only in accordance with the situation. These military tactics were used even in ancient times. In large wars, the government used to mobilize more troops and they would capture strategic areas and erect garrisons. They would advance further after examining their own condition as well as the situation of the enemy's force.

Military training

In general, all the recruits of both cavalry and infantry had to undergo training in the art of using swords, short spears, axes, iron hooks, nooses, javelins, firearms and other fighting tools, coupled with other fighting skills. There were three types of javelin-throwing practice based on the target distance. The training also included on-target slingshot, boulder shot-put, long-jump, marathon, crossing rivers, wrestling, boxing and other martial arts needed on battlefields. All these different types of physical trainings had originated in Tibet a long time ago, not copied from any foreign countries. In Tibet, horseracing, shooting from horseback, weapon fighting and other traditional Tibetan sports are still popular and conducted during festivals nowadays. From this it clear to us that the Tibetan military training has a long history.

Chapter Five

Tibetan Army during the Time of the Thirteenth Dalai Lama

❖

Size and organizational structure of different regiments of the Tibetan army

In addition to the Simpa Regiment created by Desi Sangye Gyatso as referred to in the fourth chapter, during the time of Desi Phola's son Gyurme Namgyal, 3,000 men were recruited from U-Tsang to form a permanent army, besides maintaining many reserve-soldiers. In 1912, when the Tibetan army purged all of Lu Chun's troops from Tibet, the Tibetan government mobilized a large number of local militias to help the government's army. Thereafter, many soldiers were recruited based on the old Tibetan conscription system to serve as bodyguards of the Dalai Lama, a member of the frontier force, or a member of the police force. The government created a recruit quota system to U and Tsang regions based on their size; U was divided into 1,000 units of *dmag-rten* land and Tsang was divided into 2,000 units of *dmag-rten* land because Tsang was twice the size of U. Five hundred troops were collected each from U and Tsang based on the *nyina*[1] and *shina*[2] conscript system, and a bodyguard regiment was established. Thereafter, the government continuously drafted soldiers based on various conscription systems; the *shina* system, collecting one soldier each from every four soldiers, the *gyena* system, recruiting one soldier each from every eight soldiers, and *drugna* system, conscripting one soldier each from every six soldiers. With these soldiers, nine additional regiments were created and each was named from the Tibetan alphabet from "Cha" to "Pha". In times of emergencies, the government raised more troops by collecting men from the four regions of northern Tibet *(byang rigs sde bzhi)*, Shotarlhosum[3], Powo, 39 Hor states, Rakarsogsum,[4] Khyungpo Karnagsersum[5], Richabpasum[6] and Mardragosum.[7]

---

1 Nyina (*nyis sna*) is a system of collecting one soldier from every two soldiers to serve in war.
2 Shina (*bzhi sna*) is a system of calling one soldier from every four soldiers to serve in war.
3 Shopando, Tar Dzong and Lho Dzong
4 Ragshul, Kandze and Sog Dzong
5 Karu, Nagru and Sertsa
6 Riwoche, Chamdo and Pashopa
7 Markham, Drago and Gojo

Besides local militias, many volunteers would come from monasteries as well as lay people to help the government. Regarding the system of mobilization of troops in times of emergencies, the government would send orders to different district headquarters across the country to send a fixed number of troops to a particular place, and if necessary, the Tibetan Army Headquarters would send military instructors from any regiments to give trainings to them.

The Thirteenth Dalai Lama realized the need for changes in the Tibetan military system in general, and military parade, drill commands and uniforms in particular. In 1912, the Tibetan Army Headquarters was established. Appointing Japanese veteran Yajima[8] as a military instructor, the Japanese style of military training was taught to one of the Tibetan regiments. The barrack of the Bodyguard Regiment was constructed in Japanese style. Sogpo Tenpai Gyaltsen, who was well trained in the Russian military system, was appointed to teach Russian military system to another Tibetan regiment. Another two Tibetan regiments were trained in the British military style and the traditional Tibetan military system. Altogether, four different styles of military trainings were given to four different Tibetan regiments. After training, a four-day military sport events was held on the ground of Chensil Palace at Norbulingka, in the presence of the Dalai Lama, Tibetan civil and military officials, and many spectators from Lhasa and Shol. The events included parade, drills, equestrian, swimming, identification of weapons and their parts, and manual dexterity for detaching and assembling different types of new and old guns. At the end, the Dalai Lama adjudged the British military style the best and made it the model for the Tibetan Army.

Thereafter, some bright and young soldiers from different regiments and some government staff were sent to the British army camps at Gyantse Changlo as well as to Shilong and Guwahati states of India for military training, including training on mortars and machine guns. Upon arrival back after training, they were sent to different Tibetan regiments throughout the country to share British military trainings. The uniform, emblems, insignias and colours of all the Tibetan army units were all made based on the British style.

The Tibetan military flag was red with brownish edges, two snow lions at the centre, facing each other in the manner of lifting crossed-vajras together. In those days, the national flag and the military flags of Tibet were similar in design, except for their emblems—the national flag had flaming jewels instead of crossed-vajras. A military law was codified and announced throughout the country. The flags were flown permanently at the Army Headquarters and they were flown or carried during all official ceremonies. In his memoir[9], Eric Teichmen, who spent many years in

---

8   For more details, see *The Rising Sun in the Land of Snows: Japanese Involvement in Tibet in the Early 20th Century*, Berry, Scott.

9   Namgyal Wangdu might be referring to Erich Teichman's *Travels of a Consular Officer in Eastern Tibet*, 1922

Chengdu as the British consular officer in China, describes the Tibetan national flag having a yellow background, with snowy mountains on which two snow lions face each other. However, some Tibetan veterans told me that the Tibetan national flag had a red background with light brown edges, with two snow lions facing each other at the center, in the manner of lifting the flaming jewels. This is the real description of the Tibetan national flag, and some samples of old Tibetan national flags can still be found in army stores in Tibet. In fact, the Tibetan national flag and military flags had the same background color, but the national flag had the flaming jewels and the military flag had the crossed-vajras as its emblem. In Markham in those times, there were several Christian missionaries and Red Cross agents from western countries. They were given road passes and the Tibetan national flag by the Governor-General of Kham Jampa Tendar to travel in the region. They carried the documents and flags wherever they went and pasted them on walls, and the local people treated these documents and flags with great respect.

The government imported different types of automatic guns, machine guns, Lewis guns, Sten guns, mortars, and hand grenades, and distributed them to different army units and deposited the remaining in the government's armories.

Each Tibetan regiment had its own band party, the size ranging from four to eight squads, depending on the strength of the regiment. Their instruments were different types of British trumpets, drums, bagpipers, and flutes, etcetera. The band parties would sing military songs and two kinds of patriotic songs in praise of the country. Their duties included sounding bugle calls thrice daily; the wakeup call in morning, the return call at sunset, and the good night call at night. Some larger regiments had musical groups composed of about 10 soldiers at their assembly tents *(dkyil sgar)*. Their duty was to sing and play Tibetan trumpets, clarinets, flutes and drums during parade marches performed thrice daily—morning, midday and night.

It was also the duty of the band parties to make bugle-calls during parades to summon soldiers, form lines, and breakup, etcetera. During a war, their responsibilities included giving signals to their soldiers by means of different kinds of bugle-calls, mirror reflections, and flying flags of different colors on the battlefields. These methods of secret communication were taught and made the standard in all the Tibetan regiments. The military system was also improved during the time. Inviting Sonam Laden-la from Darjeeling who was well trained in the police system, the soldiers of the Dadang Lhangam Phunsum Regiment were given police trainings. Thereafter, the regiment was put under the Lhasa Mayor and assigned the responsibilities of security and cleanliness of the city, which will be discussed in detail later. Each of all the Tibetan regiments was given a Tibetan alphabet in order as its name (ka, kha, ga, nga, etcetera.). For ease of understanding, I have given a list of regiments below, the sources of their soldiers, and the quota of recruits required from each source:

Regiment Name	Recruitment Sources	Number of Soldiers	Notes
Ka	U & Tsang	1,000	U was larger than Tsang under the military tax system. Therefore, U was reserved for 1,000 and Tsang was reserved for 2,000 soldiers. At that time, 500 troops from U based on nyina system and 500 from Tsang based on shina system were summoned to serve as bodyguards of the Dalai Lama on a rotation basis.
Kha	U	1,060	The soldiers of this regiment were conscripted from U, Lhoka, Phenpo, Jara, Dagpo and Nyemo, collecting one man from each unit of land under military tax system.
Ga	Shigatse	1,000	This regiment was composed of 750 soldiers from Shigatse—one soldier each from a unit of land under military tax system—and 250 soldiers from Labrang (Tashi Lhunpo), one each from one military unit
Nga	Gyantse	526	444 soldiers from Gyantse and Wangdupasum—one man from each unit of land under military tax system, and 82 from Lhoka under the Governor of southern Tibet.
Ca	Dingri (upper Tsang)	526	The members of this regiment came from Upper Tsang and Lato areas, including Dingri and Shelkar.

Cha	Simpa	500	This regiment had three units: exterior, interior and middle. The exterior and middle units were later joined and this created the Artillery Regiment. The interior unit was retained and assigned the duty of traditional Tibetan army parades and performances during the Monlam Festival every year.
Ja	U	500	Its troops were collected based on the military tax system.
Nya	U		As above.
Ta	Tsang	500	As above.
Tha	Tsang	500 800	As above.
Da	Lhangam Phumsum (Lhatse, Ngamrin and Phuntsokling)	500	The soldiers for this regiment were conscripted from Lhatse, Ngamring and Phuntsokling that were under the jurisdiction of Tashi Lhunpo. After receiving police training, they served as Police Force for many years.
Na	Lhasa and Shol	500	The members of this regiment were drafted from Lhasa and Shol communities. They received a salary and uniform from the government, as other soldiers did. There was no any reserve conscription sources for this regiment.
Pa	Agriculture Department	500	The Agriculture Department used to employ many men to collect grains from people. Five hundred workers from well-off families were selected for this regiment. The weapons were provided by the government. This regiment had no any particular recruitment sources.

| Pha | Well-to-do families | 700 | This regiment was founded by the Dalai Lama's favourite attendant, Thupten Kunphel. Its members were drafted from well-off families and it comprised two brigades. Yuthog Se Tashi Dhondup and Taring Sumtsen Wangpo were appointed its first leaders. |
| Ba | Kongpo | 500 | The soldiers of this regiment were conscripted from four districts of Kongpo based on the conscription system. |

Ancient Tibetan weaponry, machinegun training and the foundation of the Phadang Drongdak Regiment

(This article on ancient Tibetan weaponry, machinegun training, and the foundation of the Phadang Drongdak Regiment by former Tibetan minister, Kasur Taring Jigme Sumtsen, is found among the collection of documents related to the Tibetan Army).

Development of weaponry

In Tibet, during the Stone Age period before the discovery of iron and the arrival of the Tibetan Buddhist kings, slings were used in place of guns and catapults *(rdo rgyogs),* and staff slings *(rdzogs rdo)* and so forth were used in place of cannons as war weapons, as in England and other Western countries. The sling was made with chords prepared from yak's hair and it could shoot a stone a distance of about 200 steps[10]. The catapult was made from wood with strong strings made from yak's hair. It could project a large stone, as big as a man of average strength could lift with his two hands, a distance of 100 steps. The projectile stones were kept on the balcony above the gate of a fortress. When an enemy approached the castle, the defenders would shoot stones with the help of catapults. During the 6th and 7th centuries, when the Buddhist kings ruled Tibet, the Tibetan army used bows and arrows, swords and spears as weapons when fighting against the Chinese. It is unknown whether these weapons originated from the East or the West. Old

---

10 Lack of standard measuring instrument, footstep was used as a measurement unit in Tibet.

Tibetan records speak about Tibetan swords with names such as *dmar stag bzhi ma*, *dmar mtsho dgu ma, nam mkha' rgyal mtshan*, and *ya ma rgan rdi*. Thereafter, with the arrival of gunpowder in Tibet, Tibetans started using matchlock firearms. As for the matchlock firearms, gunpowder and lead projectiles were put into the gun's barrel and the powder was ignited at the wick, which was kept burning. There were different types of matchlock guns, such as *sog chu bab, sog pho mo g.yas bcus, sog pho mo g.yon cus*, and *sog gling bzhi ma*. Perhaps they were given such names because they were seized from the Dzungar Mongols. Later, the Tibetan government started manufacturing guns and ammunitions in large quantities. During the Tibetan-Gurkha war in 1854 and Tibetan-British wars in 1888 at Lungtur and other border places of Tibet, the Tibetan army used indigenous guns and cannons. In 1904, the year of Wood-Dragon, during Anglo-Tibetan battles at Phari, Chumig Shongko, Gyants and others, the Tibetan army also used their indigenous guns and cannons, such as Sinmo Dreshon *(srin mo gre gzhon)*, Khabarma *(kha bar ma)*, Namchag *(gnam lcags)*, Seril *(se ril)*, Kugpa *(lkugs pa)*, and Chamseng *(lcam seng)*. These cannons were also used during the Lhasa Monlam Festival.

During the Sera riot in 1948, the Fire-Pig year, I was in-charge of the Lachag Office (*bla phyag las khungs*)[11]. I received an order to report to the Drapchi Office. When I went there, Sawang Kasho and Commander-in-Chief Gyabumgang Khendrung Ngawang Namgyal, appointed me the leader of the artillery unit of the Tibetan Army. When we went to suppress the Sera riot, the monks fired cannons from the monastery's main gate, and the shells reached as far as the Tsesum ground, which was approximately one mile away from the monastery. I saw them with my own eyes. Around that time, all the Tibetan guns and cannons were manufactured by the Tibetan government.

Around 1890, the Tibetan government produced a cannon called Gurkha Yangchen *(gur kha yang chen)*, which had a lid (called *topi* in Nepali and *cap* in English) and it did not need an igniter. After that, the government set up arsenal near Drib Monastery on the southern bank of the Kyichu River, and started manufacturing automatic guns, such as *drib yangchen, chu tsi po* and *ushang*. The factory also manufactured cups called *drip kar (grib dkar)*, meaning the "cups made by Drip factory". Later, in 1900, the factory moved to Yamen in Lhasa and its name was changed to Norkyil Trulsokhang. It started making arms and ammunition, as well as gold and silver monetary coins. The factory was closed after the Anglo-Tibetan war in the Wood-Dragon year (1904). The British government sent 5,000 long rifles, each with 300 rounds of ammunition, as gifts to the Tibetan government. Thereafter, the Tibetan government purchased many shotguns, Lewis guns, machineguns, Sten guns, Bren guns, 10-pound mortars, howitzers and hand grenades from the British government of India.

---

11 Lachag Office was responsible to manage fund and expenses of the Monlam Festival held every year.

Training in machinegun and the foundation of the Drongdrak Regiment

In 1932, the Water-Monkey year, Ma Pufang of Sining led military incursion into Tibet from its northern border, ransacking the villages and killing many people. The Tibetan government felt the importance of improving and increasing the strength of the Tibetan army and weaponry. Led by Kashag's steward Kadron Yutok Se, one platoon from the Bodyguard Regiment along with 20 government mules, was sent to the British army camp at Changlo in Gyantse to receive training in Lewis guns and hand grenades. At that time, I was just back home from India after finishing my study. I received an order from the government to go with them to act as their interpreter as well as to do training with them. In its order, the government had promised to pay me 50 *srang* money during the training period. The trainer was a Major Marshal and I served as interpreter and trainee during the training time.

After becoming well trained in firing, detaching and assembling machineguns and using hand grenades, all the trainees left for Lhasa in the twelfth Tibetan month. When we arrived at Chushur, we met a Dalai Lama's horse servant who had been sent to us from Norbulingka, with an order that we should go there on an auspicious day after our arrival in Lhasa. From Nyethang we went to Lhasa by way of Shun Dongkar, where we spent the night. When we reached Lhasa, we loaded the machine guns on mules. All of us, officers and troops, dressed up in army uniform, and marched in line towards Norbulingka, but we received an order to halt our march at Kyitsel Luding until we received further order. We then stayed at Shun Dongkar for one day, and spread all the machineguns and saddles on ground and cleaned them. The next morning, we marched to Kyitsel Luding and waited there for an order. A stable keeper of the Dalai Lama came to us, with an order that we should arrive at the Dalai Lama's Chensil Palace from its northern gate. We proceeded from Kyitsel Luding towards Norbulingka and when we reached near Sertam Bridge, we could see the Dalai Lama watching us through binoculars.

Upon arrival at the northern gate of the palace, the Dalai Lama's favoured attendant, Kunphen-la, instructed our leader, Yuthog Se, to report to the palace's courtyard where the *drungja*, the monk officials' morning tea ceremony was being held, and to perform a complimentary parade march to the Dalai Lama. Accordingly, we marched on and when we were passing through the middle gate of the security room, we saw the Dalai Lama watching us from his balcony. After performing the complimentary march and salute to the Dalai Lama, we fetched all the machineguns and arranged them in line on their three-leg stands. Wearing a *jozha* hat and a shawl, and accompanied by his attendants, the Dalai Lama came down to the ground to observe the guns. Since it was the first time for Tibetans to see machineguns, the Dalai Lama, looked at the guns with smile and joyful expression on his face, and asked Yuthog Se some questions about the weapons. He ordered Brigadier Nangkarwa of the Bodyguard Regiment to deposit all the guns at the Bodyguard Regiment. We, the officers and troops, were allowed to take rest for about seven days. After that, the troops did military exercises and machinegun firing practice on the ground at the western side of Chensil Phodrang every morning. The Dalai Lama, with his attendants, visited the training site several times and watched the training with great enthusiasm.

After that, in the Water-Bird year, after the Great Monlam Festival was over, the Phadang Drongdak Regiment was established in accordance with the plan[12]. An edict was issued, ordering that one boy each from three families in U and Tsang should be sent to serve in the army and the Drapchi Office registered the recruits. In the same year, a new regimental barrack was constructed at the western side of the Drapchi Office. Colonel Phurbu Dorje of the Bodyguard Regiment supervised the construction. On ground of his efficiency, he was made the supervisor of the construction and it was completed after about four months. Yuthog Se and I were made the leaders of the new regiment. Until the barrack became ready, all the recruits lodged at the Yamen army camp, and their hair was cut and their trainings started. Ngabo Se Ngawang Jigme, Derge Se Kalsang Wangdu, Samling Gyanpa, Dedrug Chondze Wangdu and a Gurkha veteran named Choje sent from Darjeeling by Legden Dzasag (Laden-la) were appointed our instructors.

In the fifth Tibetan month, all the soldiers were moved to the newly built barrack, and the unit was named Drongdrak Regiment, meaning, "the regiment of well-off families". There were 1,000 soldiers in all. Yuthog Se was appointed as *dapon* (brigadier), Taring as *datsab* (deputy brigadier), Ngabo Se and Derge Kalsang Wangdu as *rupon* (colonels), and Samling Gyanpa and Dedruk Chondze Wangdu as *gyapon* (captains). The uniform of Dapon Yuthog and Deputy Dapon (Datsab) Taring were ordered at the Ring.ca Company in Calcutta, and their badges and crossed-vajra insignias were made at the Drapchi Office. The uniforms of the colonels, captains, and the soldiers were prepared by the Drapchi Office and were khaki in colour. The summer uniforms were cotton and winter's was woolen. The army's helmets, leather belts and leather boots (gora boots) were ordered from India through Pomda. The new regiment participated in the parade march with other regiments during the Great Lhasa Monlam Festival in the Water-Bird year.

Thereafter, some of the 25 troops who previously received training at the British army camp in Gyantse were selected and sent to teach military trainings to different Tibetan regiments. At the Drapchi Regiment, about eight young government officials, including Lhalu Se, Numa and Kharna, were given training

---

12 According to the Dungkar Lobsang Trinley's great dictionary, the Drongdak Regiment was created in 1914, the year of Wood-Tiger, but dissolved after the death of the Thirteenth Dalai Lama. It was reestablished in 1948, the year of Earth-Rat.

in machineguns, with Deputy Dapon Taring as the instructor. Dapon Yuthog selected several soldiers from different regiments and gave them training in the 10-pound mortar artillery under the instructorship of Dingpon Dingja Lhakpa, who had received training in artillery. After their training, the best trainees were then sent to Kham to give training to the Tibetans armies stationed there. Under the instructorship of Captain Choje of the Drongdak Regiment and Colonel Dorji of the Bodyguard Regiment, the soldiers performed drill practice and exercise thrice daily. In the Water-Bird year (1912), in the presence of Gould Sahib, the Political Officer of Sikkim and Colonel Neam, a high-ranking British army officer, the Tibetan army demonstrated military exercises and drills in mortars, machine guns and Lewis guns. The Dalai Lama watched the events through binoculars from the balcony of the Drapchi Electrical Machine Office.

Kunphel-la looked after the Drongdak troops with great love and care. They had better uniforms, food, band instruments and other facilities than the troops of other Tibetan regiments. The Dalai Lama also gave special interest in the new regiment. The Lhasa people therefore nicknamed the new regiment "Chensil Magar," meaning the "Favoured Regiment."

On the 30th day of the tenth Tibetan month of the Water-Bird year (1933), the Thirteenth Dalai Lama passed away, ensued by bitter internal struggle for power within the government. On the third day of the eleventh month, which was an army holiday, Lungshar lied to some senior members of the Drongdrak Regiment, such as Shitse Tsogse Tojang Omdor, Lugra and Shoshar that their soldiers were holding a meeting on the field near Mondor Bridge, not far from Ramoche. The leaders immediately went to see them and met some soldiers leaving, carrying their luggage. The leaders checked their bags and found that they were carrying all their belongings, including cooking stuffs, food, and dress, etcetera. The soldiers who were aware of what was happening had left their boxes filled with bricks and stones in their rooms, while those who did not know what was going on had left all their belongings in the room.

On that day, Yuthog was on leave until the next day and I was at the barrack. At 10 am, I went to him and reported the incident. He said that it was better to report the matter to the Kashag. When we were heading toward the Kashag, the soldiers were running towards Norbulingka through the Willow Grove as if "cows are being driven out by a thief."[13] When we arrived at Norbulingka, the main gate had been closed so Yuthog asked the gatekeeper to open the door. When the gate was opened, the soldiers rushed into it with great force and went straight to the Kashag to submit a petition. The Kashag was in session and we explained the matter to them. The

---

13 Tibetan proverb: *rkun mas ba 'khrid pa,* meaning "to go somewhere without knowing why and where one is going.

Kashag called the Chief Abbot Official and Kunphel-la to the meeting and discussed the matter. Drapchi officer Khendrung Thupten Kunkhen and the salary officer, Nangsey, were instructed to bring four machineguns from the Drapchi Office to be given to two of us. We were instructed that those soldiers of the Drongdrak Regiment who had left the barrack should not be allowed to come back to the barrack, and 200 troops with weapons should be deployed at the Drapchi Office and the Drongdrak Regiment. Yuthog and I returned to our barrack. After receiving the machineguns and six boxes each containing 1,000 rounds of ammunition, we instructed the Bodyguard Regiment about the arrangement of security at the Drapchi Office and the barrack of the Drongdak Regiment. The Drongdak soldiers sat on the ground of Magar Sarpa, waiting for a reply from the Kashag. Those who had no relatives in Lhasa faced great difficulty in getting food and as a result, had to beg.

The Kashag issued an order that only 250 soldiers should be kept and the rest should be sent home. Yuthog Se and I were fined with 10 gold *srang*s and 6 gold *srang*s money respectively, on grounds of not knowing what was going on around us. Soon after, Dapon Nangkarwa of the Bodyguard Regiment was appointed the Commander-in-Chief and Yuthog Se was appointed to his place. In the meantime, until all the Drongdak soldiers were sent home, Yuthog remained as their leader. Since the soldiers did not have routine training sessions, they were assigned the task of digging up a well inside the compound of the Army Headquarters, as both the Drapchi Office and the army camp got their drinking water from Drapchi Monastery. The well greatly benefitted all of us.

Once complete, all the remaining Drongdrak troops were sent home. The soldiers of the Chinese trained Khadang Regiment at Drapchi were moved to the barrack of the Drongdak Regiment.

A brief discussion on the origin of knives in Tibet

All peoples in this world have their own unique weapons of fighting bearing their own characteristics. As human society progressed, the tools used by humans also improved, and various types of tools with different qualities were invented. We use some of them in our day-to-day life for domestic purposes. Similarly, many unique instruments were invented in Tibet many thousands of years ago. One of the earliest instruments that appeared in Tibet was the knife that we use in our everyday life, although it is difficult to know the exact time of its origin. According to historians and archeologists, many hundred thousand years ago, during the period called the Stone Age, Tibetans once used simple tools, such as blades and axes made from stone, to protect themselves against dangerous wild animals. Those tools were the foundations of the modern Tibetan weapons.

The first Tibetan reference to swords is found in the *Five Chronicles*. According to this source, before Nyatri Tsenpo became the first king of Tibet, the country was ruled by non-humans. During the rule of the nine Masang Brothers *(ma sangs spun dgu)*[14], weapons first appeared in Tibet. In other sources, it is said that during the rule of Nojin Nagpo, different kinds of weapons such as axes, knives, catapults, blades, pointed bones and so forth became popular in Tibet. During the period of the Tibetan royal dynasty, Tibetans started making knives. Regarding this, the *Great Annals of Tibet and China,* authored by Taktsang Dzompa Paljor Sangpo in the 14th century says:

> *Dgu zi* is a Tibetan knife. It was invented in the time of Drigum Tsenpo by the nine *mig zin po* brothers in the land of Zi 'du. Regarding the meaning of *dgu zi*, *dgu* refers to the nine brothers and *zi* is a part of the name *mig zin po*. Thereafter, all the knives made by them became known as *dgu zi*.

In the *A Wish Granting Treasury for Chinese and Tibetans (rgya bod nor rdzas spyi don yid kyi 'dod 'jo)*, it says:

> *Dgu zi* is a Tibetan knife. It was made by nine *mig zin po* brothers in the country called 'Zi du in the time of Drigum Tsenpo. The biggest one could cut the celestial rope. Other ones had labels of sharpness. Nine brothers had their own trainees who spread knives in Tibet. The knives were called *dgu zi* because they were made by nine brothers called *mig zin po*.

In the Gold Rosary: A Tibetan History (bod kyi gyal rab gser gyi phreng ba), it says:

> During the reign of Drigum Tsenpo, raw iron, raw silver and raw copper were discovered (in Tibet). Using coals, they were smelted to get iron, silver and copper.

It is clear from the above sources that knives became popular in Tibet during the reign of King Drigum Tsenpo, the first of the Two Upper Kings. This confirms that metalwork had already spread in Tibet since Tibetans started using iron axes, knives, and blades, etcetera. As the saying goes, "Hammer, pincers and bellows are the three main tools of a smith"; these three tools were the earliest tools used by Tibetan smiths. During the Tibetan imperial period, with the discovery of the technique of smelting raw iron, people started making different types of metal knives. There are different Tibetan swords with different names based on the methods of how they were made. Some examples are *dgra lha'i gar chod* (knife that can destroy the enemy's war-deities), *gong khra dgu chod* (knife that can slash a hawk), *gnam mkha' spu chod* (knife that can kill a flying bird), *chu nang nya chod* (fishing knife), *gal rga'i jo chod* (knife to cut a snare), *bye ne'i gdong chod* (knife to kill a *jena* bird) and *ngan tho'i skas chod* (knife that can destroy evils). From these, it is clear that different kinds of high quality swords were produced in Tibet during the Tibetan imperial period until the empire collapsed.

---

14 They were non-humans who once controlled Tibet before human beings emerged in Tibet.

The epic of King Gesar of Ling is very popular among Tibetans and clearly depicts the picture of political, military, cultural, economic and social conditions of Tibet of the time. Therefore, I think it is quite correct to say that King Gesar's epic is like a mirror that reflects the early Tibetan society. As mentioned above, the reference of *chu gri* (razor-knife) used in prehistoric period and *dgu zi* invented during the period of a Tibetan Dharma king are found in some Tibetan annals. However, we will hardly know the story of these swords after the fall of the Tibetan empire unless we consult the Gesar epic. In King Gesar's story called *Ja rong 'bru rdzong*, when describing how King Gesar set off to the battlefield, it says:

> To the handle of sword "*btab pa lan med*",
> A white scarf of a cubit length was tied.[15]

From this, it is clear that the sword was one of the "nine kinds of weapons". We can also understand from Gesar's epic that there were different types of swords, such as Dri Azi Dugral Bawa (*gri a zi dug ral 'bar ba*), Drichung Shelgi Yudar (*gri chung shel gyi yu dar*), Kyedri Jigten Chunyul (*sked gri 'jig rten chu myul*), Guzi Regcho (*dgu zi reg chod*) and Sindri Barwa Tsenon (*srin gri 'bar ba rtse rnon*). The following are some names of swords made in Tibet: *gri chung* (dagger), *ko gri* (leather knife), *mar gri* (butter knife), *rum gri* (scalpel), *gtub tri* (chopper), *dpa dam* (swords), *nywa gri* (fishing knife), *spu gri* (razor), *sha gri* (butcher's knife) and *ltebs gri* (folding knife). Their names were derived from their uses, quality, material, and size, etcetera.

Since everyone may encounter attacks by an enemy at any time, there is a Tibetan saying, "Knife is an ornament of men; turquoise and coral are ornament of women."[16] Therefore, there was a time in Tibet when most men used to carry knives at their waists for the purpose of self-defense. However, knives were also used as ornaments. Some people used to make silver sheaths decorated with gold, silver, copper inlays or ornamented with patterns of leaves and flowers using turquoise, coral, onyx or any other precious materials.

---

15 ral gri btab pa lan med la//
    dar dkar dpa' lung khru gang btags//
16 Gri chung stag shar gyi rgyan cha// g.yu byur bu mo'i rgyan cha//

Chapter Six

The Headquarters of the Tibetan Army

❖

A. Tibetan army headquarters

The Tibetan Army Headquarters was established in 1913, the Water-Ox year, by the Thirteenth Dalai Lama, after he arrived back from India following the expulsion of all the Manchu Lu Chun's troops from Tibet by the Tibetan army. There was no army headquarters in Tibet before that. In ancient times, military responsibilities were given to an army general under the leadership of a king or a minister, whoever was in power. When the Tibetan Army Headquarters was founded, Khendrung Jampa Tendar was appointed Commander-in-Chief, with the title of *Kalon Lama*. He was the first Tibetan Commander-in-Chief and was appointed in recognition of his excellent military service in the past. Tsipon Trimon Norbu Wangyal was appointed Deputy Commander-in-Chief and Chensel Namgang Dasang Dradul Assistant Commander-in-Chief, with the title of *Dzasak*. Later, Jampa Tendar was appointed the Governor-General of Kham, and Dasang Dradul was made Commander-in-Chief in consideration of his remarkable military achievements. The details regarding successive Tibetan Commanders-in-Chief are given in the second part of this volume.

The Tibetan Army Headquarters was located at the centre of the building adjoining of Dorjeling Armory on the ground floor of the Potala Palace. On the western side of the building were an armory of ancient Tibetan weapons and the quarters of the armoury staff and guards. On the eastern side of the Headquarters was a chapel of the War Deity. At the base of the building was an armoury where arms were kept, arranged in the order of their serial numbers written in the Tibetan alphabet. The Tibetan national flag was flown permanently in the centre of the rooftop of the Army Headquarters.

The Army Headquarters was staffed by the Commander-in-Chief, two Deputy Commanders-in-Chief in the rank of *dzasak*, two army secretaries, two office assistants and several army officers in the rank of lieutenant as clerks, couriers and cleaning staff. Whenever necessary, the Headquarters would send an order to any regiment to send a fixed number of personnel to serve at Headquarters. In the office, all the files, properly indexed in the Tibetan alphabet, were kept separately on the shelves in proper order. The files contained documents, such as proposal documents, lists of regiments and soldiers, correspondence, petitions and others related to military affairs. The daily jobs of the Army Headquarters included submitting petitions to the Kashag and other high offices of the Tibetan government on behalf of all the army regiments, sourcing and supplying grain to the different units of the Tibetan army on time, and obtaining the sanction of the government for pack animals, riding animals and road passes for army regiments whenever they had to go to collect summer and winter uniforms or go on expeditions. The Headquarters also handled the issue of arms and ammunition to different regiments in consultation with the government. Whenever a vacancy occurred in a regiment due to the death of a soldier, retirement or desertion, the Headquarters would instruct the regiment concerned to recruit a new soldier and send him to the Headquarters for a recruitment test. The Tibetan Army Headquarters therefore had certain administrative powers within the ambit of military affairs.

B. Shodrung Nornangpa's article on the Tibetan army

Shodrung Nornangpa served as army secretary at the Tibetan Army Headquarters for several years before he left for India on an official mission in 1959. He remained in India permanently and settled at Rajpur, Dehradun, where he lived for many years before he passed away. The following is the full transcription of his eyewitness account of the Tibetan Army Headquarters and the Simpa Guards, preserved among the collections of documents related to the Tibetan Army.

1. Army headquarters

I shall relate here from my memory as much as I can of what I saw and did during my more than ten years of service as army secretary at the Army Headquarters:

> At that time, the Army Headquarters was staffed by Commander-in-Chief Khenchung Kungo Tenpa Jamyang and Dapon Nangkar of the Bodyguard Regiment. After that, Dapon Chapelwa of the Ngadang Regiment was appointed to the Army Headquarters, and his title was *Rimshi,* the title for a fourth grade official. A few days after I got an investiture audience *(sarjel)* with the Dalai Lama for my new appointment, Shodron Khenrab Palden, a steward at the Sho Office, was appointed to the Headquarters on the *letsenpa* (staff) post. He was dressed in Mongolian clothing when he came to the office to start his duty. These two were the first *rimshi* and *letsenpa* ranking government officials to be appointed to the Army. Ragtsiwa was one of the two army secretaries. He succeeded Rongdrakpa Tanag, who was made *Yakpon,* the chief in-charge of the government's yaks. Phulung Surpa and Rongdrakpa Tanag were the first Sho officials to serve as army

secretary. Tsedrung Woeser was also a staff member of the Headquarters at that time. Khenchung Tenpa Jamyang and Tsedrung Woeser were the first Tsedrung officials to be appointed to the Army Headquarters.

Including myself, there were seven main staff members at the Army Headquarters. The fourth *rupon* of the Gadang Regiment was the treasurer of the Headquarters. There was one captain and 50 soldiers from the Tadang Regiment at the Headquarters as armoury guards. The Headquarters also had four lieutenants whose job was to draft letters and one lieutenant whose duty was to look after the cleanliness of the office. The Headquarters had the authority to appoint its own staff, selecting from any particular regiments, without having to consult with the Kashag, except for the armoury guards, consisting of one captain and a platoon, who could be selected from any regiment only after prior consultation with the government.

During my tenure as army secretary, some reshuffles occurred in the staff of the Army Headquarters. Tsedrung Woeser Ngawang was appointed the Lhapu district officer, and his post was filled by Tsedrung Sholkang Richoe Thupten Choephel. Commander-in-Chief Khenchung (Tenpa Jamyang) was elevated to the post of *khendrung* (third rank). [He and Dapon Nangkarwa] were thereafter were called Magchi Drungda Drelpo[1]. Thereafter, Khendrung Tenpa Jamyang was made (Kalon) and the Senior Commander-in-Chief. So he and Dapon Nangkarwa were together called Kada Drelpo[2], and they served as the Commander-in-Chief jointly for many years.

After Nangkarwa passed away, Dzasak Dokharwa became Commander-in-Chief. After that, the two Commanders-in-Chief were together called Kadza Drelpo[3]. When the Kalon Lama died, Khenchung Kalsang Tsultrim was appointed Commander-in-Chief. He and Dzasak Dokharwa were called Dzakhen Drelpo[4]. Soon after that, Khenchung was raised to the rank of *dzasak*. The two were then called Dzasak Serkya Drelpo[5]. During their term, Letsen Khenrab Palden passed away, and a man called Lhundup-la, who had been stationed at the eastern gate of Shol, was appointed to the vacant post in the same year. When Tsedrung Sholkang Richo Thupten Chophel was transferred to another office, Tsedrung Tsetrog Tsultrim Gyaltsen was appointed to the post of Commander-in-Chief. Thereafter, army secretary Ragtsiwa was appointed as district officer of Chongye, and his army post was filled by Shodrung Dingja Shonpa.

Ragtsiwa was my colleague; we worked together for many years. He was proficient in the way he performed his duties in the office, including letter drafting and maintaining accounts. He was calm and gentle by nature. He was a simple

---

1 Magchi Drungda Drelpo (*dmag spyi drug mda' sbrel po*) means a *khendrung* official and an army Dapon jointly acting as the Commander-in-Chief.

2 Kada Drelpo (*bka' mda' sbrel po*) refers to a *kalon* and a *dapon* jointly serving as the Commander-in-Chief.

3 Kadza Drelpo (*bka' dza sbrel po*) means a kalon and a *dzasak* official sharing the post of Commander-in-Chief.

4 Dzakhen Drelpo (*dza mkhan*) is two officials of *dzasak* and *khenchung* ranks together acting as the Commander-in-Chief.

5 Dzasak Serkya Drelpo (*dza sag ser skya sbrel po*): a monk and a lay officials, both with the dzasak title, sharing the post of Commander-in-Chief.

man, just like a yogi—he did not have even the slightest trace of ego or selfishness. He was one of the best *drungkhor* officials. For me in particular, he was my teacher, who always guided and cared for me with love, like my parents.

After that, in the Fire-Dog year, I was transferred to Saga as its governor, and Shodrung Junpa Bu was appointed to my army post. In the presence of my colleague, I handed my charge and office goods over to my successor in accordance with the list. I never returned to Lhasa after that, so I do not know who joined and who left the Army Headquarters after I left.

The office items that I handed over to my successor included a large roll of documents of proposal and petitions submitted by the Army Headquarters and signed by the Thirteenth Dalai Lama; one big roll of petitions and proposals submitted by the Headquarters to the government during the regency of Reting and Taktra; four thick registers of weapons and other items of military equipment deposited at Dorjeling Armoury; a thin booklet of rules and regulations of the Army and a large roll of papers that contained the list of soldiers in the different regiments. The registers had brocade covers. It was the responsibility of the army secretaries to take care of all these documents and to open and close the doors of the Headquarters every morning and evening.

To access any of these documents, other staff of the Headquarters had to first seek permission from the army secretaries; no one was allowed to open them at their own discretion. Besides the above, there were other files, containing edicts received from the Kashag, receipts, bills and orders issued by the Headquarters. Many such big bundles of documents would come out every year.

Regarding how the files were preserved at the Headquarters, there was a cupboard of appropriate size in the office to keep the files. The office was a room with six pillars. It had about six windows, all facing towards the south. There was a large cupboard wedged between two pillars opposite the windows. The cupboard had many separate shelves, each with double doors. Each section had a label written in the Tibetan alphabet in sequence. It was therefore not difficult to keep the files properly.

As regards the job profiles of the seven staff of the Army Headquarters, they had no particular permanent jobs—they had to do different types of work every day. There were some tasks that had to be done repeatedly. The Headquarters would often receive petitions from different regiments, requesting them to send a new soldier to fill the vacancies left by soldiers who had retired, died, become sick or deserted. When such requests arrived, the Headquarters would send an order to the appropriate recruiting source to send two young men, a first choice and a substitute, aged between 18 and 30 who were trustworthy, healthy and physically and mentally fit, to the Army Headquarters on such as such date for military service. When the recruits arrived at the Headquarters, the two Commanders-in-Chief would examine their physical fitness and height. After the physical examination, either the first choice or the substitute would be selected. After that, the caretaker *(gad pa)* would bring some sealing wax *(la bzhu)*. The chief security guard would bring the seal from the office. The recruit had to kneel down on the floor. The two Commanders-in-Chief would bring a bangle of a sort made from twisted wool chords and put it tightly around one of the recruit's wrists. After that, the seal was placed under the ring and pressed hard, so as to leave the impression of the seal on the soldier's wrist. The recruit now became a registered soldier. The Commanders-in-Chief would give him brief instructions about his duties and then hand him over to the regiment concerned.

Every month, when the salary day approached, the regiments based in Lhasa would submit lists of their soldiers, excluding sick or dead soldiers or deserters, to the Headquarters, signed by their Dapon, and if the Dapon was not present, the Rupon or Gyapon. The Headquarters would prepare a pay slip for each regiment and get it sanctioned by the Kashag. The original copies of the pay slips were given to the salary collectors. The Headquarters would give a supporting letter to each salary collector, detailing the regiment's name, the number of personnel and the amount of grain or money to be given. They were sent to the Shol salary office to collect the salaries.

Every year, every regiment based within or outside of Lhasa used to send its representatives to collect cash or grain as compensation for uniforms from their respective regions. At that time, each regiment would send two officers, a lieutenant and a captain, each with three assistants, to the Headquarters to get a road pass and authorization letter. The Headquarters would draft the authorization letter and the two Commanders-in-Chief would carry it to the Kashag for approval. The Headquarters would put its own seal on the list of items authorized for collection. Later, when the government decided to use gray *nambu* cloth for the army's uniform, the Headquarters issued each regiment with a piece of genuine *nambu* cloth and a length of chord as the standard sample of cloth and measuring unit.

The Army Headquarters would receive all kinds of requests from different regiments. The request had to be made to the Headquarters by sending representatives. The Headquarters would examine the petitions and write comments on them. If the petitioner accepted it, it would be finalized. Some requests entailed complicated follow up procedures. For example, once an army unit stationed in Domey for border duty sent us a request, saying:

"The long-barreled British rifles that issued to us are now either lying damaged or breaking down easily due to frequent use in many wars in the past, and there are not have enough for all the soldiers. Since border defense is very important, the risk is too great to all of us. Therefore, kindly send us 500 short-barreled rifles along with ammunition and allow us to deposit the old rifles in the government's armoury in Domey."

The regiment concerned had sent its representatives to Lhasa to submit the petition and collect the weapons. They approached the Kashag, who acknowledged their petition by putting the date of its arrival on it and forwarded it to the Army Headquarters for follow up. The two Commanders-in-Chief read and verified the petition. Having found it reasonable, they sent a petition to the secretariat office of the Regent through the Kashag for permission to issue weapons to the regiment, quoting the reasons. The Regent granted permission. The Headquarters chose a date to hand over the weapons. It informed the personnel who came to collect the weapons that they should come to the Headquarters on a certain day to receive them. The Headquarters sent a request to the Kashag, Tse Office and Regent's office to send their representatives to witness the process of issuing the weapon on the day that had been fixed. On that day, seats were arranged on the balcony linked to the Headquarters. The armoury was slightly dark inside, so a few oil lamps were lighted to brighten the room. All other necessary arrangements were made there. When the government's representatives arrived, the two Commanders-in-Chief showed them the Kashag's sanction letter and explained the procedure of issuing weapons. The representative from the Tse Office had brought with him the stamp of the Tse Office; the stamp was in a pouch, which had been sealed. The pouch was checked as to whether its seal had been tampered or not. The pouch was found properly sealed. So it was opened and the stamp was taken out. The army secretaries brought the armoury register and presented it to the two Commanders-in-Chief, who checked the serial number of the last rifle issued from the Shol Armoury. They then went to the armoury. The main gate of the armoury faced to the east, opposite the doorsteps of the Army Headquarters. The officer in charge of cleaning the Army Headquarters handed the stamp and key of the armoury to the Tse Office representative, who checked the key pouch as to whether its seal was broken or not. Finding it properly sealed, he opened the pouch, took out the key and unlocked the door. Directly opposite the door was a spacious room with many pillars, resembling an assembly hall. Inside the room were many cupboards along the sides. The officer in charge of cleaning gave the keys of the cupboards, sealed in a case, to the Tse official, who opened the cupboards with the keys. Starting with the serial number after that of the last issued rifle, the exact number of rifles was taken out. There were many soldiers standing in a line along the staircases up to the balcony of the Headquarters, and the rifles were passed along the line one by one to the balcony. When the required quantities of guns, ammunition, oil tins, cleaning threads, etc., had been taken out, the armoury was closed and a triangle-shape stamp (*gling gsum ma*) was impressed on the bolt and the door was then locked. After that, the same stamp was embossed on the main gate of the armoury and the gate was locked. After that, the keys were put in the pouch, which was also sealed. Finally, all the officials gathered on the balcony.

Regarding the wax-seal, though some experienced people may know about it, those who are hearing about it for the first time will wonder what it is. The representative of the Tse Office would carry with him either the silver-seal or the *lingsuma* seal. Whichever it was, the official would bring it wrapped in a cloth, and including a red wax and a spatula to apply wax on the seal. When the red wax is smeared on the face of the seal, it is called *zhal-tshal*. I am just describing it here.

After that, all the representatives as well as the two Commanders-in-Chief put their signatures on the bottom of the register. A receipt was prepared, which read as "As per the proposal put up the Army Headquarters, ...x....quantity of British short-barreled rifles, ...x...boxes of bullets, ...x... boxes of oil-tins, ...x... bundles of wiping cloth, ...x... rolls of cleaning threads and ...x... wooden boxes were taken out from the Armoury. The doors of the Armoury were thereafter locked and sealed, and the keys were handed over to the Caretaker of the Army Headquarters." On the bottom of the receipt, the weapons collectors and the two Commanders-in-Chief put their signatures and the seal of the Tse Office. The register was then handed over to the two army secretaries. The seal was put back into the pouch, which was sealed and handed over back to the Tse official. The procedure of issuing the weapons was now finished. After that, a lunch was served to all the members.

The next day, the weapons collectors came to the Army Headquarters. A written guarantee was taken from them. The guarantee read: "I/we, (name/names), received ....(item names) as mentioned in the receipt, from the government, and I/we promise to hand them over to the regiment, without delay, immediately after our arrival in Domey."

As per the rule, the complete serial nos. of all the rifles had to be written one by one in the receipt, instead of writing briefly, for example, "from this serial number to this serial number." The two Commander-in-Chief after that went to the Kashag to obtain a road pass for the weapons collectors for their return journey. They at the same time gave the guarantee taken from the weapons collectors to the Kashag. The Kashag gave them a letter to be given to the regiment concerned by the weapons collectors. The letter stated: "As per your request and in accordance with a recommendation made by the Army Headquarters, weapons, as detailed in the receipt, have been handed over to the weapons collectors...x.... Immediately after they arrive, you must receive the weapons and care for them just like your own property and make sure that you are able to return them later. Regarding the old guns, you should hand them back to the armoury of the Governor-General of Kham from where they had been issued to you."

The guarantee taken from the weapons collectors was given to the army secretaries, who put it in the file containing documents concerning agreements, promissory notes and others. Until the weapons collectors could arrange for horses to carry them, they kept the weapons on the balcony of the Army Headquarters, guarded by security guards at all times. After they had got the horses, they set out on their return journey, with the weapons, starting from the gate of the Army Headquarters.

As seen above, in order to use the government's weapons, first of all a requisition had to be submitted to offices of various levels for their approval. The withdrawal and issuing of weapons must be done in the presence of all the representatives of the Tse, Sho and Kashag and the two Commanders-in-Chief—no one was allowed to take out or issue weapons at their own discretion.

We had many other tasks besides such secretarial jobs. Whenever the two Commanders-in-Chief assigned a task to any of us five staff members, whoever was the most suited to it, we used to help each other.

In those days, we did not have typewriters and other mechanical equipment, as we have nowadays. We had to write by hand. Sometimes, if we were not able to finish an important letter during office time, we used to take it home to finish.

Regarding the office hours, all the staff had to report to the office at nine in the morning and they were not allowed to leave the office before 4 pm. This rule was uniform to all the government's offices. Except on official holidays and Saturdays, the office was open every day.

As for the income for the Tibetan Army Headquarters, it did not have any source of income, such as agricultural or nomadic production. Once many years before, the government had recruited soldiers from northern Tibet, but they faced difficulties with the new weather and environment of Lhasa. Therefore, later they were excused from military service and made to give *dmag dod* (money or goods paid in lieu of military service). This system seemed to have started several years before. The total money collected from 39 Hor tribes, Khamdol Targo Lagyab, Kharta, Shingyer, Drongpa Lhojang, Gyertse and Gyerge of northern Tibet came around 1,000 Tibetan *tam* coins.

Initially, the Army Headquarters had only two army secretaries as office assistants. Their salary was small. Therefore, the *dmag dod* collected from northern region of Tibet in place of military service was granted to the two army secretaries as a part of their salary. I heard that when Phulung Surpa was serving as an army secretary, he used to hire men to collect money for him. After I joined the Headquarters, Kungo Tenpa Jamyang sent his representatives to collect *dmag dod* during his lifetime. Even after his death, his family sent men to collect *dmag dod* for two or three years, reasoning that they had some pending works to be completed. I do not remember who collected *dmag dod* thereafter.

During my time, when the *dmag dod* collectors arrived back, they would hand over the money to the treasurer of the Army Headquarters, the post held by a *rupon* officer. Though the main financial responsibility of the Headquarters was on the two Commanders-in-Chief, the task of maintaining accounts and cash was entrusted to the treasurer appointed by them. The money was used for the Summer Picnic of the Headquarters and the salary of the two Commanders-in-Chief and other staff of the Army Headquarters. An account book was maintained and all the income and expenditure were recorded properly, and all kinds of transactions were supported by bills and receipts, verified and approved by the two Commanders-in-Chief. At the end of every year, the two heads of the Headquarters used to present the account statements to the Kashag for audit. The accounts were audited annually and closed, rather than accumulating accounts over many years. From the money collected as *dmag dod*, around 200 *tam* were loaned on interest to people to generate income for the Headquarters. Therefore, the money did not go to waste.

One thing that I remember is that during the time of Khenchung Tenpa Jamyang and Nangkarwa as the Commanders-in-Chief, it was decided to Tibetanize all the English military commands and terms of the Tibetan army. Though initially the English military commands seemed impressive, gradually the pronunciation of the English words degenerated and sounded very funny when used by the troops. If people who knew English heard them, they would laugh. If they were in Tibetan and both the speakers and listeners were Tibetan, they would find it easy to understand and learn them. Therefore, the Headquarters planned to translate them into Tibetan gradually. It was also planned to Tibetanize the uniform of the Tibetan Army. A proposal was submitted to the government to change the British uniform of the Tibetan army into Tibetan and make *nambu chupa* as the new uniform as the cloth was available in the country. The government agreed. However, the idea of translation of the English military terms into Tibetan could not be put into practice at that time.

As regards how the Tibetan army uniform was Tibetanized, the Tibetan Army Headquarters purchased white *nambu* cloths. They decided to make the army uniform gray to make it distinct from their civil dress. They sent the *nambu* cloths to the Nepalese Dry house to colour them. From the cloths were made two kinds of *chupa*, one with a multicolored collar and one with a single coloured collar, two different hats and shoes. The Two Commanders-in-Chief dressed the gatekeepers in the new army uniforms and took them to the Regent Reting at his residence to show him the uniforms. He chose the *chupa* with the coloured collar as the army uniform. As for the uniform hats, the summer hat was gray with a conical shape, resembling the mouth of a big clarinet, and could be folded from the back. The winter hat was the same as the summer hat, but it had earflaps with lamp skin liners. The shoes had thick soles and long angles, made from gray *nambu* material.

Before that, every regiment used to send a team to collect money for uniforms (*dmag chas kyi dod*). After that, a system of collecting brown *nambu* cloth instead of money was made. Each regiment was given a piece of original *nambu* cloth as the sample and a length of thread, each end bearing the stamp of the Army Headquarters, as the standard of measure. Whenever *dingpon* or *chupon* officers from a regiment went to collect *nambu*, they had to take with them the *nambu* sample and the measuring thread. An edict was circulated throughout the country to this effect.

Not long after that, the following things happened. When the Tibetan Army Headquarters was established, the impression of the old round seal was removed from the hands of all the soldiers and the impression of the new seal was put on. Later it was discovered that some retired soldiers of U-Tsang, the Khadang Regiment, Shigatse and Gyantse still had on their hands the impressions of old army seals of different designs. When investigated, it was found that their deputy *dapon* officers had done them. In order to prevent such things happening in future, the Army Headquarters made a new seal embossed with the words "Tibetan Army Headquarters" in Tibetan *uchen* script and decided to emboss the new seal on the hands of all the army members, both officers and soldiers. The Headquarters kept one seal for its own office to use for the soldiers who were in Lhasa at that time. At that time, the Shigatse soldiers and *gyena* reserves had been granted recreational leave and they were in Tsang. Instead of summoning them all to Lhasa, Dapon Kyipugpa Junior of the Thadang Regiment was sent to Shigatse, while the two army secretaries—Nornangpa and I—were sent to Tsang, with the new seal and an edict, to change the seals of the Tsang soldiers. We first went to Shigatse. There we called all the soldiers residing in and near Shigatse and changed the seals on their hands. After that we went to Gyantse, where we also called all the soldiers and officers residing in Gyantse and nearby districts and changed their seals. We received an order from the Headquarters that we should summon the soldiers posted for border duty in Dromo to Gyantse in two groups instead of going there. We did as we were ordered. After we had finished sealing all the soldiers and officers in Tsang, we returned to Lhasa and gave our work reports to our heads of department. After that, the seal on the hands of all the Tibetan army members became uniform.

The Tibetan military and civil laws were different. Cases of soldiers fighting or breaking the law in towns had to be reported, along with the offender/s, to the Army Headquarters. Minor cases could be handed over to the regiment concerned for investigation and a decision. If a regiment was not able to deal with a particular case, it had to refer the case to the Army Headquarters, which would judge the case and pass a verdict in accordance with the severity of the offence. Military legal cases were handled only by the Army Headquarters, not by the Lhasa Mayor, Shol Security Office, or Shalngo Office as in the case of Lhasa Monlam Festival.

Since the Tibetan Army Headquarters was founded during the time of the Thirteenth Dalai Lama, some people may think that the institution of the Tibetan army came into being only with the creation of the Tibetan Army Headquarters and that the Tibetan army had no head office before that. I will clear up this misconception. In the past, Shol Dorjeling Armoury was the oldest as well as the main base of the Tibetan army. I have found many pieces of evidence to prove this. For example, in the middle storey of the armoury building, where the Army Headquarters was based, there was an office for the *dapon*, a room supported by six pillars. Below the *dapon*'s office were the offices of the *rupons* and *gyapons*. The names of these offices were still used in those days. From this we know that the building was the meeting venue for the army officers of U-Tsang. Moreover, on the balcony, there was also a chapel of two official protector deities called red and black Dharma protectors erected for both religious and political purposes. In the chapel were images of Palden Lhamo and Chamsing deities, but I don't know how to identify who was black and who was red. One monk from Dorga Monastery was appointed permanently to perform ritual functions in the chapel. The government had given him a letter authorizing him to draw his wages, ritual equipment and offering materials from his monastery. The Army Headquarters did not provide him with a salary. This further shows that the armoury existed before the foundation of the Army Headquarters.

During the Monlam Festival held every year, private horse racers used to borrow costumes from the government's armoury. The representatives of the Tse Office, the Kashag and the Sho Office acted as the witnesses when the costumes were lent. In the armoury, helmets were kept in one corner in stacks, while shields, armour, mirrors were kept in more than 2000 leather boxes stacked in another corner. This proves that the building had been the headquarters of the Tibetan army in the past. There were many other military tools in the armoury, such as the cavalry costumes worn by the Yasor cavalry and the soldiers of the eight camps of Dham during the Great Monlam Festival when they were performing in procession with the Black and Red Dharma Protectors of Tibet. Their costumes had been put in leather boxes, but two complete costumes worn by the bearers of the images of the two Dharma protectors had been put in two boxes made from tiger skins. All the helmets and armour shone, without a speck of dust or rust on them. The edges of the waist belts and mirrors had been ornamented with different patterns such as chains of flowers engraved with gold. One of the helmets had on its front five or six Urdu words, similar to those written by a calligraphic pen, engraved with solid gold. All these articles had an excellent finish without the slightest trace of hammer or solder.

There was a type of armour called *a-khrab*, or Mail, made up of thousands of interlocked little iron rings. There was a helmet called *sog rmog*, or Mongol helmet, made of iron. They were for the cavalry soldiers. As for the Simchung soldiers, they used to wear *byang khrab*, or Lamellar, which were made up of overlapping small iron plates. The helmet was designed in the same style. They were for infantry soldiers. So the cavalry and infantry had different armour and helmets.

The used shells fired during the *torgyag* ceremony of the Monlam Festival were collected by some young men from Shol. The shells were shown to the representatives of the Tse and Sho offices on the same day to request new zinc to make new shells for the following year. The government would grant a few lumps of zinc from a government store. In the store, there were many Simpa's regalia hats called *sba sgor* hanging in a line on wooden rods. There were more than 2,000 leather pouches containing big and small bullet shells of Tibetan homemade guns made from black stones hanging on rods. There were also leather cases called *ko-tho* containing shells, in the same quantities and stored in the same way as above. In one corner, there were stacks of zinc material, enough to make many sacks-full of bullets. Bullet material was taken from here whenever a need arose. Regarding the fuel used for smelting and making bullets, coals were fetched from an armoury behind the Chakpori hill called Menchu Gozo (*sman chu go mdzod*), which was earlier called Menchu Sekhang (*sman chu rdzas khang*) when I was small. So, it appeared that there was a large arms factory. Because of these reasons I say that Dorjeling Armoury had been the base of the Tibetan army headquarters since the early days.

I have not seen any ancient military equipment such as arrows, bows, swords and spears in the armouries that I have visited. They must be in other armouries.

Arrows, bows, sword, spears and slings were the only Tibetan weapons in ancient times. Later, Tibetans started making a gun called bod mda', or the Tibetan indigenous gun, which became popular throughout Tibet. After that, many kinds of guns and swords spread through Tibet. According to Tibetan oral tradition, there were swords with names such as dmar stag bzhi ma, dmar mtso dag ma, rla nam mkha' rgyal mtshan, so gri ya ma 'gan di, dmar pad ma can, sla rgya mtsho ma and so on. As for Tibetan guns, they had such names as *sog dar ma chu 'bab, sog g.yas gcud, sog g.yon gcud, sog sgam mda' ma, hor nya mig ma, sog gling bzhi ma, 'dzam grags* and so on.

The Tibetan troops used Tibetan home-made weapons such as swords and guns during the Anglo-Tibetan battle at Chumig Shongka in the Wood-Dragon year. As noted above, the Tibetan weapons were made by the Tibetans themselves using their own skills. The materials for ammunition were granted by the government. Doubtlessly Tibet was independent and self-sufficient, without having to depend on any foreign countries. However, due to our inability to move ourselves forward towards modernity, our country lagged behind, and our weapons became obsolete. During his reign, the Thirteenth Dalai Lama set up an arms factory at Drip, on the southern bank of the river Tsangpo, and started producing a gun, with 13 bullet chambers, in a large quantity in order to improve the strength of the Tibetan army. Soon after that, the factory was shifted to Lupukgang in Lhasa and was named it Mikyi Trulsokhang, meaning "Joyful Machine Factory," and some lay officials and monk officials were appointed to manage the factory. In this way, Tibetans started making weapons again. I saw some of the guns produced by that factory.

Around that time, the Chinese used to make frequent incursions into Dokham from different sides and caused harassment at border areas in order to invade Tibet. The Dalai Lama was compelled to think about how to suppress the invaders. At that time, Tibet's closest friend was the British government of India. The Tibetan government bought large quantities of various weapons from the British government of India. In addition, the Tibetan government produced many shotguns and bullets at the Drapchi Factory, modeled on the British shotgun, using Tibetan's own techniques and skills. I heard that the guns were issued to some regiments for their use. The factory also produced cannons and shells. It was said that the gun makers gave demonstrations of target firing of the weapons. After the Drapchi Factory was founded, the Mikyi Factory at Drip was shifted to Drapchi and combined into the Drapchi Factory.

Even after the Thirteenth Dalai Lama passed away, the Tibetan government purchased many different kinds of weapons needed in war from the British government of India. The weapons included a large cannon called a Howitzer, 10 pound Tank, 3-inch motor, machinegun, Lewis gun, Bren gun, Sten gun, shotgun, long-nozzle rifles, ammunitions, spare parts, handguns with different shape and capacity, etc. I do not know the exact quantities. There were about 20 regiments in Tibet, each having sufficient weapons. The government had weapons in its arsenals sufficient for more than 50, 000 soldiers.

The Tibetan government's main armouries were Dorjeling Armoury at Shol, Dradulkhang at Tse Potala, Shol Armory, Tsedeyangshar Armory, Norbulingka Armoury and Menchu Armory at Chakpori. There were other government armouries at different district headquarters, including one in Chamdo under the Governor-General of Kham, one under the Governor of Western Tibet, one under the Governor of Northern Tibet, the armoury of Shang Ganden Chokor Monastery and the armoury of Lhatse Dzong. In around 1949, when Shodrung Kyipugpa and I were serving as the Gyantse district officers, the government sent us a large quantity of bullets for the British shotguns. We put them in the government's large barn at the back of the fort and we sealed the barn. That was also an armoury.

As regards how the weapons were kept in an armoury, Shol Dorjeling Armoury, for example, had wooden boxes of different sizes for keeping weapons. Weapons which did not have cases were wrapped in tarpaulin. There were many wooden cupboards to keep guns. The rifles were arranged vertically with their tips up on the shelves. To prevent rusting of all kinds of weapons, they were properly oiled. They were kept with great care. Similarly, all other armouries kept their weapons properly.

At the entrance to the Tibetan Army Headquarters, there was a room whose door faced towards the west. In it were 500 British shotguns, many boxes, each filled with 1,000 bullets, wiping cloths, oil-tins, cleaning thread and so forth. This room was not an armoury. These arms were reserved to be used in time of emergency, and they were under the care of the Headquarters. They were arranged on the shelves nose upward, as in the Shol armory.

At ground floor, there was another room with many windows where the army leaders met and worked. The room contained many damaged Chinese guns; these guns had been seized from the Chinese troops when they surrendered to the Governor-General of Kham Jampa Tendar after they suffered defeat in the Water-Rat year war with the Tibetan forces. At that time, the damaged Chinese weapons were sent to Lhasa for repair. Three of the guns had sharp cuts on them, allegedly made by knives thrown by Tibetan soldiers. There were about five 6-guns; I do not know whether they were Tibetan or Chinese. These guns were not in the account of the armoury, but in the account of Headquarters. These are just what I have seen.

History of the Simpa Guards

The interior division of the Simpa Guards had many ceremonial activities to do on the Monlam Festival every year. First of all, when they arrived in Lhasa, they had to make an arrival report, which was to be done in a peculiar manner. On the 21st day of the 12th Tibetan month, both the leaders and soldiers of the Simpa Army had to gather behind Kani stupa near Shol Drago. The two army secretaries [of the Army Headquarters] also had to be present. The two armoury-keepers of the Headquarters also had to attend, carrying both the white and the yellow military banners. The dress of the Yeru section of the Simpa was a white *nambu chupa* and that of the Yonru section was yellow *nambu chupa*. They wore the same *barkor* hats. The two flag bearers would stand behind the stupa and look at the Potala Palace frequently [to see whether the Namgyal Monastery's monks were appearing to blow conch-shells], and remain alert. At around 9 am, two monks from Namgyal Monastery at the Palace would sound conch-shells. The flag bearers of the Simpa Army would immediately raise their flags. The flags had to be raised immediately the conch was sounded. If this was done, their arrival report was correct. On one occasion, the secretariat at Potala summoned the two army secretaries there and rebuked us, "Yesterday, when the Simpa army made their arrival report, they raised their flags before the monks blew conch-shells. Why, give us the reasons."

After that, the Simpa troops would march in parade formation in two columns, led by the flag bearers, followed by the two army secretaries, two armoury guards, four government's archers, Tsochen Umdze, *dingpon*s and Simpa soldiers in order. The march would go through the main gate of Shol village and stop at the government's stable, where the two officers in charge of the armoury had arranged a *chemar*[6] and *changphu*[7] as well as mattresses and tables. Everyone would sit down on the mattresses. Tea and *chang* would be served to them. The *dingpon* would give a list of soldiers under his command at the march to the two armoury keepers, who would read out the names one by one. Each soldier had to say "present" when his name was read, and go clockwise and stand in line on the left side. After all these events were finished, the troops would go to receive their ceremonial costumes from the two armoury keepers, who had collected them from the Shol Mint. However, I have not witnessed how it was done.

Two armoury keepers were appointed by the *Dapon* of U. From the next day until the until the Monlam Festival finished, the *dingpon* officers of the Simpa regiment would wear *skra lcog* (the hairstyle of lay government officials) and the Lhasa people used to call them one-month government officials.

---

6 chemar: a mixture of roast barley flour and butter used by Tibetans as an auspicious offering during the New Year celebrations.

7 changphu: first pouring of chang, usually offered to gods, as religious or ceremonial offering.

After this, a *dingpon* officer would come to the two-army secretaries every morning to ask whether they had to do drill practice on that day. The venue of the practice was the circumambulation path near Menthang, to the opposite of Langkhang and behind the Potala Palace.

There were two types of parade march—*'bu khrid* (worm style) and *zhag sgor mo* (intestine pattern). The *zhag-sgor* was called the full parade march and the other one was called the brief parade march. The *zhag-sgor* got the name probably because of its similarity to the intestine in shape. Regarding the full march, firstly some men were sent to stand at suitable locations on the path as the marks where the marchers were to pass through. After that, a government's archer, brandishing a sword in the air, walked in a slow and graceful manner. Immediately, the bugle men would blow their bugles. After this, the Simpa soldiers would start marching, with equal steps, without breaking lines. They were to march in a clockwise direction around the men standing on the path and appear from the left side, in two columns. In *'bu 'khrid* march, the soldiers did not need to go round and round; it was a single round, just as a snake moves on a ground.

On the actual day of the military display, the Simpa members were in full warrior dress. Firstly, the four Uchen, carrying spears in their hands and wearing back shields decorated with red and black yak's hair around them, would perform military acts, shouting and acting like warriors, such as doing a demonstration of throwing spears.

After that, the archers would march, carrying arrows and bows and shields. From two sides, the Uchung would give a military display, shouting at each other and finally acting as if they were fighting.

After this, the troops carrying *zamdrag* guns marched in two columns. In their right hands, they would carry matchlocks with the wicks lit. The guns were carried slanted and the matchlock wicks were raised high. Their knees were raised high while marching. With fearful facial expressions, walking in an exaggerated manner, their leaders would do heroic acts and shout boastful words. At the end of their military demonstration, they would fire nine shots.

As noted above, when the leaders finished their acts, the bugle players would blow their bugles together and then shout "ki hi·hi". This complete practice was repeated four times.

For the Tse Gutor Ceremony, the Simpa members had to gather in the morning at the Deyangshar, a large balcony on the Potala Palace. They had to make prostrations at the bottom of Dyangshar before they went up. The two army secretaries would sit on brown cushions spread for them. The Simpa members, including the storekeepers, were seated on long mattresses, below the clarinet players of Namgyal Monastery. The Potala's cook would bring in a silver teapot and serve tea to all the assembled members. After that, the Simpa members would perform military drills. They would fire nine shots (*dgu shog*) at the end of their performances. Nine shots means the firing squad had nine men, each of whom would fire one shot.

On that occasion, Namgyal Monastery normally organized a *torgyag* ceremony. The Simpa soldiers used to follow the *torma*, which would pass through the Phuntsok Gate, until the *torma* reached the torma ground at the outer stone pillar, while firing guns that produced a quacking sound. After the *torma* was thrown, they would fire nine shots and returned to their place.

On the occasion of the great visit by the Regent, the Simpa soldiers and Shol staff would jointly clean the roads, arrange white painted stones on the roadsides, draw auspicious signs on the road and burn incense on the sides of the road where the Regent would travel, beginning from Shalkhar Ngadong to the eastern side of the Willow Grove. Many people would wait in a queue along the road to greet the Regent. The Simpa army had the responsibility of security and order during the visit. The Lhasa Mayor and other officials would lead the Regent with burning incense. This road was supposed to be the border between Lhasa and Shol.

For the invocation ceremony of the Palden Lhamo deity, the Simpa members, including their leaders, had to do ceremonial duties on the hills of the Palden Lhamo and Pehar deities. The Uchen and Uchung would perform military acts, and after each dialogue, the bugle men would blow their bugles. At the same time, the two army secretaries and leaders of the Simpa Army had to raise their swords and shout "ki hi hi".

Not long after I joined the Army Headquarters, most probably during the time of Regent Reting, the Regent and Kashag ministers went to the Barkor to watch the Butter Ceremony of the Monlam Festival. On that occasion, we two army secretaries and the leaders of the Simpa Army stretched ropes along the narrow streets of the Barkor to prevent the public from causing security problems. Sometimes people would not care about the ropes and would rush into the streets. In some areas where there were large crowds, people would sometimes throw stones, shout or push against the ropes. Some people would also hurl bad words. It was better for us to behave as if we were deaf, or else they could easily have charged and beaten us. Since it was not possible for us to control the crowd by the ropes alone, we requested the two Commanders-in-Chief to send the government's soldiers who had arrived in the Barkor to perform a complimentary parade march to help us control the crowd. Our request was granted. After that, it became customary for the army regiments to help the Simpa Guards in managing security in the Barkor during the Butter Lamp Ceremony. After that, even during the Dalai Lama's visit to the Butter Lamp Festival, the security arrangements were done in the same manner.

On the day, the two army secretaries went to meet the two Shalngo, the officers in charge of security of the Lhasa Monlam, at their residence, and told them, "The Regent and the cabinet ministers will be coming to witness the Butter Lamp ceremony tonight, and there is also a military parade. Therefore, a large crowd of people will gather there. Not a single monk should be allowed into the Barkor until the Regent and ministers have finished their visit, and you should instruct the monks accordingly." The two Shalngo told us that we had already given clear instructions to the officials and house masters of all the monasteries, and not to worry about this. They said the monks who were to bear the butter lamps and *tormas* had been instructed separately. The teachers and their assistants would patrol the area. In this way, a strict order was given so that there was not a single monk to be seen in the area.

On the 18th day (of the 1st Tibetan month), there was an archery contest called Chogye Thogda (*bco brgyad thog mda'*) on the picnic ground at Dzongyab. All the leaders and the soldiers of the Simpa would gather there. The armoury keepers of the Army Headquarters had prepared seats inside the grandstand on the ground. The two army secretaries, dressed in their official yellow costumes, would sit in the grandstand, where normally the cabinet ministers sat, in a dignified and pompous manner. There was a display of arrow-shooting from horseback, in which the Julangpa and government staff members would participate. After that, about 20 men from the Yeru and the Yonru sections would run a race. This was followed by a long-distance archery contest. The participants were the four government archers and several archers from the common people. Each archer would shoot two arrows in the first round and one *ju* arrow, which was heavier and longer than a normal arrow, in the second round. During the contest, all the contestants would sing aloud "come to receive the arrow-letters," in a long and melodious tune. The two *dingpon*s of the Simpa would stand up on tables and shout archery words. The archers had to mark their arrows with their own names and marks with the help of the two army secretaries. During the archery contest, no one was allowed to go near the target or onto the contest ground. Some Simpa soldiers were sent to supervise the contest. They would watch from a distance. After the end of the competition, the two armoury keepers, the four official archers, Tsochen Umdze and two senior *dingpon* officers would visit the target to inspect the marking. They would discuss from a distance and judge the arrows' positions, before the seeing the names on the arrows, and decide the first, second and third positions.

After that, there were wrestling matches between two teams of Yeru and Yonru. The wrestlers would be naked, covering only their male organs. There were two referees, who would check whether the wrestlers had applied oil on their bodies or had sharp fingernails. To win the game, one should not only able to throw the opponent down, but be able to make his back touch the ground. During the match, the wrestlers were not allowed to grab each other's hair or twist each other's legs. After the matches, the team members would put *chupa*s on their wrestlers. The armoury keepers would put scarves on the winners. This was a friendly match as a preparation for the final wrestling match between the Simpa and Dam Gyeshog teams to be held on the Ramoche ground on the evening of the 23rd day after the Drapchi stocktaking was finished.

The two armoury keepers, the four government's archers and *dingpon*s of the Simpa Guards—dressed in new winter uniforms—and the Umdze, Uchen, Uchung and other members of the Simpa, in their civil dress, would assemble there, carrying arrow-cases. The buglers would carry their bugles with them. As a rehearsal for the final day, the Tsochen Umdze, Uchen and Uchung brandished their swords in the air, as the Umdze sang an epic ballad (*ljags brkyangs*), while the four Uchen sang in chorus. At the same time, they would walk, while dancing.

Regarding the meaning of "*ljags brkyangs*", it is a long ballad describing and praising the landscape of Tibet and the heroic achievements of the Tibetan kings and the ministers, and praying for the progress of the Tibetan government and its future success, and so forth. Between each interval, the buglers would sound their bugles, followed by shouting "ki hi hi".

The winner of the long-distance archery contest and the first three positions in the running race were presented with tri-coloured silk scarves and all other participants with ordinary scarves. I do not know how these expenses were met. At the end, everyone would participate in the incense-burning ceremony and shout, "May the gods win!"

On the 23rd day, at around 4 pm after the audit of the Drapchi Office was over, there was a wrestling contest between the Simpa and Dham Geshog teams behind the Ramoche Temple, organized by Dham Gyeshog. There were ten men from each team. The wrestlers were naked, covering only their male organs. The wrestling took place in the presence of all the leaders of the two sides and was watched by many spectators, and the way the event was organized was similar to the archery contest held on the 18th day. The winner would be congratulated by presenting them with *padar* flags.

The 24th day was observed as the Torgyag Ceremony. At sunrise on that day, all the Simpa leaders and soldiers assembled at the exterior stone-pillar at Shol. The two army secretaries, clad in the Gyalu costume, had to arrive there on time. The two officers in charge of the armoury at Simpa and the four government's archers also had to be present. Their dress included a yellow shirt, a brownish woolen garment, a golden coloured scarf (*kyerag*), *jalam* shoes and a *bogto* hat. They would also wear knives at their waists and carry whips in their hands. The Dingpon officers had to wear the Gyalu costume. The Tsochen's dress included a dark blue gown with many plaits, similar to the non-ceremonial dress of the Simpa soldiers, and a shirt made from multicolored silk (*gos chen*) cloth. They had a rainbow-coloured upper garment, shoes made from leather, whose edges were ornamented with green *thornam* cloth[8], and a *bakor* hat. They wore red shawls on their shoulders. A sword, *khugdra*, and seal case were hung from their waists on the right side. On the right side of their body they held bow and arrow cases. The ordinary soldiers would wear the complete set of armour and carry *khorsum* weapons. The buglers would carry copper bugles with them. They would conduct a roll call, after which they would perform weaponry drills. After that, they would form two lines and march back, led by the flag bearers, followed by the two army secretaries, the two officers in charge of the armoury, the four official archers, dingpon officers, Tsochen Umdze, Uchen, Uchung and the rest of the Simpa soldiers. The Uchen and Uchung would perform chivalric acts as they marched. The march had to go up to the Shide Yulkha Teng through the eastern side of Gonseb from the east of Willow Grove. There, the Yarsor officer, his servants, Gyansangma and deputy *dapon*s and others had pitched a large tent. The flag or the banner of Simpa Yeru had white flaps and that of Simpa Yonru had brownish flaps. The Yeru's costume was a white *chupa* and the Yonru's was a brownish *chupa*.

The Yarsor and his cavalry also had to participate in the event. Until they arrived at the Barkor, the cavalry and the Simpa Guards had a length of time for rest. On that day, it was customary to fire the cannon called *lugma dongsugma*[9] when the *torma* was being burnt. The junior Datsab, the junior army secretary, the two armoury keepers, the government's archers and two or three *dingpon*s, with two assistants, who were to carry the shells, went to the lower end of Tsedrung Lingka Park, near Kalsang Bridge. Datsab had a riding horse, but others did not. They rode the horses of Yarsor's servants, saying that it was customary. Sheldrong Namchag Shal ngo was an experienced cannon firer. A master carpenter took measurements of the spot and drew a line on it to position the cannon. Some young men from Shol village had brought the shells. There were different kinds of cannons with different nicknames. The biggest one was called Kugpa, meaning "dumb". The next biggest was Khabarma, followed by Chamsing, Sinmo Kudrey and Sinmo Kushon. The two smallest ones had no nicknames, because they did not have shells. A list had been given to the armoury keepers detailing the number of shots to be fired from each cannon. The deputy *dapon* instructed the master carpenter and the two Namchag Shalngo that they should conduct the event successfully.

After that, they returned to Gonseb Shar. By the time they reached there, the Yarsors had just finished their ceremonial performances, according to tradition. They had deployed two men at the Tsuglakhang temple to inform them when the procession should leave for the Barkor. When the Yarsors received the message

---

8 Thornam (*thor snam*) is a cloth imported from Torgo country.
9 Lugma dongsugma (*lugs ma mdong gzugs ma*) means a cast metal artillery weapon in the shape of a tea-churner

to proceed, they immediately told the procession to be ready to leave for Barkor. The first line in the procession was the deputy *dapon*-s and his servants mounted on horses. After them were the leaders and soldiers of the Simpa Guards, followed by the bearers of the images of the two Dharma Protectors. A distance of 4 or 5 arm-span was kept between each group. After that, there were two Yarsor officers of the Dham regiment dressed in rich attire, followed by the Master Chamberlain and cavalry who were costumed similarly to the Yarsors. After them, following at a distance of 4 or 5 yards, came the main Yarsors and cavalry. The march started from the gate of Tsemonling, went through Shesar Gang from the right side of Yabshi Phunkhang's residence and finally reached the Barkor.

Regarding the Simpa Guards' march, the bearers of the flags were in the first line. They were followed by the two army secretaries. After that there were the two armoury keepers, followed by the government's archers, Tsochen Umdze, Uchen, Uchung and *dingpon* leaders, leading their own soldiers. While marching, the Uchen and Uchung made heroic gestures and fired quack-making guns in the air several times. They halted their march at a corner of the Shingra fence. There, led by the two Datsab officers, all the leaders of the Simpa, including the two army secretaries, offered prostrations near the willow tree called Jowoi Utra towards the Dalai Lama's Palace. They again went around the Barkor. By that time, the Yarsor officer and his cavalry, the last group in the parade, had finished their first circumambulation of the Barkor square. While the Yarsor and his retinue prostrated at Jowoi Utra, his cavalrymen waited at the eastern and southern sides. After that the Yasor officer and his cavalry made another circumambulation of the Barkor. Then the Simpa Guards (coming from the Barkor) performed at Jowoi Utra all the ancient military drills they had practised earlier. Having done this, they again went around the Barkor for the third time. Meanwhile, the Yarsor officer and his cavalry arrived from the Barkor and received scarves at Thonpa.

The Simpa Guards waited at Sabog Gang until the time came to follow the *torma*. In the meantime, the two deputy *dapons* rested below the gate of the Shingra fence. Many local people came to offer scarves to them. Sometimes, the Ragshag used to invite the leaders of the Simpa Guards to his lower residence, where he had arranged tea and *chang*. At that time, the manager of Ragshag's estate, carrying a long scarf, would make a request to the Simpa leaders, saying, "The guardian of our residence is very strict. As usual, do not let the Yonru fire the guns until the marchers pass their house." Therefore, even during the actual Torgyag Ceremony, only the Yeru would fire five or six shots in the air when passing through the Ragshag's residence. However, it is difficult to know whether they did so in fear of the protector deity of the house or the house itself.

After that, *torma* bearers, flag bearers, monastic heads, monk officials and monk-musicians from Nampar Gyalwa Phende Leksheling Monastery and Drepung

Tantric College arrived at the Torma ground near Lupug, with a grand procession. By that time, the Yarsor cavalry had finished the third circumambulation of the Barkor and marched quickly after the monks. The Simpa guards, who were at Sabogang, stood in formation facing toward the north. The two deputy *dapon* officers, the two army secretaries and the leaders of the Simpa Guards stood in the front line in the order of their ranks, ready to march forward. In the meantime, the Nechung oracle entered into a trance at Menying Chog and proceeded to the Jowo Utra, two willow trees near Jokhang Temple, where he performed a *dgu 'cham* dance. After that, he turned towards the Simpa guards and lifted his right foot slightly up in a dancing mode. After that, led by the two deputy *dapons*, the army secretaries and other Simpa leaders raised their swords in the air and shouted, "Lha Gyalo! (May the gods win!)" and "Ki hi hi!" While doing so both the Nechung oracle and the Simpa team ran towards each other in a very joyful fashion. After this, the oracle sat on a chair and gave an audience to all the Simpa guards. He then proceeded after the *torma*. If he walked too slowly, his attendants would ask the Simpa guards to fire a shot in the air to awaken him. When two or three shots were fired, the oracle would come to his senses and quicken his walking pace. After that, when the *torma* was burned, the Oracle shot an arrow at an effigy, and then returned. The Simpas fired nine-shots (*gu shog*). After they left, cannons were also fired. After that, the Yasor officer and the cavalry left in a manner called *ru 'dzings* or "mix lines", so that the Yeru went from the right side and the Yonru from the left side. Following the Simpa's procession, there were two cavalry men with spears. Both the men and horses were in full armour. The armour was borrowed from the armoury through the help of the two armoury keepers. The two men were the two duty men at Shod Office during the Tibetan New Year. The horses were provided by the government's stable at Shol.

On the 25th day, an image of Maitreya was brought out. Early in the morning, five or six Simpa guards were deployed on the racecourse that passed through Shol Drago Kani, Yuthog Lingka Park, Yuthog Bridge, Luguk Gate, etc. Their task was to see if there were any people hiding near the racetrack with an intention of hitting any private racehorse that ran in front of the government's racehorses during the horserace. Once during a horserace event during the time of the Thirteenth Dalai Lama, the Shalngo, who was a horserace participant at that time, secretly employed someone to hit any private racehorse that ran in front of the government's horse. During the race, the man hit the horse that was ahead of a government horse and the horse fell down. The Dalai Lama came to know about this and reprimanded the Shalngo for his mischief. After that, the Dalai Lama instructed the Simpa Guards to supervise the horserace.

The Great Closing Ceremony was held on the 27th day. On that day, the two army secretaries, the officers in charge of the armoury, four skilled archers representing the government, the *dingpon* officers and his attendants, Tsochen Umdze, Uchen, Uchung and all the members of the Simpa Guards, all dressed in the archers' costumes that they had worn for the archery competition on the 18th day, gathered at the picnic ground at Dzongyab. The ministers had already arrived there and were seated in the grandstand. Tsochen Umdze, Uchen and Uchung emerged on the ground to perform their ceremonial acts. The Umdze recited aloud a ballad in praise of the country, while the Uchen and Uchung chorused after him. The three went around the ground, walking with dance steps. After that, all the Simpa members would gather at the centre of the ground to make prayers, and the people from Shol village served tea to them. At that time, the clothes or anything that the participants in the horserace a few days before had dropped on the ground and which had been picked up by Shol residents were returned to the owners. The owners sent street children to collect them. Before the clothes were handed over, the children were sent to the Simpa guards assembled on the ground. The Simpa guards put *tsampa* on the children's faces, lifted them upside down and smacked their bottoms as punishment. After that, the horse-racer's articles were given to them. In the evening, after song and dance performances, the ministers returned to their homes. The Simpa guards escorted them to their residences, while singing aloud on the way. That was the final activity of the Simpa guards prescribed for the Monlam Festival of that year.

On around the 23rd day of the 2nd Tibetan month, the army secretaries, dressed in Gyalu attire, and all others in their civil dresses, had to make departure report to the Dalai Lama's secretariat office at the Potala Palace. After having an audience with the Dalai Lama, each of us was given 1 tea-cake and 4 or 5 rolls of cloth as well as cash-money in envelopes as a farewell gift. We left the Potala in line. On arrival at the inner stone-pillar (*rdo ring nang ma*), we raised our army flags and marched through the Main Gate and Shugtri Lingka up to Kalsang Bridge. This was a way of indicating that we were returning directly to our homes from the Potala Palace.

Chapter Seven

Institutional System of the Tibetan Army

Conscription system

According to the Tibetan conscription system, the government, noble families and monasteries that had landholdings in Tsang and U had to send one man from each *dmag rten* land (recruit source)[1], which was an average of 10 acres in Tsang and more than 10 acres in U, to do military service. The nomadic regions in northern Tibet were also required to provide compulsory military service. However, the reserves of the Agriculture Department, the soldiers of the Drongdrak Regiment and local militias were not drafted based on the said recruit system. An average of 10 acres of land in Tsang and more than 10 acres in U owned by the government, noble families or monasteries was fixed as a *dmag rten* for one soldier.

The government had issued a decree that each land holding family or recruit source must send a young, intelligent, healthy man to do military service, and the order was always obeyed. If a recruit source family had no qualified man to send, the family would send someone else and they would give him a salary during his service term. Generally, everyone was happy with the army tax. In times of peace, except for the government's permanent troops, all reserves were sent home to avoid putting an extra burden on people. In times of war and emergencies, the government sometimes recruited one or two extra men from each recruit source's estate to serve in the war. People were not happy with the army tax in such times. If any estate became ownerless or had no eligible men to send to do military service, another aristocratic family or a monastery would take over ownership of the estate, and send men from among their own subjects to do military service.

If a soldier deserted or was dismissed from the army as punishment, the owner of the soldier had to pay a fine. If the deserter was caught, he was either punished and kept in the army or expelled at the request of the owner.

The Tibetan recruitment system at that time was appropriate to the time and social condition of the country; no one can say that it was outmoded. Just as all other military systems in the world changed with time, the Tibetan government

---

1 A unit of land under the military tax system.

made modifications to the system of the Tibetan army continuously until the country was invaded by the Red Chinese. This is clear from the historical records.

Structure of the Tibetan Army

Each brigade (*mda' khag*) had two battalions (*ru shog*), which in turn had two companies (*brgya shog*). Each company was composed of five platoons (*lding shog*). Each platoon had two sections (*bcu shog*) and five workers. Each platoon had 26 personnel, including its leader, the Lieutenant (*lding dpon*). Each company had 231 soldiers, including the Captain (*brgya dpon*). Each battalion had 263 personnel including the Colonel (*ru dpon*). Each brigade was made up of 527 personnel, including its leader, the Brigadier (*mda' dpon*). This was the general organizational structure of all the Tibetan army regiments, although the number of their soldiers might not be exactly the same.

Distribution of arms and ammunition

Before the Chinese army of Lu-chun was driven out from Tibet in 1912, each regiment of the Tibetan army had a few Tibetan cannons called *seril* (*se ril*) and several automatic guns called *dribyangchen* (*grib yang can*). In the Water-Rat year (1912) when the Chinese troops surrendered, some weapons were seized from them, including guns called *bcu bog* and *brgyad chang*. The main weapons of the Tibetan army were Tibetan guns, swords, axes, spears, slings, etc., and they were issued to different regiments through their respective district headquarters.

In 1914 during a tripartite convention held in Simla between Britain, Tibet and China for a peace treaty, the Chinese maintained a policy of aggression against Tibet. For the defense of the country, the Tibetan government purchased many long rifles from the British government of India and distributed them among the different army units. Outdated weapons were collected and handed over to the district offices. Later, machineguns, Lewis guns, 2-inch mortars, 3-inch motors, 10-pound mortars and howitzers, along with ammunition, were dispatched on mules to different army regiments in various parts of the country. A separate artillery regiment called Chadang Simchung Regiment was created. A few cannons were also issued to the Kadang Bodyguard and Khadang Drapchi regiments.

In 1917, to improve the weaponry of the Tibetan army, British model short-range guns were issued and old long-barrel rifles were withdrawn and deposited at their respective district armories to be used in future when required. The weapons were strictly protected against misuse, and a rule was made that except on official missions no one was allowed to carry any guns for personal use.

General system of the Tibetan army

When any regiment was in U or Tsang, it was under the jurisdiction of the Tibetan Army Headquarters and when in eastern Tibet it was under the command of the Governor-General of Kham. On minor matters, the regimental leaders had the authority to make decisions.

Since antiquity, it had been customary in the army to treat the officers and elder soldiers with respect. Soldiers were obliged to obey the orders of the government. Drinking, gambling, taking French leave, quarreling and fighting, raping women, stealing, robbing and any unlawful activities were strictly prohibited. Whoever violated the laws, irrespective of whether he was a leader or ordinary soldier, the offender would be punished in accordance with the gravity of the crime.

Training system and appointment of leaders

New recruits were required to undergo various types of training for several months. They were taught various military drills, skills in dismantling and reassembling different types of weapons and identification of the different parts of guns. There were tests after the completion of this training. After that, they were trained in the use of weapons, and learned the secret codes of bugle calls as well as the rules and regulations of the army. Finally, there was battle training in which the soldiers were taught how to fight an enemy using code signs of bugles, flags and hand gestures. Even after finishing their training, they had to practise their battle skills occasionally and undertook regular military drills. These were regarded as general duties in the army.

As mentioned in the second part of this volume, during the reign of the Thirteenth Dalai Lama, after Lu-chun's troops were expelled from Tibet in 1912, the Tibetan army adopted a new military system. At that time, the Dalai Lama appointed Russian, Japanese and British military instructors to teach their styles of military training separately to different Tibetan regiments. During the training sessions, the Dalai Lama personally visited the training grounds and carefully inspected each training method. As mentioned in his biography, the Dalai Lama finally chose the British military system as the model for the Tibetan army, and the uniform, weaponry and training were modeled on the British style. This marked a new phase of improvement of the Tibetan army. Many young officials and soldiers were sent to the British army camps in Gyantse and India to receive British military training. The newly groomed military instructors were sent to different Tibetan army regiments throughout the country to teach British military drills and exercises, thus making the training system uniform throughout all the regiments.

The organizational structure, band party system and uniforms of the Tibetan army were changed to the British style. All the words of command and military terms, including the names of weapons, were taught in English. Regarding the uniform, it consisted of gray cotton trousers, a gray tunic, a felt hat in summer, a woolen hat in winter, shoes with leg fasteners and a leather belt. The Bodyguard Regiment's uniform was the same, except for its helmet. The ceremonial dress, which consisted of a yellow tunic and blue cotton trousers, was not changed.

Regarding the Tibetan army's flag, as mentioned above, it had a red background with yellow crossed-*vajras* as the emblem. The name of a regiment (ka, kha, ga, etc.) was written in the top corner of the flag. All the regiments had their own regimental flags, whose colours differed from one another. There were also small flags used for giving secret signals on the battlefield.

Regarding the rank insignias, a *chupon* (section leader) had one red chevron on the right shoulder epaulet. An instructor had two red chevrons, the senior instructors had three and the deputy lieutenant had four red chevrons. A lieutenant had a half *vajra* badge on the cap. A captain had one single *vajra* badge on the cap. A colonel had one and half *vjaras* on the cap. A brigadier had one crossed-*vajras* on his cap. The Commander-in-Chief had one crossed-*vajras* enclosed by two regimental flags. The Senior Commander-in-Chief had a badge of a pair of snow lions lifting a crossed-*vajras*, with two army flags, enclosed by two wheat straws made from precious materials. The caps of all other officers had a copper snow lion with snowy mountains as background and a small *vajra,* inscribed with their regimental names, the group's name and a number to indicate the number of soldiers under his command.

Except the official uniform of the officers, the caps and dress, cap ornaments and horse's ornaments of the brigadiers, colonels, captains and lieutenants were the same as those that had been introduced during the time of Desi Pholawa's son.

Regarding the appointment and removal of officers, any capable soldier would be sent for training in any particular field according to his choice, and he would be then promoted according to his skill and service years. Any personnel who served with great dedication and performed excellently in war would be nominated for promotion and his name would be sent to the government for consideration. A Brigadier had the authority to appoint subalterns such as Section Leaders, but he could appoint or remove any higher officers, such as Instructors only through consultation with the Army Headquarters. To appoint any officers above the sixth grade, such as a Colonel, the Brigadier had to submit a list of nominees to the Kashag through the Army Headquarters. Army officers above the rank of Captain had the privilege of attending the morning tea at the Potala or Norbulingka with other government officials. They were also required to attend any official ceremonies, in their full official attire, whenever they received order from the Army Headquarters.

Whenever they had to leave for an outstation, they had to report their departure or arrival at the secretariat office at the Potala and the Regent's Office, as well as the Army Headquarters, just like the secretaries of the government.

If any member of the army was promoted to a subaltern post, such as Instructor or Section Leader, he had to have an investiture audience with an image of the Dalai Lama at his own regimental headquarters. If promoted to the post of Lieutenant, his investiture audience would take place at his own regimental camp as well as at the Army Headquarters. If appointed to the post of Captain, the officer had to conduct his investiture audience at his own regiment, the Army Headquarter, the Kashag, the secretariat offices at the Potala and the Regent's Office. When a promotion took place at an outpost, the investiture ceremony was done at the outpost and other ceremonial functions were conducted in the same manner.

As far as ordinary soldiers were concerned, they could gain promotion through the ranks up to the level of Colonel. Officers above the rank of Brigadier were appointed directly by the government, selecting from among the government officials. Regarding the grade system of commissioned army officers, the Commander-in-Chief who held the minister's post was on the third grade, a *dzasak* official acting as the Commander-in-Chief held the next third grade, Deputy Commander-in-Chief was on the fourth grade and *dapon* or brigadier was on the fourth rank in the government's grade system. Rupon or colonel was on the fifth rank; captain the sixth and lieutenant the seventh. There were also majors and section leaders.

From Darjeeling, the military systems expert Sonam Ladenla was invited to Tibet. He gave police training to the soldiers of the Dadang and Nadang regiments, who were thereafter made a Police Force. The police system that had been previously instituted had deteriorated by that time, so the police system was improved. Though its responsibilities and duties differed slightly from the other army regiments, the institutional system was the same. Thereafter, four young government officials, with Lungshar as their guide, were sent to England for training in different technical fields. Among them, Gokhar Bu Sonam Gonkyab received training in the British military system, and this greatly benefited the Tibetan Army.

The system of issuing weapons and uniforms and remittance of salary

The Army Headquarters issued new weapons or exchange weapons at the request of the regiment. concerned. Regarding the uniform, the regiment concerned had to request the Army Headquarters for new uniforms, and the Headquarters would issue a written permit and specify the quantity of material to be collected from their source families. The regiment would send its soldiers to collect the uniform materials from their source families through the respective district office. After getting the materials, they would tailor their uniforms. During parades, the troops wore the British uniform, issued by the government or made by their own regiments.

The salary of the army was revised from time to time in accordance with the time and situation. Apart from the compensation from their source families, each soldier, instructor and section leader used to get 2 *khal* measures of grains, 1 tea-ball and 1 *nyag* measure of butter as the monthly salary. The salary of a senior instructor and a lieutenant was 4 *khal* measures of grains, captain and colonel 6 and 7 *khal* measures of grain respectively. They also used to get salt, baking powder, firewood, fuel, etc. as a part of their salary, but I will not detail here the series of changes on the salary to avoid too much detail. I will discuss these in the latter chapters of this volume.

Regarding the collection of salary, a regiment had to submit a salary sheet to the Army Headquarters before the salary day, as described above. The Headquarters would give a sanction letter, informing the regiment from where the salary should be collected. The regiment could approach the salary office directly. Sometimes the government would instruct any regiment to collect grains from any specific grain store at any particular place. In such cases, after obtaining the sanction letter and permit, the salary collectors would go to that particular grain house to collect the grain. The sacks of salary-grain would be properly sealed and handed over to the regimental office.

Every year each regiment used to send five or six soldiers to the Medical College in Lhasa to receive training in medicine. The regiments would send along with each student grain or money, amount equivalent to the annual salary of captain, to the head teacher of the Medical College as school fee. During the time of Lungshar as the Commander-in-Chief, all the regiments were issued with tents, cauldrons, fire-barrows, ladles, snow goggles and so forth, and they were in service even after his time.

Travelling and transportation

When any regiment received a posting order and road-permit from the government, the regiment had to leave promptly for the destination to which they were being posted. In order to avoid creating too much burden on the government and people, the regiment had to remain at the outstation for three to seven years continuously, without replacement. Soldiers were allowed to take a one-day leave to go and meet their relatives; however, only a very few soldiers would take the one-day leave, because it was difficult for them to return to their camp by nightfall, due to long distances and tough roads. In times of peace, about 20 percent of officers and troops would bring their family members along with them, and they would stay at nearby villages. However, during expeditions, no one was allowed to bring any members of their family with them.

The government used to provide horses and mules to the regiment to carry weapons and military supplies. The government would give them an edict, authorizing them to collect a fixed number of horses and mules from the villagers along the roads in case they needed extra. Regarding the quota of riding and pack animals entitled to the officers, instructors, section leaders and ordinary soldiers were allowed to carry a half *khal* of luggage on a mule. A Senor Instructor was entitled to 1 pack animal and 1 riding horse. A Lieutenant could use 2 pack animals and 2 riding horses, while a Captain had the right to take 3 pack animals and 3 riding horses. A Colonel was entitled to 5 pack animals and 4 riding horses. A Brigadier could enjoy 10 pack animals and 7 riding horses. The quota of horses and mules for the officers above the rank of brigadier and for the official transportation purpose were fixed by the government.

Regarding reception and lodging arrangements, before leaving, the army would send men in advance to inform the respective district officer about their arrival and, the army staff would, with the help of the district officer, arrange reception and lodging.

With regard to the travelling, except the family members of the soldiers and the soldiers who were leading the pack animals, all personnel, carrying their weapons, would march in their respective groups, without mixing with others. The main leader would ride and lead the march. Regarding the order in the line, the national flag bearers were at the front, followed by regimental flags bearers, then by cavalry. At intervals, the marching band would play their music. On arrival and departure, a gun salute would be made in honor of the leader. At the camp the band would play music and perform dances. The local monasteries would grant blessed chords to the soldiers, and greet the army with religious musical instruments. At places where there were big populations, many people, dressed in their best clothes, used to come to greet the army. Sometimes, at the central tent, there would be dance performance. Army officials and local dignitaries would host parties for one another. It would appear that they enjoyed a very close relationship.

In times of war and emergency, as per the order from the authority, the troops had to travel straight, with due care and cautiousness, and no one was allowed to be careless or loiter on the way.

Duties and living styles during outpost duty

The army would set up its headquarters at the place where they were posted and their regimental flag would be erected. The brigadier and several colonels and captains would remain at the headquarters to work as regular troops. In Markham Gartog, Khyungpo Sertsa and Hor Drachen, houses were available for the use of the army. In other places, tents were pitched in lines. Company, platoon and squad would be posted around the border of the country for duty according to the location. They would be replaced each year. Their main duties were to protect their territory, to prevent infiltrations from outside, to spy on the enemy, to patrol the area and to maintain law and order in the area.

The regiments based in Drapchi and Dingri had to serve as bodyguards of the Governor of northern Tibet on a rotation basis. To defend Dromo, the regiments of Shigatse and Gyantse were sent in turn by turn. A similar rotation system occurred with the regiments based in Dromo, Shigatse and Gyatse.

Reports on the situation in the area was sent through horse-messengers to the superior officers. Except on days off and official ceremonies, there were drill and exercises daily, with an emphasis on battle training in accordance with the training methods designed by the authorities. The band would rehearse every morning, and blow trumpets as a wake-up call every morning and bed-call every night. Trumpet calls were also used to summon or exchange security guards, to announce meetings and assemblies, and were blown at sunset to honor the day. After the morning trumpet calls were sounded, the band party would play drums and flutes for ten minutes one after the other.

At the Regimental Headquarters, brigadiers and officers would meet frequently. There were roll calls and prayer sessions every evening, without fail. Every half-moon and full moon day, official ceremonies and the third day of every month were rest days. On the 13th day of the fourth month of every year, there was a ceremony called the Great Summer Festival, which was celebrated as the Founding Anniversary of the Tibetan Army. On that day, all the troops would stand in line and evoke the local deities with loud prayers. A grand picnic was organized over several days.

Army members would visit local monasteries of any traditions to make offerings and prayers. If any army member died, lamas would be invited to perform rituals. The troops would also receive teachings and empowerments from lamas. If requested by a monastery or local people, the army would send any required number of volunteer troops to work in the renovation of temples or monasteries. In this way, wherever the troops were posted, they had the feeling of being part of the community and a sense of loyalty to the people. Due to their long contact, troops and the local people enjoyed strong relationships. Many soldiers would marry local women after gaining permission from the concerned local chiefs. When the soldiers returned home, they would take their wives with them. At the time of troops' departure, the local people would feel sad and come to farewell them.

In the past, Manchu and then later on the Kuomintang Chinese tried hard to destroy the unity of the Tibetan people and to create hostility between the people and the Government and between religious different religious sects. They sent spies into Tibet and lured people with money, with the intention of destabilizing and invading Tibet. Though some ignorant Tibetan people and army members cooperated with the Chinese and helped them do unlawful activities, the majority of the masses remained loyal and supportive to the government and the army. This does not need further explanation here.

Duties of the soldiers at their regimental camps

When a new regiment arrived at the outpost, the regiment on duty would hand over responsibility of the garrison to the new troops and return to their regimental headquarters. When the troops arrived back home from outpost duty, the local people, dressed in their best clothes, carrying delicious food, would go to receive them. Both the troops and people would be overcome with mixed feelings of joy and sadness. The troops would rest at the district headquarters for a few days. A required number of troops were kept at bigger army camps such as Shigatse, Dingri, Gyantse and Drapchi, and the rest of the soldiers were sent home, although they were required to report back whenever they were ordered to do so. The weapons were deposited at their armories. One platoon was stationed at the armoury as its security guards.

When the troops were at their regimental headquarters and not on border duty, they would receive their salaries from their regiment. When they were on outpost duty, they would be paid by the government.

During the Summer Festival every year, all the troops and officers used to gather at their respective district headquarters, where they practised drills, held discussions, made new plans, and so forth. They would revise their membership list and make a new register. On the final day, a *lhasol* or deity invoking ceremony was organized and a military parade and other ceremonial activities were performed, more elaborate than that usually done in Lhasa. After that, the troops would return to their homes. They would collect grain from the lands granted by the government. The officials in charge of the army's income would submit their report to a committee annually, and a new manager would be appointed.

Every year, each regiment sent a fully authorized leader to Army Headquarters in Lhasa to submit their annual report. Each regiment had to station a platoon or company at their own regimental barracks. When at regimental headquarters, if the brigadier was not present, a deputy brigadier would take his place at the district headquarters.

When a regiment received a posting order, the *dapon* or brigadier would inform all the officers and troops under his command to report to their own district headquarters. Once they had gathered at the district headquarters, they would receive weapons and make preparations for their journey. On the day of their departure, the local people would organize a grand send-off party for them. Both the troops and local people would feel sad at parting from each other. They shared advice and gifts. The people would pray for the success of the troops on their mission. The manner of their departure was always the same.

Duties of the soldiers in Lhasa

When posted in Lhasa, the soldiers were assigned various kinds of tasks by the government from time to time, besides regular military drills and training at their own camp. They were sometimes given patrol duties or policing duties. They were also sent to work on construction or renovation projects. They had to parade whenever the Dalai Lama travelled and whenever a high Tibetan official or a foreign dignitary arrived or left, as well as on all official ceremonies. The security of the Dalai Lama as well as his residence and premises was the responsibility of the Kadang Bodyguard Regiment, except in times of emergency when the troops were assigned different duties in accordance with the situation.

In the morning and evening of the three-day Shoton or Yoghurt Festival held from the 2nd to the 4th day of the 7th Tibetan month at Norbulingka, there were military parades by all the regiments present in Lhasa on the ground in front of the grandstand of the Khamsum Silnon Palace. On the ground all the troops would stand in formation in their respective regiments, which were arranged in alphabetical order. The Dalai Lama and his two tutors would arrive and sit on the grandstand under a pavilion. Behind the Dalai Lama were seated the Prime Minister, cabinet ministers, high lamas, *trulkus*, foreign dignitaries and Tibetan government officials in the official seating order. The spectators including monks would sit on the ground near the gate of Norbulingka, facing towards the grandstand. The Commander-in-Chief would give the commands aloud: "Group attention!," "Bayonet!," " Shoulder arms!" and "Present arms!" one by one, and all the troops would respond in unison to the commands. After that, the Tibetan National Anthem was sung by the Army Band and the Tibetan national flag was raised simultaneously. The military flags and regimental flags were also raised at the same time. Thereafter, the army officers above the rank of colonel would remove the bayonets from their rifles, while the troops held their rifles vertically in front of them. After the National Anthem was finished, the Commander-in-Chief would command aloud: "Arms down!," "Arms slow!," "Remove bayonet!," "Right turn!," and "March on!" Led by their officers, all the regiments would do a march past one by one. When passing near the grandstand where the Dalai Lama was seated, the regiments would make a right turn towards the grandstand and salute. They would then return straight to their respective camps.

During the three-day Yoghurt Festival, there were military parades every morning and evening. The soldiers would make camp in the compound of Norbulingka and picnic there during the festival. The army officers and civil officials used to organize parties and exchange invitations among themselves. All the army members used to thoroughly enjoy the festival.

In the evening of the 15th day of the 1st Tibetan month, the last day of the Great Prayer Festival, all the regiments based in Lhasa would parade through the Barkor streets and salute to the Dalai Lama, or the Prime Minister or any other high official on the occasions when the Dalai Lama was absent. After that, they would return to their camps.

Traditionally, the Nechung and Gadong oracles were invited during every Summer Festival. The army officers above the rank of colonel, in full uniform, would go and invite them. The Nechung and Gadong monasteries would host a luncheon for the army officers. The army officers would organize a weeklong picnic.

Regarding the organization of the military parade, the band party would go first, playing different kinds of drums, bugles, flutes, etc. After the band party, the bearers of the national flag and military flags would march. After that, all the regiments, each with four columns, would march one by one in alphabetical order. Their uniform would be the same. A senior instructor, in a loud voice, would conduct a roll call. Thereafter, the Commander-in-Chief would give a command and all the troops would march in unison in a very graceful manner. The gracefulness of the parade march would overwhelm the spectators, who would hold their hands in devotion and pray:

> May the Dharma flourish!
> May the Government progress continuously!
> May the God's Army of Tibet be the winner!

This clearly shows their extreme love and loyalty to their country, people and army.

Chapter Eight

Tibetan Military System during the Period of the Fourteenth Dalai Lama

Tibetan army uniforms and drill commands

Whether the Tibetan military system and weaponry underwent any changes during the periods of the Regent Reting and Regent Taktra is not known. In 1945, soon after the end of the Second World War, the Tibetan military uniforms and drill commands, which had been in the British style, were changed to Tibetan, except for the Kadang Bodyguard Regiment which retained the British uniform. The new Tibetan uniform consisted of a white or gray shirt, trousers and *chupa,* cotton in summer and woolen in winter. The *chupa* had multicolored stripes around the collar and a red border. The shoes were leather boots, either knee or ankle length depending on the weather. The soldiers wore felt hats in summer and grey caps in winter. The *chupa's* tie (*sked rags*) was red. The style of *chupa* was uniform to all the regiments. The *chupa* of army officers above the rank of *dingpon* (*ding dpon*) was of better quality, although the color and design were the same as that of other ranks. Badges and insignias of rank were worn on caps and shoulders. The military flag was the same as the old one. The Tibetan national flag was modified and flown at the Tibetan Army Headquarters and all the regimental barracks at all times, and carried and flown during all military parades, as in the past.

In Tibet, the Tibetan National Anthem was sung at all official ceremonies and functions. Later, the lyrics were slightly revised, but the tune was left unchanged. The Tibetan army used to sing songs such as "*dpon sar gus 'dud* (salute to the official)", "*phyags na pad mo* (epithet of Avalokiteshvara)", "*rab dkar ke la she* (glittering white Kailash)" and so on which are nowadays popular in all Tibetan schools in exile and at the Tibetan Institute of Performing Arts (TIPA) based in Dharamsala.

The Tibetan government appointed a translation committee to translate the army's English military terminology into Tibetan. The committee, which consisted of the great translators Gendun Choephel, Kashopa, Dapon Kharnawa and Dingpon Kagyin Gokye of the Drongdrak Regiment, translated several hundred English drill commands and other military terms into Tibetan. Rupon Trinle Migyur of the Kadang Bodyguard Regiment, who was an expert in military drill, demonstrated each physical movement of the drill one by one and the translation committee recorded them in Tibetan. The draft translation, along with the English version, was presented to the Dalai Lama, who approved it. The Tibetan terms were carved on woodblocks in the Tibetan *tsugchung* script and many booklets were printed. The Tibetan Military Headquarters sent drillmasters with an edict and the booklets to all the army regiments throughout the country, to teach the Tibetan version of military terms and drill commands. Gradually the entire military terminology was Tibetanized. In this way, the Tibetan government improved the Tibetan military system in general and weaponry in particular, and had plans to make further improvements for the protection of the country.

From that time on the Tibetan military terminology was widely used by the Tibetan army until the country was invaded by China. After that, it was no longer used in Tibet, although it is occasionally used in Tibetan schools in exile. Even a copy of the original booklet of Tibetan military terminology published in Tibet is not available nowadays. I think if we do not document the factual history of Tibetan military terminology in general and drill commands in particular, and hand it down to future generations, it will be a great loss. Therefore, of the military words that I learned during my long-term service in the army in Tibet, I will write down as many as I can remember. Because of not using them for many years, I have forgotten the terms for different hand-signals, whistles and bugle calls used in war. It would be excellent if we could obtain a copy of the original booklet and reprint it. If not, we should approach the Tibetan veterans and record any of the military words they can remember.

1. Military drill

In the Tibetan army all military activities in general, and military parades and drills in particular, had to be performed in accordance with the commands given by higher authorities; it was forbidden to perform any military activities arbitrarily and in a disorganized manner. Whenever there was a drill or a military parade, as well as during training, soldiers had to perform all the sequences of actions correctly and uniformly, in accordance with the cadence counts. The command voice was required to be loud, clear and forceful.

Drill Commands

No.	Commands	Actions
1	*ru sgrig* Fall in	The soldiers should form a formation in the "at ease" position.

2.	*blo sgrims* Attention	The soldiers should stand upright by stamping their left feet close to their right feet.
3.	*bag lhod* Stand at ease	The soldiers should move their left feet away from their right feet and stand in the "at ease" position.
4.	*g.yas stod sgral shibs* Dress right	Movement in which individuals except those on the extreme left side raise their left arms parallel to the ground and turn their heads sharply to the right in order to get the proper distance from each other.
5.	*lta stangs mdun* Eyes front	The group should return to the position of "attention", turning their faces straight forward.
6.	*kheb rgyab (thad drong)* Dress front	Group members have to adjust their positions with others in front in the File.
7.	a) *cha ya ang rtsis* Count off pairs b) *grangs rtsis* Count off through	a) The soldiers in the Rank count in pairs, "one" "two." b) This command is used to count the soldiers in the Rank in numerical order. This will confirm the number of personnel in the front and back Ranks.
8.	*bzhi sgrigs* Form four	Odd-numbered personnel have to move three steps back to form four lines.
9.	*g.yas su sgyur* Right turn	The soldiers have to turn right in two counts.
10.	*g.yon du sgyur* Left turn	To turn left in two counts.
11.	*rgyab tu sgyur* about turn	The group should make a 180 degree turn in two counts.
12.	*skyar stabs* as we were	This command is used to order the soldiers to return to the immediate previous position.
13.	*grangs 'dren bzhin* cadence counts	The manner of teaching drills step by step, in counts, to the recruits.
14.	*mgyogs stabs* without counts	The recruits should perform all the drill movements one by one continuously, without counts.
15.	*gus 'dud* salute	The soldiers should salute with their right hands on the first count.

16.	*phyed bsgyur* face right/left	The soldiers should twist their bodies right/left.

2. Marching without weapons

This is the simplest method of marching irrespective of the size of the squad. Here, all the movements should begin with the left foot.

	Commands	**Action**
1.	*gom spos* march past	On this command, the group should start marching.
2.	*dal bzhin 'grul* slow march	The group has to march with slow steps.
3.	*stabs snyoms* mark time	To march in place
4.	*mdun skyod* forward march	To march forward, in uniform steps, after two making stamps.
5.	*g.yas / g.yon* Right/ Left	At this command, the soldiers shall turn right/ left in one count and move forward.
6.	*rgyab bsgyur* About turn	The soldiers should make "about turn" in four counts and move on.
7.	*bzhi sgrigs/gnyis sgrigs* Form four/Form two	To make four/two lines Those who comprise the odd numbers in the ranks shall remain at the "attention" position in two steps, while those who comprise the even numbers shall turn right or left to form 4 or 2 ranks.
8.	*g.yas phyogs lta stangs* Eyes right	The parade turn their heads to the right for six steps. (In ceremonial parade, the parade leader salutes while looking in the direction where the official stands).
	g.yon phyogs lta stangs Eyes left	Similar to the "eyes right" except that the parade looks to the left.

No.	Commands	Actions
9.	*g.yas phyogs gus 'dud* To the right, Salute *g.yon phyogs gus 'dud* To the left, Salute	The parade leader salutes with his right hand, while the soldiers turn their faces to the right for six steps. (The officer also salutes in return.) This is the style of saluting a senior officer.
10.	a) *sde mtshan g.yas su sgrigs* Group, fall in right b) *sde mtsan g.yon du sgrigs* Group, fall in left	a) The parade falls into formation in two ranks to the right of the instructor. b) The parade falls into formation in two ranks to the left of the instructor.
11.	*krong sdod* Stand still	The group stands upright; movement is allowed.
12.	*mgyogs 'grul* Quick march	To march with quick steps.
13.	*gom spos* Forward march	This orders the parade to start marching.
14.	*ru rkyang sgrigs* March in one	At this command, the two lines should merge and the parade should march in a single line.
15.	*ru gnyis sgrigs* March in two	To march in double lines.
16.	*mdun du gom xx phye zhig* Move xx steps forward	The group should move xxx steps forward.
17.	*rgyab tu gom phye zhig* move xx steps back	The group should move xxx steps backward.
18.	*ru gyes* Fall out	The group turns right in two steps, takes three steps forward and falls out.

Marching with arms

No.	Commands	Actions
1	*gom spos* Forward march	To march forward, placing the rifles on the left shoulders.
2	*go mtshon brjes spos* Change arms	To change the side of the body that the rifle is held on.

3	a) *go mtshon 'phred bzung* Port arms	a) The rifles should be upright touching the legs.
	b) *go mtshon brjes spos* Change arms	b) Change hands in two counts.
4	a) *go mtshon chan stabs* Under arms	a) The rifles should be brought down from the shoulders
		b) Change the sides in three counts.
	b) *go mtshon brjes spos* Change arms	
5.	*mchan bzung* Under arms	The soldiers should carry the rifles in the right hand, with a finger in the trigger guards.
6.	*gus 'dud* Salute	a. If the rifle is on the left shoulder, the right hand should be placed on the rifle for six steps, then hold the rifle upright. b. If the rifle is in the "under arm" position, the left hand shall hold from the rifle's barrel and walk six steps, then hold the rifle in an upright position.
7	*mtshon chas btud* Present arms	The soldiers should hold their rifles in front and walk six steps.
8	*tshon dpung gzhol* Slope arms	Shoulder arms. The rifles should be thrown down from the shoulders and held upright in both hands.
9	a) *krong sdod* Halt	a) To stop marching and stand still
	b) *ru mtshon phab* Order arms	b) To put down the rifles with their butts on the ground on the right hand side.
	c) *bag lhod* Stand at ease	c) Stand at the "at ease" position
	d) *blo sgrims* Attention	d) To stand in the "attention" position, with eyes front.
10.	*mtshon gur phub* Pile arms	The two ranks turn to each other and put their rifles at the centre, making a tent shape.

No.		
11.	*g.yas phyogs la gyes stangs* Fall out at right	Both the front and back files move back on the left foot in two counts and turn right in two counts
12.	*ru mtshon sta gon* Inspection arms	The front and back files come to the previous position in two counts
13.	*g.yon phyogs la gyes stangs* Fall out at left	Both the front and back files move back on the left foot in two counts and turn left in two counts
14.	*ru gyes* Fall out	Fall out
15.	*mtshon gur bkrol*	Pick up one's rifle

4. Rifle exercises

No.	Commands	Actions
1.	*blo sgrims* Attention	To stand in the "attention" position, holding the rifle vertically by the right hand, with the butt on the ground and close to the right leg.
2.	*bag lhod* Stand at ease	To stand in the "at ease" position, holding the rifle by the right hand, with the arm outstretched.
3.	*mtshon dpung gzhol/ rjes spos* Slope arms/Change arms	
4.	*ru mtshon 'phred bzung/ brjes spos* Port arms/Change arms	
5.	*ru mtshon mchan stabs brjes spos* Under arms/Change arms	
6.	*ru mtshon mchan bzung*	
7.	*ru mtshon 'phred ston* Port Arms	
8.	*gus 'dud* Salute	

9.	*mtshon chas btud* Present arms	a) Whether or not the rifle has a bayonet, the rifle should be held in front of the face from the "order arm" position in 4 counts. b) The rifle should be held horizontally under the armpit, with the barrel facing forward, whether the rifle has a bayonet or not.
10.	*srung stabs sdod stangs* Secure arms	

5. Ceremonial parade march

As soon as the commanding office sent an order to any regiment for parade, giving the date, place, dress, arms and other requirements, there would be a bugle or whistle call.

	Commands	**Actions**
1	*ru 'dren gral bsgrigs* Fall in	On this command, the soldiers fall in to form a single file on the right side of the Instructor, standing in the "attention" position, followed by dressing and counting.
2	*ru 'dren dang po cam sdod/ byings rnams rgyab bsgyur ru dbar phye* First line, others fall out	Except for the first man, the rest of the soldiers should perform an "about turn" and take six steps forward, leaving a gap of six steps between each other, and then turn back.
3	*sde tshogs/dpung tshogs ru sgrigs* Group march	On this command, the soldiers shall form two ranks on the left side of the Instructor, who will correct the formation and conduct counting. After that, the Instructor will salute the Senior Instructor and give the authority to him. He shall then go and stand in front of the group.
4	*sde tshogs bag lhod/ blo sgrims* Group, stand at ease, Attention	This command is given by the Senior Instructor. After that, he will give the charge to his senior officer.

5	*rnam pa rnams/snap o rnams ru sgrigs* Officers, Fall in	Any senior officer higher than the Senor Instructor will give this command. The officers above the rank of lieutenant who are already in formation on the right side will move to the beginning of the rank in proper order. The commanding officer will then call another officer, either the Colonel, Captain, or Senior Instructor, to give the command.
6	*dung mang gra sgrigs* Band Party, Ready	On this command, the Band Party and flag bearers should be ready.
7	*sde tshogs/ dpung tshogs mdun bskyod* Group, March forward	The personnel march in two or four ranks, as per the command. They have to follow the Band Party.

6. Ceremonial parade

	Commands	**Actions**
1	*'gar phye* Open line	The first person in the line takes six steps forward, carrying the rifle underarm.
2	*rtse gri* Bayonet	The soldiers should hold their rifles vertically in front, in their right hands. The left hands should hold the bayonet by its hilt. The soldiers look at the man in front of them. a. When the front man says "fix", the soldiers should unsheathe the knives and hold them ready to fix them onto the rifles. b. On the second command "fix", the soldiers should fix the knives onto the rifles on the first count, then move their hands down. c. On the third command "fix", the soldiers shall pull back their rifles, and stand at the "attention" position. The front man shall step back to his former position.
3	*'gar phye rtse gri* Open line, fix bayonet	If this command is given all together, there is no need of a front man. The soldiers should fix bayonets instantly.

4	*rnam pa rnams mdun du gral sgrigs* Officers, in formation	On this command, all the officers above the rank of lieutenant shall step forward from their respective lines. They shall stand in File, led by the lieutenant, captain, colonel and brigadier in front of their group. During ceremonies and inspections, the above procedure is followed.
5	*rnam pa rnams ral gri phyar* Officers, draw swords	In two counts, the officers should place their swords, with sheaths, on their right shoulders.
6	*dpung tshogs mtshon dpung gzhol* Group, return swords	On this command, all the soldiers put down their arms.
7	*dbyings sar mtshon chas btud* Present, arms	On four counts, the officers should perform an arm-salute. In three counts, the bayonet should be opened. The soldiers should raise their rifles with bayonets attached in "present arms". The Band Party shall sing the salutation song. When saluting the Dalai Lama, the National Anthem was sung. There was no National Anthem when saluting the Regent.
8	*dpon sar mtshon chas btud* Present, Arms to the official	The style of making a salutation to a high official is the same. The Band Party shall sing the song dpon-sar. The official will return the salutation. After the song is finished, a) the troops shall immediately keep their rifles at the "Slope arm" position, and then b) put down the rifles to their left sides.
9	*sgrol phye* Break up	Personnel at the end of the front line shall take 6 steps forward.
10	*rtse gri* Unfix bayonet	
11	*sgrol phye rtse gri* Break up, unfix bayonet	
12	*dbyings/dpon sar gom bdun du bcar* Move 7 steps to the officer	This command is used during elaborate ceremonies when there are large numbers of soldiers. The troops shall move about ten steps forward. This is done when the officer has instructions to give.
13	*dpung tshogs g.yas sam g.yon bsgyur* Group, turn right/left	The group shall turn right or left according to the command; the leader shall lead the group.

14	*dpung tshogs gom spos* Group, march	Preceded by the Band Party, the group will move ahead.
15	*g.yas phyogs gus 'dud* Salute to the right	When they reach the officer or leader to be saluted, the leaders of the groups, when their names are heard, will turn their eyes to the right. If they are carrying swords, they should salute with swords in three counts. The flags of each regiment are to be held horizontally.
16	*blta stangs mdun* March straight	The soldiers are to march facing straight ahead. (This is followed by group formation and break up.)

7. Drill with arms

	Commands	**Actions**
1	*sde mtshan ru sgrigs* Squad, fall in	The instructor shall call the soldiers into formation and then call the leader of the group to give drill commands.
2	*lang nas 'phangs chog* Standing position	The soldiers should twist their bodies to the right, with legs slightly stretched, and hold the rifle in "port arm" position, pressing the butt against the shoulder in two counts. After that, if there is the command "order arms", the soldiers should put the rifles down to their sides.
3	*mde'u brdzogs* Load cartridges	This orders the soldiers to load cartridges into their rifles
4	*sdig* Aim at the target	On this command, the rifle should be placed against the shoulder and the finger should be placed on the trigger. When the instructor gives the distance and target, the soldiers should aim their rifles at the target.
5	*'phangs* Fire	The soldiers should fire. (The instructor will tell them how many shots to fire.)
6	*phab* Port arms	Put down the rifle and hold it in the firing position.

7	*spor dkrug/mde'u 'then* Open bolt, remove cartridges	Remove the cartridge from the rifle by opening the bolt, and stand at the "attention" position.
8	*zhib 'bul ru mtshon 'phred ston* Inspection arms	The soldiers should hold the rifle, pull the lock plate, and put the right thumb inside the barrel.
9	*zhib 'bul* Ready, Port arms	The soldiers should hold the gun horizontally straight. The drill master or officer concerned will examine each rifle to see whether they are clean. After the examination, the soldiers will lock the plates and trail down the rifles.
10	*pus btsug 'phags chog* Kneeling position	At this command, the soldiers should turn right, put the right knee down on the ground in two counts and hold the rifles in the shooting position on the other leg, and then fire.
11	*bsdad nas 'phangs chog* Sitting position	This orders the soldiers to turn right in two counts, kneel down and hold the rifles in the shooting position, and then fire.
12	*nyal nas 'phangs chog* Lying position	The soldiers should twist their bodies to the right, lie down on the ground in two counts and hold the rifles horizontally.

B. 35-Code Military Law

As a result of the self-manifestation of the five degenerations (*snyigs ma lnga*)[1], it had become necessary to expand the strength of the Army in light of the times and the changing situation in the country. For this, both the provisional and full Tibetan National Assemblies submitted a proposal (to the government), bearing their four seals, to make a new military law, and thereafter the Full National Assembly submitted a detailed version of the proposal. In the Iron-Tiger Year the Tibetan Army Headquarters was instructed to submit a draft of a new law. Accordingly, the Army Headquarters submitted a proposal: "Though highly advanced foreign countries have their own written military laws, it is very difficult for us to obtain copies of them and immediately translate them into Tibetan. Moreover, it is not

---

1 5 degenerations/corruptions – 1) degeneration of view (*lta ba'i snyigs ma*), 2) degeneration of conflicting emotions (*nyon mongs kyi snyigs ma*), 3) degeneration of sentient beings (*sems can gyi snyigs ma*), 4) degeneration of time (dus kyi snyigs ma) and 5) degeneration of lifespan (*tshe'i snyigs ma*).

possible to base on them all the features of our army, including the foundational structure, pay scale and so forth. It is therefore preferable in the interim to make a draft of the law in accordance with the time and situation of our country, and then make changes and improvements to it with reference to the military laws of other countries."

In response, the Dalai Lama issued the following edict:

"All the people of Tibet and Greater Tibet, who are subjects of the Heavenly Appointed Ganden Phodrang Government, especially the army officers and soldiers, leaders and people of all the districts and estates throughout the country, should pay attention to the following:

This land of snow, which could not be conquered by other Buddhas and bodhisattvas, is owned by the great lord of compassion, Avalokiteshvara, whose power of compassion and patience is inconceivable and whose body is as bright as the conglomeration of millions of moon. Therefore, all the beings born in this land are innately peaceful and compassionate; they always engage in virtuous activities for the benefit of their future lives rather than the present ones, taking less interest in worldly activities in general and military activities in particular. Because of this, the country has only a civil law called the *13-Code Law*, but there has been no separate military law. Therefore, the following 35 codes have been adopted as military law until and unless further changes or amendments are made in the future:

1. Great changes are taking place in all countries in this world, just as a great fire of the end of samsara burns down the trees of happiness to ashes. However, ours is different from other countries because it is the place where Vajradhara has performed innumerable miraculous deeds of the Three Secrets and where the Three Buddhist Kings, ministers, panditas and siddhis performed their excellent activities. Most important, it is the place where the successive reincarnations of the Dalai Lama, the master of vow-observers, have appeared and delivered all the beings of the land into the realms of happiness through their religious and secular deeds. Due merely to their kindness, there have been no wars and famine in the country so far, and all the people, irrespective of whether they are of high or low status, are living freely and happily. We have obtained this excellent happiness due mainly to the kindness of the Dalai Lamas, who are perceived as the real Buddha. For the longevity of the teachings of the Buddha, which is the source of wellbeing and happiness, depends upon the success of the political activities of the Ganden Phodrang Government, the protector of Budhadharma. As a manifestation of the five degenerations, the Buddhadharma and the Government might face attacks from evil-minded uncivilized people. Since it is the tradition of Buddhist kings not to make offensives against the enemy,

and it is the tradition of worldly kings not to ignore offensives by the enemy, it is necessary to prepare the armed forces for war. Nevertheless, our nation is not like foreign countries, the aim of whose military is to invade other countries, in the way big insects eat small ones. Although mobilization of troops entails enormous expense, great hardship and risk of life in wars, the service is purely for the benefit of Buddhadharma. Therefore, one's precious life never goes to waste and he will surely attain Buddhahood in the long run. His virtuous deeds will earn far more merits, as can be proved by referring to the scriptures and using one's reasoning. Therefore, one should not consider military service as a burden, but should perform one's military duties with the aim of protecting the Dharma, with a correct attitude and a sense of joy, devotion and happiness.

2.   In order to protect religion and polity, first of all the army must be powerful enough to overpower an enemy. Therefore, when soldiers are recruited, it is important to examine them to make sure that they are physically fit, without any chronic disease, and their eyes and ears are sound; only those who are really physically fit should be recruited.

3.   Soldiers will come from different parts of the country. Therefore, some unwise young soldiers who have not received good guidance and care from their parents or relatives might behave roughly and crudely. Some of them might even consume harmful food and engage in unhealthy practices which endanger their wellbeing, thus ruining their precious lives. Therefore, the army leaders should always take care of their soldiers and provide them with necessary medical treatment. They should give advice to their soldiers regarding their behaviour, actions and duties.

4.   Some inexperienced soldiers might think that military training and exercises are irrelevant on the battlefield. However, regular training will greatly help the soldiers enhance their stamina, physical strength, maneuvering skills and so on. Therefore, there should be two hours of military exercise daily, except on weekly rest days, government and military ceremonies and functions, and *sang* offering ceremonies. All the officers and soldiers should use the military commands which have been translated from English into the Tibetan language in all military training.

5.   Bugles, flags and mirrors are extremely important instruments by which to give secret signals from one part of the army to the other on the battlefield. Young intelligent soldiers should be taught how to use these instruments. Moreover, everyone, from the brigadier at the top to the lowest ordinary soldiers, must learn all the bugle codes thoroughly and be able to pass a test.

6.   Since Tibet has mountainous and rocky terrain along its borders, guerrilla warfare can be effective against the enemy in the event of war. Therefore, the

leaders and troops should, carrying pack food, do war training and practice on steep mountains, in valleys and other tough terrain, as well as training in crossing narrow paths and rivers without boats. However, no one may exploit the local people by forcing them to provide horses, pack animals and labour, or harass nomads and travelers in the name of training. They may not cause the slightest harm to any animals, large or small.

7.   There shall be a prayer session every evening to remove obstructions and earn merits for the benefit of others and oneself; all personnel should assemble and recite aloud the long life prayers of the Dalai Lama and the Panchen Rinpoche as well as the prayer of the 21 manifestations of the goddess Tara.

8.   When at regimental headquarters, all personnel should busy themselves with training and practice according to their own capacity during the 8 hours free time, and they may not go outside during that time. The gatekeepers should make sure that no one goes out. If anyone has to go out for some important personal or official work, he should obtain permission from his regimental leader, *dapon*, or any other officer in charge. The officer concerned should give him a wooden board, bearing the reason for his outing and the office's seal, and the soldier should carry it when he goes out.

9.   Whenever a soldier takes personal leave, he should hand in his weapons to the section leader, lieutenant or any other officer; he may not take the weapons away with him. Whether at their own regimental base or travelling on an official mission, soldiers must always keep their weapons with them, day or night. The leaders, in order of seniority, may conduct a roll call at any time, day or night, and check if any soldier is missing. When the bugle call is sounded for roll call, all the troops should, with their weapons, assemble at their camps immediately.

10.   All the weapons and items of military equipment are the valuable property of the government; they should be kept and handled with due care, as if they are personal belongings. Using them for personal purposes or lending them to anyone outside the army is forbidden.

11.   Soldiers should keep all large and small weapons issued to them in a place where there is no moisture, dust and smoke. They should often clean them with cleansing oil, just as if they were caring for their own eyes. All the soldiers must perfect the ability to assemble, dismantle and use their weapons.

12.   All the soldiers must learn to perfection all types of target firing and bayonet fighting prescribed in the military training of foreign countries, as well as sword fighting, which is the most important traditional fighting technique of the Tibetan army. There should be occasionally target-firing practice in the field.

13.   The successful functioning of the Army for the benefit of the government depends on military law. All personnel should therefore memorize and know the meaning of all the provisions mentioned in the army's law. A soldier should be "as gentle as a cat at home and as fierce as a tiger in front of the enemy".

Anyone who is found missing during a roll call will be punished with 30 leather whips to the face. Anyone who maintains his equipment carelessly, if he is an officer above the rank of lieutenant, shall be fined 8 to 30 *srang* money in accordance with the seriousness of the case, as punishment, and the amount shall be deposited in the Army's fund. If he is an ordinary soldier, he shall be given 8 to 30 leather whips to the face in the presence of all other troops.

Soldiers must maintain discipline and moral behaviour. They should respect their superiors of different ranks and older soldiers, even if they are equal to them in rank. All the soldiers should live in harmony, and fighting and quarrelling are prohibited in the Army. If found doing so, each will be given 30 lashes, irrespective of whether one is at fault or not. Anyone who is found having immoral relations with woman other than his own wife, or engaged in drinking and gambling, shall be given 38 lashes. If a soldier who has obtained permission to take leave fights with a monk or in a market or village, he will be given 28 lashes, regardless of whether he is at fault or not. An investigation committee, comprising both civil and military officials, will investigate the matter to know who started the fight and who struck the first blow. The offenders will be punished in accordance with the severity of their fault, based on the traditional law of justice.

14.   Regarding those soldiers who behave in an extremely unruly manner and disregard the orders of their superiors, and cowards who run away from the battlefield during a war to save their own lives, by ignoring the kindness of the heavenly appointed government; if the respective leaders have no authority to investigate and control them immediately, it will prove very dangerous. Therefore, if such things happen near Lhasa, the Military Headquarters should report them to the Kashag. If outside Lhasa, the Governor-General of Eastern Tibet, if not the Commanders-in-Chief, or brigadiers, if there are no Commanders-in-Chief, have the power to punish such offenders under their command, to the extent that they can even amputate their limbs as punishment.

15.   A soldier who excels in military training and adheres to the military law can rise through the different grades of rank up to the rank of *rupon*. Anyone who repeatedly commits serious mistakes shall be punished and discharged from the army, or will be debarred from promotion despite having many years of

service. Whoever maintains discipline well and performs with distinction on the battlefield shall be promoted to the next rank of seniority irrespective of his age. Those who contribute excellent military service, including those who perform bravely in wars at the cost of their lives, and those military spies who give useful information about the enemy during wars shall be promoted, without having to wait for promotion through service years. All soldiers therefore should behave well, take care of their equipment and perform to the best of their ability.

16. Whenever a vacancy falls in an officer's position, a new one will be appointed to the post, taking into account his service years, capability, education, past performances and majority's choice, after obtaining approval from the government. There shall be no place for nepotism, favoritism and bribery in the selection of leaders, as this could cause mistrust among the people and failure in the functioning of the army.

17. The army leaders must have the quality of being both feared and loved by the soldiers, as in the relationship between a parent and child. The leaders should deal immediately with those who behave badly and violate the military law with strict punishment, without sympathy. They should look after those who are disciplined to see that they get proper food and clothing. Soldiers who are ill should be given timely medical treatment, with as much care as if they were one's own brothers or sons.

18. When any member of the army dies, all his belongings should be handed over to his parents or wife and children, and compensation should be given to his family members. Whatever remains from his belongings should be spent for his funeral ceremony, and everything should be done transparently to the satisfaction of all the members of the army.

19. Without instructions from the regimental leader, no officer is allowed to keep soldiers as his servants or force them to do labour works for others to earn money or name; instead they ought to treat their soldiers with kindness and love.

20. If a regiment has a common fund, it cannot be kept by any individual officer. The amount should be invested or loaned out for the generation of profit, through discussion and unanimous agreement among the troops and officers. The proceeds should be used for useful purposes, such as improving the facilities of the regiment and for the benefit of its members, just as "the medicine of eye disease is used to cure the eye disease". The accounts should be audited annually in the presence of the regimental leader and other junior leaders, and the statement of accounts should be presented to the Army Headquarters.

21. Soldiers whose families live near their regimental headquarters may take a vacation of seven days, excluding travel days, after every six months.

In addition, a leave not exceeding seven days can be granted on special conditions, by the most senior officer present at the time at the regimental headquarters. When granting such leave, the officer concerned should give the soldier a board bearing the seal and the reason of the leave. To obtain leave of more than seven days or to go to a long distance, permission should be sought from the Governor-General of Kham, or the Army Headquarters, the Governor of Northern Tibet, the Governor of Dromo or any other officials with real authority. The authority who gives the leave should give a slip to the soldier, writing in detail the duration of the leave and the reason clearly. In times of emergencies, no one is allowed to take or grant even a half-day leave.

22.   As was traditionally done, all the regiments should send a team of lieutenants or section leaders on a rotation basis to collect the army's salary. The regiments can decide the selection of their salary collectors. Apart from this, all requests, including leave request, must be made through the most senior officer present at the camp at the time, not arbitrarily. It is forbidden to approach a lower ranking officer if a superior officer is present at the regiment, for example approaching a *rupon* while the *dapon* is present, and approaching a *gyapon* despite the presence of a *rupon*.

23.   To ensure that all the officers and soldiers maintain proper discipline and moral behavour, the *dingpon* leaders shall conduct a roll call among their soldiers once every day, the *gyapon* leaders should conduct a roll call among the soldiers under their command once in every week, and the *rupon* leaders should do so quarterly. The *dapon* shall conduct a roll call once every month. The roll call must be accompanied by examination of the soldiers, weapons and living quarters. The Army Headquarters shall visit different army camps occasionally to check the situation. If the army is administered, controlled and trained properly in this way, it will prove strong and effective against an enemy and there will be harmony and respect among the soldiers.

24.   If the army leaders and soldiers are gentle and pleasant in their behaviour and speech, the enemy will feel emotionally overwhelmed, and our own people, lay and ordained, will appreciate and voluntarily give support and cooperation for our common goals. Therefore, both army officers and soldiers should respect those who are superior to them in accordance with the traditional codes of respect, treat appropriately those who are equal to them, and speak politely to those who are under them. Everyone should always strive to win the love of others, and should never do unbecoming and foolish things that show their own negative qualities. Moreover, despite belonging to different regiments, all army members are the same in that they are the soldiers of the same nation. Therefore, soldiers should respect any

army leaders, including those who are not from their own regiment, as if they were their own leaders, and the leaders should treat all the soldiers with love and kindness. The soldiers should live in harmony among themselves with a sense of brotherhood. No officer or soldier may engage in mindless acts, fighting and quarreling over the name of their regiment. If anyone does so, strict punishment will be given, regardless of rank.

25. Regarding the dress code—the hat should be worn properly, the belt should be fastened at the appropriate level and the shoelaces should be tied tightly. Everyone should get up early in the morning and be asleep late at night. Faces, hands and hair should be washed daily and kept clean and tidy, so as to maintain personal comfort and present a good appearance to others.

26. Whenever making a journey, all personnel must march straight, without loitering on the way, and in a disciplined manner. Whoever is met on the way, whether of high or low status, no personnel may give them any kind of military information, such as information about soldiers, weapons and activities, except what is necessary for the performance of the mission. If anyone gives military information to outside people, if he is a leader, his half-month's salary will be deducted, and if a soldier, he will be given 20 lashes as punishment.

27. It is said that some officers and troops steal and sell weapons to outside people secretly, or carry them for personal use. If anyone is found doing this, if he is a leader, his salary for one year will be deducted, and if he is a soldier, he shall be given 78 lashes and the cost of the item will be taken.

28. During parades on important occasions, all personnel must wear their dress properly, whether it is Tibetan or Western uniform. Examples of the wrong use of dress include clothing with buttons not fastened properly, and leg-straps not worn properly and uniformly. Some soldiers carry needle cases and matchboxes in their uniforms. Of those who wear cloaks, some wear both sleeves, while others wear one sleeve, either right or left. Caps are worn in different styles. There should be uniform rules regarding the dressing style, including the way of wearing sleeves.

  Soldiers are prohibited from allowing civilians, young or old, to join a parade. Laughing, shouting, waving and looking around at others are forbidden during a parade. All soldiers must maintain discipline and decorum so as to create a pleasant sight for the spectators.

29. Whether at the regimental base or on outpost duty, all the army members should try to help monasteries and people, instead of harassing them. If members of the army hurt the feelings of the people, it will cause great danger, both at the present time and in the future.

  Whenever the government gives a posting order, the regiment concerned must leave within ten days for their destination. If the officers do not have servants for their horses and if the soldiers have no potters, they can request the government permission to requisition horses. The government will examine the situation and decide how many riding horses and pack animals are required. It will give money to hire horses and pack animals at the rate of 3 *sang* for each riding horse for one day's journey and 1 *sang* and 5 *zho* for each pack animal for one day's journey. However, the army may not take money from people to pay for horses and pack animals. During the journey, the leaders should go in front or behind to make sure that all the troops march straight without loitering on the way or straying into villages. All the officers and troops should march as a group in a dignified manner and should always remain together.

During a long border duty, there is no restriction on the troops staying with their families. However they are not allowed to take their families along with them when they go to fight a war, as it would create great difficulty for the soldiers in carrying out their duties on the battlefield.

30. Whether going on a journey to an outpost, to collect new materials for uniforms or to collect the salary for the troops, the government has allocated a maximum of 12 load-packs, and the regiment is not allowed to take more than this. All the packs should be properly sealed and labeled. It is forbidden to cause unnecessary trouble to people by blaming them for losing luggage and asking them for compensation.

31. All members of the army must pay respect to Buddhist monasteries, large or small, belonging to any sect, immediately they see them, by taking off their caps and folding their hands in devotion, which is the basic characteristic of all those who were born in this land of Dharma. If soldiers meet a monk, including a person wearing robes with red or yellow patches, not to mention high lamas, they should perceive them as the Sangha Jewel (*dge 'dun kdon mchog*) and honour them with great respect and devotion.

32. No army member may enter any stranger's house. Whoever does so will be given 19 leather whips to the face.

33. Anyone who immorally harasses a woman will be flogged 28 times in front of the victim.

34. No army leader or soldier may let their horses and mules graze on fields, to steal crops or pull wood from the fences built around the fields, in violation of the law of the country. Anyone who does so, if he is a leader, his half-month's salary will be cancelled, and if he is an ordinary soldier, he will be given 18 leather whips.

35. All the members of the army should always live like the "four harmonious brothers"[2]; the soldiers should respect and obey their leaders sincerely, and

---

2 Mthun pa mched bzhi, also called mthun pa spun bzhi (four harmonious brothers): elephant, monkey, rabbit and *sreg pa* bird

the leaders in turn should look after and control their soldiers with kindness and love, without selfish feelings. Whenever there is war, everyone should remember the kindness of the Ganden Phodrang Government and make combined efforts with the determination to sacrifice their precious lives to destroy the enemy. In short, the Tibetan army, which is called "God's Army of Tibet", must be strong enough to protect the government and the people of Tibet, which is being governed jointly by religious and political systems, against the enemies. The army must be in all respects, including discipline and moral behaviour, pleasing to the eyes of both monastic and lay people, for the benefit of their present and future lives.

Therefore, the leaders of all the regiments, while adhering themselves strictly to the above rules, must always maintain discipline in the army to make sure that all their soldiers adhere to the military law. The Army Headquarters should send an inspection team from time to time to observe if any army member is transgressing the law, whether at the army camp, outside the camp or in any other way. Any army member, high or low, including the leaders, who is found violating the army law, shall be investigated and punished. Therefore, if any army member breaches the above rules, no matter where, it should be reported immediately. If a local leader connives or tries to favour any offender, the local leader concerned shall be punished. Hence, all the civil and military leaders should keep in mind that they must do what is right and avoid what is wrong by adhering to the above rules.

On the xx day of the xx month of the Iron-Tiger Year."

As mentioned above, the Simpa Guard was created during the time of the Fifth Dalai Lama, based on the traditional military system of Tibet established by the Tibetan Buddhist kings. However, many Tibetan regional armies gradually adopted the Mongol system because of their long-term association with the Mongols. Later, as Pholawa the ally of the Manchus, brought Manchu troops into Tibet, many characteristics of the Manchu army were assimilated into the Tibetan armies. After Pholawa's death, his son instituted a government army that bore the characteristics of both the Chinese and Mongol armies. The Simpa Guard and local armies remained the same as before. Then during the time of the Thirteenth Dalai Lama, the Tibetan government's army adopted the British military system as its model. When the Fourteenth Dalai Lama assumed the leadership of Tibet, efforts were gradually made to Tibetanize the Tibetan military system. This is the story how the Tibetan army evolved through time.

Part II

Chapter One

Wars in Ancient Times

—•◦•—

Many centuries ago before the system of "ruler and subjects" had developed, the people in this land of snow lived or moved from one place to another in tribal groups. These tribes often fought among themselves, using stones and sticks as their main weapons. Gradually they developed from barbarism to civilization and started living in organized social groups and taking up different types of occupations for their livelihood. Soon they started making weapons to fight and created armies as well. During this period, the subjugation of one group by another began.

According to some sources, Tibet was first ruled by seven Masang brothers, followed by 25 major kingdoms, 12 minor kingdoms and 40 principalities in succession, before the first Tibetan king (Nyatri Tsenpo) arrived. Those petty kingdoms were in a constant power struggle. In the *Feast for Scholars (mkhas pa'i dga' ston)*, it is said,

> These petty kingdoms were based on fighting and killing. They recognised no difference between right and wrong; anyone who criticized was imprisoned.

In circa 127 BC, Nyatri Tsenpo became the first king of the whole of Tibet. His dynasty had 27 kings up to Lha Thothori Nyentsen. They were grouped as the Seven Kings of the Sky *(gnam gyi khri bdun)*, two Kings of the Upper Realm *(stod kyi steng gnyis)*, six Good Kings of the Middle Sphere *(bar gyi legs drug)*, eight Earth-Bound Kings *(sa'i sde brgyad)* and four Kings of the Lower Realm *('og gi btsan bzhi)*. A few generations after Lha Thothri, Songtsen Gampo was born. Although Tibet surely had many military accounts before Songtsen Gampo, Tibet had not yet developed a writing system in those times, so the military accounts of the country before him were preserved orally and passed down from generation to generation through oral tradition. After Tibetan writing was invented, Tibetans started documenting some historical events. According to some old Tibetan records, Drigum Tsenpo, the seventh king of Tibet, was hostile to the Bon religion, while his minister Longam was a staunch supporter of the religion. Both of them decided to fight against each other. The king sent a woman to spy on Longam, but Longam knew it and made a clever plan. He killed the king with a sword during their fight. *The Feast for Scholars* explains, "The king had a female dog that could understand human language. He sent it to spy on Longam, but Longam knew about it. The king's strategy failed." From this, we know that even in ancient times spies were employed to obtain secret information about the enemy.

In about 617 , in order to fulfill his father's wishes, King Namri Songtsen sent a force of 90,000 troops to conquer the kingdom of Singpoje. Singpoje was killed in the battle and Mangpoje fled to Drugu. All the areas between Phagyi Yungwa and Kongdre fell under the control of Namri Songtsen. The Dunhuang documents related to Tibetan history say,

King Tri Lontsen sent a force of 90,000 troops (to invade Singpoje). Nyang Tsegu and Non Tronpo were sent on a reconnaissance mission. We Yitsab and Tsepong Nagseng advised (Originally invited) the king (Tri Lontsen). The river was dried and the banks were leveled. The castle (of Singpoje) was destroyed and Gutri Singpoje was captured.

Mangpoje Sumbu fled to Drugu. All the areas below Phagyi Yungwa and above Kongdre were handed over to the king (Tri Lontsen).

Namri Songtsen conquered the kingdom of Singpoje with the help of Nyang Tsegu, Non Dronpu, We Yitsab and Tsepong Nagseng. He made them his ministers and granted to their families many serfs as rewards. From this, we know that there existed in ancient times a system of giving rewards to those who performed well in military campaigns. In the Dunhuang documents on Tibetan history, it is said,

> The subjects of the father rose up in opposition, and the people of his mother's homeland revolted. Revolts broke out also in Shangshung, Dzo Sumpa, Nyanyi Dakpo, Kongpo, Nyangpo and other areas. Father Namri Songtsen was killed by poison.

It is clear from this that revolts broke out in the above regions during the time of Songtsen's father, Namri Songtsen.

Chapter Two

The Tibetan Army during the Reign of Songtsen Gampo

—◆:◆—

In circa 619, Songtsen Gampo was enthroned. There were many independent tribes in Tibet at that time. These tribes gradually realized the need for a central administration for the unity, peace, stability and progress of the country. Songtsen Gampo also found it necessary to unify and consolidate all the tribes in the country under his rule. First he subjugated through diplomatic means Dakpo, Kongpo, Sumpa and other regions which had refused to accept the rule of the Tibetan king in the time of his father. According to the Tibetan records discovered from Dunhuang, after the death of King Tri Lontsen (Namri Songtsen), his son Tri Songtsen, Nyangpoje Shangnang (Nyang Mangpoje) conquered the entire kingdom of Sumpa by diplomatic means, without harming the people or livestock, and won the people's support and willingness to pay taxes.

At this time, Shangshung, a kingdom in northern Tibet, was militarily powerful. The Tibetan king conquered it by establishing a matrimonial alliance with it. The Dunhuang Tibetan history says, "Songtsen extended matrimonial relations to Shangshung Debu with the aim of conquering it. The king offered his sister Semakar to King Lekmi of Shangshung as a bride." Semakar was well aware of her brother's plan. Enduring great hardship, she collected and sent secret information about the military situation of Shangshung to Songtsen several times. Songtsen accordingly made his war plans and sent his ministers with a force to invade Shangshung. The Tibetan force subjugated the kingdom, encountering only minor resistance.

After this, in order to conquer the neighboring kingdoms, Songtsen decided first to unify the whole country of Tibet under his rule. He therefore subjugated all the remaining small kingdoms within Tibet. During his time, many Tibetan ministers who were brave and skilled in military and secular affairs emerged, such as Minister Shang and Minister Gar. The king himself was wise, brave, strong and powerful. The *White Annals* say,

> In the manifestation of the One God, Padmapani,
> Like a mighty Maheshvara, who dictates the two-fold system,
> Songtsen Gampo, victorious over the three worlds,
> Subjugated the kingdoms of the four frontiers.

They also say,

> By decree of the Great Monarch,
> Like a wild horse goaded by the crop of immeasurable bravery,
> The army of the red faced Tibetan barbarians
> is known to have conquered two-thirds of the world.

In around 635, Songtsen sent a delegation to China for the first time in Tibetan history, beginning the tradition of exchanging gifts between the Tibetan kings and the Tang emperors. In 636, when Songtsen heard that Tokiki, king of Uyghur and Drugu (Tuyuhun), had requested the Tang Emperor (Tai Zong) to give his daughter Wencheng Kongzhu in marriage, he immediately sent a large force of cavalry under the command of his minister Gar, with gifts, to China with the same purpose. The Emperor refused and the Tibetan cavalry returned empty handed. Offended, Songtsen dispatched four columns of 20,000 troops by way of the northern route to attack Drugu and the Jang kingdom.

Before that, the Tibetan army had invaded Nepal. It is said that there was a stone pillar installed by the Nepal king Narendra, bearing an inscription about Nepal paying tribute to Tibet. In 635, Nepal King Amshawarma (605-621 CE) offered his daughter to Songtsen as his bride. Ministers Gar Tongsen and Sambhota, with around 100 cavalry, were sent to receive her. Fearing that Tibet would launch military attacks, the Nepali king decided to give his daughter (Bhrikuti Devi) to the Tibetan king. Three years later, in 639, the princess proceeded from Nepal to Tibet. With her she brought a statue of Mikyo Dorje (Manuvajra) as her dowry. The Ramoche Temple was constructed in Lhasa to enshrine the statue.

There is no consensus among scholars about how long the Tibetan troops remained in Nepal. Nepal revolted [against the Tibetan army] during the time of Duesung Mangpoje or before that. According to an old Tibetan record discovered from Liyul, King Trede Tsugten was in Nepal in a Horse year. From this, it is clear that Nepal had been under Tibet's rule since the time of Songtsen until Trisong.

According to both the old and new Chinese Annals, having had his throne seized by his paternal uncle, the Nepali king Narendra Dewa fled to Tibet and requested the Tibetan king to help him regain his throne. The Tibetan king helped him retake his throne from his uncle. Nepal thus became a part of Tibet. In his *A Short History of Nepal*, Nepalese scholar N. B Thapa says that Nepal's king Harsha Vartanta offered his daughter Bhrikuti to Songtsen Gampo, the king of Tibet in the north, in order to maintain friendly relations with him. There were many pieces of evidence proving that the Tibetan army remained in Nepal for many years. For example, in Nepal there are many Tibetan clans, such as Tsang, Lama, Sharpa and Tamang, which are said to be descended from Tibetan soldiers who once lived in Nepal.

As mentioned above, Tuyuhun or Drugu and Xinjiang or Jang submitted themselves to Songtsen Gampo. Consolidating about 200,000 troops from Qiang, Bailang and Tangshan, the Tibetan army attacked Chinese cities, causing heavy destruction and casualties. They seized Songzhou (in Sichuan). The Tibetan king again sent a mission with gifts to the Chinese court, with the message that if the Emperor did not give him his daughter, he would continue to attack China. The Emperor dispatched his commander Hanbe with a small elite force to encounter the Tibetan army, but was badly defeated. The Emperor again sent his commanders Hou Chunji, Cheli Sili and Nyeuchu Dali, with separate detachments, to confront the Tibetans. Commander Liu Len, with 50,000 cavalry, was sent to attack the Tibetan garrison at Songzhou. They fought the Tibetans for many days, killing more than 1,000 Tibetan soldiers. The Tibetans pulled back to some distance, and both sides remained inactive for several days.

Songtsen again sent a delegation to the Chinese court, with the message that he wanted to have friendly relations with China and that the Emperor should send the princess to him immediately, if not he would dispatch a large army to attack even the Emperor. Out of great fear, the Emperor agreed to give Songtsen his daughter. The Tibetan king sent his minister Gar, with a *drey*-full of gold dust and various kinds of jewellery to receive the princess. The Emperor was pleased and sent the princess, escorted by a large force, led by his minister Jiangxia Daozong, to Tibet in 641. The Chinese farewell party camped at Poho and stayed there for a few days. Songtsen himself, leading a force, arrived at Tso Kyaring Ngoring to receive the princess. Kongzhu brought along with her an image of Buddha Shakyamuni as a representation of her faith. On the way she met Songtsen and they stayed at Jyekundo in Yulshul for a few days. After that, they headed to Lhasa. The two countries remained peaceful without mutual hostilities for a brief period after that.

Some say that Kongjo brought with her seeds from China and introduced agricultural practices to Tibet, and that agriculture had not developed in Tibet before her arrival. This fairy tale is due to lack of knowledge about the real history of Tibet; Tibetans had already started raising stock and cultivating crops as their main occupation during the period of the successive Buddhist kings of Tibet, before Kongzhu arrived in Tibet. This is clear from history.

In around 648, the Central Indian king Harsha sent a priest to China to present gifts to the Chinese Emperor. In return, the Emperor sent his royal emissary Wang Yuance, escorted by about 300 cavalry, to India to deliver return gifts to the Indian king. By the time Wang and his party reached India, Harsha had died and his minister Arjuna had occupied the throne and started persecuting Buddhists. He assaulted the Chinese delegates, robbed them of all their belongings, and killed most of their troops. Wang fled to Nepal and appealed to Songtsen for help. Songtsen dispatched around 8,000 cavalry, comprising Tibetan and Nepalese troops, with Wang, to India on a punitive mission. When they arrived at Trishta, north of the Ganga, they fought Arjuna's army. After a few days, they crushed Arjuna's army. Arjuna gathered more troops to fight back, but was defeated. The Tibetans arrested Arjuna, along with his relatives. Arjuna's rival king, Kumara of Kamarupa (Assam), was overjoyed and sent a large quantity of rich gifts to Songtsen. Due to the hot climate of India and the thick forests there, Songtsen withdrew all his troops soon after that.

Greatly impressed, the Chinese Emperor (Tai-Tsung) praised Songtsen highly and offered him high titles. Songtsen promised to provide military help to the Emperor whenever he needed it. The Emperor hosted a grand banquet for Songtsen in the traditional Chinese style and sent artists expert in farming silkworms, making glass and building windmills to Tibet.

Songtsen, in order to overpower the countries surrounding Tibet, unified all the regions within Tibet under his direct rule, either by peaceful or military ways. He sent Thonmi to India (to study linguistics). Thonmi invented a Tibetan writing system. The king codified 10 virtuous commandments *(lha chos dge ba bcu)* and 16 codes of civil mark *(mi chos gtsang ma bcu drug)*. He also created several great laws related to the military. He opened the door for Buddhism in Tibet and made great efforts to spread it throughout the country. He constructed many temples, including Trulnang Temple. This king, the first of the Three Great Buddhist Kings of Tibet, was a wrathful emanation of Avaloketshevara. In his time, the prowess and fame of the Tibetan army was beyond description. Tibet's military strength was unmatched by China and India, as is mentioned in many annals and in the Tibetan records discovered from Dunhuang. No one can say these accounts are not true. Though Songtsen, who conquered many territories in his short lifetime, had greater achievements than Genghis Khan of Mongolia and Alexander the Great of the Greeks, the stories of his marvelous deeds were confined to Tibet in the form of oral narratives, and they were not published or translated into foreign languages.

If Songtsen was born in 617 and died in 653, he lived 36 years. According to the theory that he lived from 569 to 650, he lived 82 years. There is no consensus among scholars regarding the dates of his birth and death. I have treated 617 as the year of Songtsen's birth. However, further research on this subject is required.

It is said that after Songtsen's death, Chinese troops arrived in Lhasa and set fire to the Potala Palace. They searched for the image of Shakyamuni, but not finding it, they took the image of Jowo Mikyo Dorje to a distance of a half-day's march. This is not true, because there is not even an inkling of this event in any reliable Tibetan sources, Tunhuang Tibetan documents or Chinese annals.

Songtsen was succeeded by Mangsong Mangtsen to the throne. Because he was so young, his minister Gar ruled the country for 15 years. Gar created a system of holding a conference for the interior ministers, rulers of principalities and regional leaders of Tibet whenever there were important political and military matters to discuss. According to oral tradition, Gar and his troops camped and resided at the foot of the mountain called Lonpo Serchen in Domé for many years.

The Tibetan army used Domé as their main military base whenever there was war between Tibet and China. Due to their long stay in Domé, many Tibetan soldiers settled there, marrying local women. As a result, there were many old clans of U and Tsang, especially Nyang and Khyungpo, in Domé. The majority of the people of the Chone area in Amdo are descendants of Tibetan soldiers who had been posted there in ancient times.

In around 658, the people of Drugu surrendered themselves to China. Commanding a large army, Gar led an expedition to Drugu in order to restore Tibet's rule over it. Fighting lasted for about eight years. Minister Song Hurkuo of Drugu surrendered to Tibet and gave detailed information about Drugu's political situation. Prince Muyung's army and his Queen Hunhu Kongzhu fled to Liangchou (Kansu). Drugu was once again made a part of the Tibetan empire.

In around 666, Gar Tongtsen returned to Lhasa from Domé and died after a prolonged fever. Gar was illiterate, but he was intelligent, self-controlled, brave, strong and expert in military affairs. He was very popular and highly regarded by everyone. It is said that Tibet's military prowess was extended through his efforts, and this is true.

Gar had four sons; the eldest Gartsen Nyadombu succeeded his father as the senior minister. The younger sons became military leaders and the Tibetan army became stronger than ever. After the Tibetans defeated Drugu, many people from Drugu fled to Liangchou as refugees. The Tibetan army prevented them from seeking refuge in China. In 670, Tibetan forces raided many regions of China and seized 12 major Chinese castles. The Chinese Emperor convened a meeting and summoned the senior ministers Chang Khe and Yan Lipen and General Chipi Holi to make plans about how to drive out the Tibetan troops. The meeting however did not reach any unanimous decision.

Following this, the Tibetan forces captured 18 large regions of China and continued their military campaigns within China. The Emperor sent his ministers Xue Jengui and Anshi Choching, with 100,000 troops, to confront the Tibetans. They twice attacked the Tibetan positions at Guchi and Dasin, leading to high casualties on both sides. However, under the command of Gar Tsen Nyadombu, the Tibetan forces guarded their positions strongly. Finding no other options, the Chinese asked Gar for peaceful negotiations. The Emperor rebuked the two ministers for failing in their mission and removed them from their ministerial posts. (In 1954 when the Dalai Lama visited China, Mao Zedong narrated to him a short account of the Tibetan army having invaded China.)

In around 676, the Tibetan army attacked Shanzhou and Kuozhou in Gansu province, killing the leaders and robbing the people. Hearing this, the Chinese

Emperor (Tang Gaozong) dispatched his minister Liu Jengui to Taoho and General Liyu to Liangchou, with troops. Before they arrived, the Tibetan army had captured the cities of Tiezhou, Mikong and Dangling of Gansu. Enraged, the Emperor summoned his army commanders and reprimanded them, saying that their failure to defeat the Tibetan forces had led to the loss of many cities in the northeast, near to Tibet. He dismissed them from his service. He appointed his political advisor, Li Qingwen, as the General and ordered him to collect more troops from Chiennan and Shannan provinces and drive away the Tibetan troops. Li Qingwen was an expert in military affairs. Unlike his predecessors, he made repetitive attacks on the Tibetan army, causing great casualties. However, the Tibetan forces retained their positions. The Chinese again attacked the Tibetan army camp of Gar Tsen Nyadombu in Kokonor, but many Chinese soldiers died or were injured in the battle. Commander Liu Shenli, aide of General Li Qingwen, lost his life because of his reckless courage on the battlefield.

Li took his remaining troops and occupied Fengli (on the eastern border of Kokonor), but they failed to push back the Tibetan forces. Owing to a rumour, all the Chinese troops suddenly fled in disorder. After this, Li's commander Heichi volunteered to fight and leading a cavalry of 500 troops, attacked the Tibetan army camp under the cover of night, causing great casualties. In the darkness, they also unwittingly killed many of their own soldiers. However, the Chinese could not crush the Tibetan army; they fled to Shanzhou and hid there. The Emperor berated Li and demoted him in rank. He convened a meeting and summoned all the ministers to discuss how to defeat the Tibetan forces. However, there was no consensus among them as to what course of action they should take. Finally they decided to place garrisons at strategic locations on the Sino-Tibetan border. After that, both the Chinese and Tibetan armies remained inactive for some time.

In 679, King Mangsong died and his son Duesong Mangje aka Trulgyi Gyalpo, who was three years old, was enthroned. The senior minister Gar Tsen Nyadombu acted as the regent. A revolt broke out in Shangshung and Tibet sent troops to suppress it. Shangshung was once again brought under Tibet's rule. In those times, Tibet had no real competition in eastern Asia in terms of military strength and it was feared by other counties. Tibet undertook military expeditions into many neighbouring countries.

In around 680, the Tibetan army leader Tsenpo Gar Triding and the Drugu minister Suhoko, leading a force of 30,000 troops, went to Holun (to the north of the Machu River). They fought with the Chinese General Li Qingwen's army at Hoshun near Longji (on the eastern border of Qinghai) for many years. The Chinese forces were defeated in a series of battles. The Chinese Emperor again sent Hechie Changzhing, with a force of 3,000 selected troops, to fight. They made a strong surprise attack on the Tibetan army camp, forcing the Tibetan general Tsenpo to flee for a while.

In the same year (680), Queen Kongjo died. Chinese delegates arrived in Tibet to offer condolences and funeral offerings for the queen. When they left, Tibet sent with them the Chinese minister Zhinsheng Yan, who had come to Tibet on a royal mission but had been abducted by Gar Tsen Nyadombu and detained in Tibet for many years.

During the time of Duesong Mangpoje, the Tang army constructed a fortress at Anwi, to the northwest of Maotsu in Xian, to repel the Tibetan troops. A man named Owu of Jang origin (from Golok) guided the Tibetan troops to capture the fortress. All the small regions of Mon on the valley (the Dali area in Yunan) surrendered themselves to the Tibetan king. Shangshung and Minyag had already fallen under Tibetan rule. The Tibetan empire in those times extended to the east as far as the border of Songzhou (Sang Fenshin in Sichuan), Maotsu (Maoxun in Sichuan), Suchou (Xia Changshen in Sichuan). It expanded in four directions, as far as Mon in the south (India); Kucha (Kucha in Xinjiang), Shuli (Kashgar in Xinjiang), Yutian (Hotan or Khotan) and Hui (Yanqi in Xinjiang) to the west and Uyghur in the north, extending many tens of thousands of kilometers *(lebar)*. It is said that there was no king of such power even during the periods of the Han and Wei dynasties. This is true.

In around 685, Minister Gar Tsen Nyadombu died and his younger brother Gar Triding Tsendro was appointed to his post. The two youngest brothers became leaders of Tibet's border forces. There were seven military leaders famous in Tibet in those times, and they were Ngog Dronshor, Ngog Lingkham, Non Gyaltsen, Pago Dongchen, Go Yagchung, Chogru Drongshor and Non Triton Yuljin. All of them were famous for their bravery, intelligence and military expertise, and it was said that they had great knowledge in the field of warfare.

In general, the Gar brothers were very brave and wise, and they gave remarkable service to the country. Out of jealousy, some people spread a rumour that Gar Tsen Nyensungton was plotting a revolt against the king. The rumour strained the relations between the king and Gar. Eventually, Gar Tsen was secretly murdered by some Tibetan soldiers. The youngest Gar brother, Sindose, was captured by the Chinese troops in 694 during a battle. Minister Gar Triding was demoted. In the following year, he was ordered to appear before the king in Lhasa, and committed suicide on his way to Lhasa. These are mentioned in Chinese records, but Tibetan sources do not mention anything about Gar Triding's suicide. Anyway, in the end, Gar's descendants were mistreated despite their great service. Therefore, there is a myth that most Tibetan government officials who made great service to the country were eventually punished as a result of the injustice done to the Gar lineage.

King Duesong Mangpoje was reportedly killed during a military expedition to Nepal and northern India to suppress a revolt. According to some Tibetan annals, he died in Jang. In the Dunhuang documents on Tibetan history, it is mentioned that he died in Mewa in 704. This means that Yunnan was part of Thailand at that time.

Tibet and Thailand shared friendly relations in those days. Thailand asked Tibet for military assistance. The Tibetan king, with a force, went to Jang or Mewa, to help the Thai king. This is probably true. However, whether it is true or not, the Tibetan king's death occurred in the same year.

Chapter Three

Tibet's Military Conquest in Asia during the Reign of King Trisong Deutsen

❖

At the dawn of the 8th century, Trisong Deutsen, also known as Me Agtsom, meaning "Bearded Old Man", ascended to the royal throne of Tibet. His mother, Trimalo, ruled on his behalf. He took several queens, one of them being Jangsa Tritsun, princess of Thailand. In 710, following in the footsteps of his grandfather Songtsen Gampo, he sent an envoy to the Tang court of China to request Princess Gyimshing Kongjo (Jincheng Kongzhu) as his bride. In fear of Tibet's military prowess, the Emperor granted the request. Trisong sent a reception team to bring the princess to Tibet, and the Chinese Emperor himself came up to Shi Pingxian (Shiban) to farewell his daughter.

In those times, there were continual conflicts along the border between Tibet and China. Minister Tara Lugong was appointed military leader and sent on a military expedition to China, with approximately 100,000 troops. After some fierce battles against the Chinese forces, they captured Feng Sihuna, a Chinese city. Chinese General Xia, with his army, arrived at the great bridge of Chang to encounter the Tibetans. In the battle, the Tibetans were defeated and Shigu city was lost to the Chinese in 748.

In those days, Tibet and Arabs had established military alliances. According to Shakabpa's *Tibet: a Political History,* in Arab countries there are names such as Tubbata and Tubbat Khan from Tibet inscribed on stones during the time of Orgon, indicating that there were close trade relations between the two countries.

About 755, King Tride Tsugtsen was murdered by his ministers Bal Dongtsen and Langmi. The two ministers also planned to kill the young king, Trisong. Minister Taktra Lugong knew about their plan. The two ministers were executed by the king (Trisong).

Trisong was enthroned at the age of 14. From his childhood, Trisong had great faith in Buddhism. Senior ministers Mashang Kyonpa Kye and Tara Lugong who professed the Bon religion created great obstructions to the spread of Buddhism. The Buddhist ministers Go Trisang and Takra Lugong removed those powerful ministers and contravened their plans. They promoted Buddhism. Ba Salnang and other Buddhist ministers were sent to India and Nepal at different times (to study Buddhism). On invitation, the Great Buddhist scholar Shantirakshita and the adept Padmasambhava arrived in Tibet and spread Buddhism in the country. Many Buddhist temples were built, including the white temple of Samye. The first Buddhist monks were ordained. Many Indian Buddhist texts were translated into Tibetan. The King was therefore very benevolent toward us.

There had been frequent conflicts between Tibet and China around this time. In 763, Trisong appointed Takra Lugong, Shang Gyal Lhanang, Shang Chim Gyalsig and Lhasang Pal as commanders and sent them on a military expedition to China, with about 200,000 troops from Tuyuhun (Drugu). They went up to the Chinese city of Qingzhou, where they defeated the Chinese forces. The Chinese governor Kaohui surrendered to the Tibetans. The Tibetan army continued with its military campaign and seized Feng Sihun in Binzhou. Emperor Dai Zong (Tai-Tsung) of China sent a large force under the command of his minister Kuo Tsiyi to encounter the Tibetans. An intense battle took place. The Chinese forces lost ground and fled.

According to other sources, the Emperor even changed the name of the place to Jincheng Kongjo in memory of his daughter.

With the help of the Chinese governor Kaohui, the Tibetans conquered the Chinese city of Xi'an with great speed. The Emperor, along with his family and relatives, fled to Shezhou. Minister Kou Tsiyi, with his family, fled to Niuxingu in the south. Regarding this, the Dunhuang Tibetan documents (folio no. 40) says:

It was the Tiger year. Shang Gyalzig, Takra, Shang Tongtsen, Shang Tsenpa and Le Chogpe attacked and seized Kangxi. The Chinese Emperor fled. The Tibetan troops crowned a new Chinese emperor and returned to Tibet.

After that, the Tibetan army invaded the Chinese capital X'ian or Ch'angan and seized the Kangxi Palace. They installed Queen Gimshing Kongjo's brother (Gaowang) as the new emperor, and gave him the Tibetan title Tashi. As per the Chinese tradition of changing the name of the era, the Tibetans announced the new era, named for Emperor Tashi. An agreement was made with the king that he would pay an annual tribute to Tibet. Fifteen days later, the Tibetan troops returned to Tibet.

The above accounts are found not only in Tibetan sources, but also in both the old and new Chinese annals, as well as in the Dunhuang documents. The rewards given to Minister Takra Lugong were also mentioned in the stone inscription installed at Shol, below the Potala Palace.

In 783, a peace treaty was signed between Tibet and China at a place called Chingshui, regarding border issues. In the agreement, Taozhou and the areas to the west of the Tatu River were included within Tibet. The Tibetan king assigned the northern area of the Machu River and eastern Gyatrak Thang (the field of Chinese blood) and Gyadur Thang (the field of Chinese graves), where the Chinese and Tibetans had fought fiercely, to different Tibetan army leaders for the defense of the country. The responsibility for the defense of the northern region was given to his nine famous generals. The king asked them whether they would be able to protect them or whether they needed additional troops. They replied that they would be able to hold the area permanently without additional troops. Hence the area got the name of Guthubthang, which means "the place able to be defended by nine." After many years, they asked the king if they should return. The king replied in the negative. As a result they settled there, leading a nomadic life; their descendants are called Kamalog *(bka' ma log)*, which means "those who received an order not to return".

Not long before that, during the time of King Pilawko and Prince Ko Lofeng of Siam (Thailand), China often attacked Siam. Siam therefore established a military alliance with Tibet. In 754, due to the invasion of Siam's area Nanchao by China, Tibet sent an army to help Siam and defeated the Chinese forces. In 778, during the reign of Siam's king Imohsun, Tibet and Siam also formed a military alliance. They jointly fought the Chinese in Sichuan. The Tibetan soldiers stayed in Siam for eight years. After this, as Siam and China had signed a peace treaty, the Tibetan troops withdrew from Siam. These accounts are found in Shakabpa's *Tibet: a Political History.*

Though China and Tibet entered into a treaty and ceased border conflicts at Kansu, they again started border conflicts a few years later. The Tibetan army captured Chingzhou, Lungzhou, Yinzhou, Shingzhou and other Chinese cities. The Tibetans and Chinese agreed to meet at the border place of Panling in Shingzhou for negotiations. Their meeting however ended without any agreement, followed by a war. The Tibetans killed several Chinese officers and arrested about 60 others, including Shuchu and Lusaye .

In 788, the Tibetan army again attacked Ch'ing, Sining, Chou and Huzhou. In 801, they captured Liangzhou and killed its governor. They destroyed the fence walls of the city. The Chinese Emperor (De Zong) sent a negotiation team led by an official named Yiwon to reconcile with the Tibetans. The delegates of the two nations met for negotiations. During the meeting, the Chinese delegates argued that the Tibetans had first breached the previous Sino-Tibetan treaty, while the Tibetans complained that the Chinese did not fulfill their promise to give a Chinese area to Tibet as reward for suppressing the rebels who revolted against the Emperor.

During the time of Trisong, the Tibetan troops conquered a large portion of China, and remained there for some time.

In order to bring relics of the Buddha from India for the White Stupa of Samye, Trisong gathered all the horses in Tibet and the time was fixed for all the troops to assemble at Phari. India's roads, villages, cities, etc. were surveyed. Following this the Tibetan army marched through the Trihti city of India. The king of the region was terrified and said to his men, "The king of the remote land of Tibet has countless numbers of cavalry and infantry troops, it is better for us to surrender before they destroy us." He placed the shoes of the Tibetan king on the top of the palace and sat below them with his retinue, and then said, "I submit my kingdom to you, the king of Tibet, and I will offer you annual tribute." The Tibetan army was said to have conquered the kingdom.

The Tibetan army crossed the River Ganges and seized Magadha. All the people of Magadha were scared and hid their wealth at Odantapuri and most of them fled to the east. Without having to fight, the Tibetan troops headed to Bodhgaya where they made offerings to the *bodhi* tree. Opening the stupa, they took out 6 *drey* measures of relics and sealed the stupa as before. They erected an iron pillar on the bank of the River Ganges, and the inscription on the pillar says (said) that all the areas beyond the pillar belonged to Tibet. A Tibetan garrison was kept there to guard the area. The garrison soldiers could not return even after many years. Hence they settled there. Their descendants are the Kuru people living at Botathang. These accounts are found in the *White Annals*.

Following this, the Tibetan king sent Sham Kyechung to Turkistan on a spying mission. After his arrival, the Tibetan king sent troops and conquered Turkistan. The land was divided into five administrative divisions, each made up of 10,000 households, and one Tibetan minister was appointed as its leader. One piece of evidence to prove that Turkistan was at one time under Tibetan rule is that the ruins of a Tibetan castle have been unearthed there. In addition, letters exchanged between the Tibetan generals and the people of Turkistan   als, various kinds of Tibetan articles, tax-registers, clay idols, murals, etc., were discovered in Turkistan. Later, archeologists from Britain, France and other foreign countries took these articles to their countries. Moreover, according to the *White Annals,* the *Tang Annals* say that many people of the areas which had been previously under Tibetan rule were forced to migrate to other places, and the people of Drugu were forced to migrate to southern Tibet. Many people of Xinjiang were expelled to Nepal. For example, in a letter sent by the Xinjiang people in Nepal to the Tibetan governor of Xinjiang, they requested the governor to help them get rights and privileges equal to those enjoyed by the Nepalese people.

Around that time, the military power of Tibet extended far into both the east and the west. In 693, during the reign of King Duesong, the Chinese attacked the Tibetan army in Anshi and captured the areas occupied by the Tibetan army. In 790, Tibetan forces retook the lost areas from the Chinese after a long fight. All these accounts are found in the Shakabpa's *Tibet: a Political History.*

About this time, Tibetan troops marched through Pamir in the west, crossing the Oxus River, into Arab lands. They stayed there for many years. As evidence of their living there, there is a small lake with the Arabic name AI-Tubbat, meaning "small Tibetan lake". This lake is said to be found on old maps. Later, the Arabs had a very powerful king named Harun al-Rashid. He established a military alliance with China and started attacking the Tibetan positions. Despite suffering high casualties, the Tibetan force defended the area very bravely, without losing it.

In *Tibet: a Political History*, Shakabpa has quoted E. Bretschneider's book, saying Tibet's military power reached its peak and it captured a large area of China in the middle of the 8th century. Later Tibet turned its military interest toward the west. As a result, China suffered fewer military raids from Tibet.

Around that time, Tibet's military strength was unmatched by any country in the world. A rumour spread that the neighbouring countries to the four corners of Tibet were planning to make a combined attack on Tibet. At that time, Master Padmasambhava was residing at Samye. At the request of the Tibetan king, he performed a magical rite to avert the enemy's attack, and the neighbouring countries suddenly changed their plans and returned to where they had come from. This is mentioned in the inscription on the stone pillar installed at the end of the bridge near Chongye Taktse. The conclusion of the inscription reads:

Tibet's borders in the four corners touched Be'u, Mu chi'u and Su chi'u in the east, the land of Brahmin *(bram ze)* in the south, the land of Islam in the west and Hor in the north; the circumference of Tibet's entire territorial boundary is many thousands of miles *(dpag tshad)*. Nobody as powerful as the Tibetan king had ever appeared, even during the times of the Han, Yu and Chi'u emperors.

Rigzin Jigme Lingpa has also praised the king Trisong, calling him "Trisong Deutsen, the King of Universe." These historical facts testify that in those times the Tibetan kings had no equals.

At that time, the Tibetan king and the Arabian Caliph formed a military alliance. They jointly appointed a king in Iran, Ferghana. After that, the Caliph found it necessary to establish military relations with eastern countries and political relations with western countries. Therefore, he allowed foreign embassies in Arabia. Hurt by this, the Khorasan king protested to the Caliph. Caliph Harun died soon afterwards. The new Arabian king Al Maimum sought a military alliance with Tibet and promised to abide by the existing treaties between them. These accounts are found in a book written by Walter Leifer.

According to AI-Ya'qubi, the Tibetan force once seized the Arabian capital Transoxania, as well as Samarkand. Maimum established military relations with the Tibetan army leader stationing in Turkistan (Liyul) and signed an agreement with him. The Tibetan army leader sent him a gift of a gold statue inlaid with different precious gems, and this statue is reported to be found in Kapala, a city in Mecca.

In 798, Trisong Deutsen died and his prince Mune Tsenpo was enthroned. In 804, Mune's younger brother Tride Songtsen, aka Sena Leg Jingyon, was enthroned.

Chapter Four

Peace Treaties Signed between Tibet and China during the Reign of Tri Ralpachen

—◆◇◆—

In 815, Tritsug Detsen, aka Ralpachen, ascended the royal throne as the fortieth king of Tibet. At that time, Tibetan forces occupied Chinese areas such as Kansu, a western mountain called Xishan, Nanchao, Xiatan and the western part of Sichuan. In those days, there used to be frequent minor conflicts between China and Tibet at the borders. Shortly after that, Chinese Emperor Xian Zong died and Mu Zong was crowned. China and Tibet exchanged envoys to offer consolation messages to the departed kings and congratulations to the new ones. Their relations improved and hostility decreased. Tibet gave back Nanjing and Yunnan to China. The two nations agreed to a cease fire and to sign a peace treaty. They exchanged correspondence several times for a few years.

In 821, corresponding to the Iron-Female-Ox year, with several Tibetan translators and *panditas* and Chinese monks acting as mediators, representatives of the two countries met at the Sino-Tibetan border area of Gugu Meru to sign a treaty on peaceful coexistence and the maintenance of their own territorial borders. After a series of negotiations, they drafted a treaty on border issues. On the signing day, some animals were killed and sacrificial offerings were made. Bonpo priests performed rites. With the Three Jewels, exalted beings, the sky, earth, mountains, the sun, the moon and stars as witnesses, the representatives of the two nations swore all together that whoever transgressed the treaty would be killed as one would kill an animal. The negotiators then, one by one, went up to the platform, took an oath and put their signatures on the treaty. The content of the treaty was inscribed on three stone pillars, one installed at Gugu Meru on the border of the two countries, the second in front of the Kangxi Palace and the third near the gate of the Jokhang Temple in Lhasa. Since the full content of the treaty is found in many sources, I will write below only the gist of the treaty to avoid too much detail:

> Tibet and China shall protect their own areas and borders of which they are now in possession. The whole region to the east is China and the whole region to the west belongs to Tibet. The two countries shall not have enmity against each other, nor attack or invade each other. Tibetans are happy in Tibet and the Chinese are happy in China.

The integrality of the treaty shows clearly that China and Tibet are distinct nations. This is an unquestionable fact. Later the Chinese manipulated the sentence in the treaty "*chab srid gcig tu mol ba* (conferred together for a solution to their political issues)" by interpreting it as "negotiated to unify the political entities". This manner of openly distorting facts and creating controversies shows clearly that China has no real evidence to claim Tibet as an integral part of China.

The sentence "*chab srid gcig tu mol ba*" has two meanings, direct and indirect. It means that the two nations conferred together in negotiations or discussions on their political issues. In short, it means that the two countries met and discussed their own political issues. Nowadays, the Chinese government misconstrues the sentence, saying the two countries negotiated to become one nation. The treaty has been inscribed on stone-pillars, which still exist. Therefore, no matter how hard the Chinese try to by-pass the treaty, they cannot take the people of the world for fools; they are instead revealing their real face as greedy colonists. This is my brief comment in passing here.

King Tri Ralpachen had a deep faith in Buddhism. He granted farmlands, pasturelands and cattle to monasteries and temples as sources of sustenance. He assigned seven households to each monk in order to support them. He created new monastic laws. In short, he did much for the benefit of Buddhism. Ministers Be Takna, Chogro Lhalo, Leg Dugtsen and others who were hostile to Buddhism banished the king's eldest brother, Tsangma, to Mon. They made a false report to the king that Minister Drenka Palyon, the most senior pro-Buddhist minister, and the queen were having a secret affair. The king ordered the execution of both of them. The queen committed suicide. Drenka Palyon fled to the north, but was caught in Nyethang and executed. An effigy was made from his skin. In 841, at the age of 36, while the king was drunk and asleep in his Maldro Palace, the three ministers assassinated him by strangling him. They installed Lang Darma Udum Tsenpo as the new king. Be Takna became his senior minister.

Around that time, Tibetans witnessed many bad omens. For example, many epidemics took place in Tibet and agricultural diseases destroyed the crops. The anti-Buddhist ministers blamed Buddhism for bringing the misfortunes, and they spread negative rumours about Buddhism. They demanded that Buddhism and the laws based on Buddhism be banned. Hoping to gain more powers, King Lang Darma said that the image of Buddha Shakyamuni (Jowo Shakyamuni) brought to Tibet by Kongju was the image of a devil and that it was causing many misfortunes wherever it was kept. He further said that Kongju was a demon who had destroyed the good landscape of Tibet, and that China was planning to conquer Tibet. He declared that Buddhism must be destroyed. By his command, the images and texts in all the monasteries and temples in Tibet, including the Tsuglakhang Temple, were destroyed. High lamas were killed, monks of medium status were banished and most ordinary monks were forcefully converted into laymen. A strict law was passed that no one was allowed to utter even a word of Buddhism. In 846, unable to bear the current affairs of State, some pro-Buddhism ministers requested the king to read the inscription on the stone-pillars installed by Tri Ralpachen near the Temple. One day, while the king was reading the inscription, Lhalung Palgyi Dorje, pretending to prostrate himself in front of the king, shot an arrow and killed the king. Lhalung immediately fled towards Kokonor.

Chapter Five

The Fall of the Tibetan Empire after King Langdar's Suppression of Buddhism

—◆—

The year after Langdar's assassination, his junior queen gave birth to a son named Woesung, "Guarded by Light". Out of jealousy, his senior queen adopted a baby and announced that she herself had borne him. She gave him the name Yumten "Protected by Mother". When the two boys grew up, a dispute developed between them about the throne. Woesung ruled Yoru, which comprised Ngari and the northern part of Tibet, while Yumten ruled U-ru (the central part of Tibet). In this way, the empire was divided. The two princes and their partisans were called the Elder Prince and the Younger Prince, Larger Faction and Smaller Faction, Gold One and Turquoise One or Meat Eaters and Tsampa Eaters. There was a constant power struggle between the two rival factions. Peasant uprisings broke out several times and the royal tombs were destroyed. As a result, the Tibetan empire broke up into many small principalities. The chiefs constructed fortified castles and kept armies to protect themselves and their own territories against their enemies.

The tax collectors and officials stationed in Tibetan border areas such as Doto, Dome, Gyalrong, Gyalthang and Lhomon during the Tibetan royal dynasty resided there permanently as rulers. As their biographies explain it, those officials were descendants of Tibetan kings and ministers.

The disintegration of the Tibetan empire was followed by frequent civil wars in the country for several years. In Dome, for example, Shang Pipi and Shang Phosher, who had been posted to eastern Tibet as army leaders during the reign of King Tri Ralpachen, became political rivals and fought in a battle at Ta Shaton. Phosher constructed strong fortifications around his army camp. Pipi's commander Pang Gesin and Manglor Silu secretly camped near the fortress of Phosher. Pang Gesin provoked Phosher by sending him an arrow and a letter containing harsh words. Enraged by the letter, Phosher went out of his fortress, leading his troops (to fight). Pang Gesin and his troops, who were lying in wait, ambushed them, killing Phosher and many of his troops. This account is found in the *Chinese History on Tibet* translated into Tibetan by Dekbar Khenpo.

According to Yarlung Jowoi's *History of Buddhism,* Jetsun Sonam Gyaltsen's *The Clear Mirror* and Nelpa Pandita's *A Garland of Flowers of Ancient Story,* during the period of political fragmentation of Tibet, local chiefs, landlords and monasteries independently ruled their own serfs or territories. They did not bother to make combined efforts for the protection of the country against foreign powers and for the overall progress of the economy, the military and the policy of the country. As a result, many areas of Tibet were lost to external powers. Between 1048 and 1089, there were regular wars between China and Tibet at Lanzhou, which had been under Tibetan rule during the Tibetan imperial period. During the wars, the Chinese general Shao Jiang killed thousands of Tibetan soldiers, and Shao himself lost his life in the war. Some Chinese records mention that Tibet and Xixia were at war in 1081 when the Sung Dynasty was ruling China. The leader of the Tibetan army at that time was Donden, son of Ngadag Tride, who arrived in the Tsongkha region of Dome and ruled the 18 regions of Dokham.

In the same century, a very powerful and miraculous man called Kyechog Lingje Gesar Norbu Dradul was born on the border of Doto and Dome. He invaded many nearby small kingdoms and promoted Buddhism. There are many tales about him, available in both the oral tradition and in the texts. However, further research is required to find out and confirm the years, locations, events and other things relevant to the stories about him. Shakabpa has also mentioned this in his book *Tibet: a Political History*.

Chapter Six

The Emergence of Regional Leaders and Civil Wars during the Period of Political Disintegration of Tibet

—◆:◆—

In the beginning (of the period of political disintegration), there emerged two rival groups of regional leaders in Dokham, Lhokha, Dakpo and Kongpo—one led by Be Phosher Lekong and six men from the upper Chim and the other led by Shupu Taktse Nyak. They had their own armies to control their subjects and to safeguard their territories.

Over time, the country broke up into 11 independent regions: Tsangto, Drampa,Lhatse ruled by the Dro and Chogru clans; Shu Nyemo, Drangkhar Jetsen ruled by the Nyang and Nang clans; Phanpo Sadam ruled by the Dro and Ma clans; Yarlung ruled by the Chim and Nyag clans; Yarlung Namo, Yartse Martse ruled by the Nyib and Shungpu clans; and Chongye and Chokhar ruled by the Shu and Nyag clans. Other regions were Dolpo, Konpgo, Nyal and Lhasa, which also had their own rulers.

The collapse of the Tibetan empire resulted in the loss of the integral power of the country. There was no government army deployed on the borders to protect the country's frontiers, unlike the situation which existed during the period of the successive Buddhist kings of Tibet. Consequently, neighbouring countries gradually started to annex parts of Tibet in the border regions. Tibet underwent a very weak period in its history. This is of course the result of the evil deeds of the partisans of Langdar (Lang Darma), who was hostile to Buddhism, and his descendants. However, some people say that if Langdar had succeeded in his mission (the destruction of Buddhism), the Tibetan empire would not have collapsed. This view is utter nonsense, because history shows clearly that due to the wide spread of Buddhism in Tibet during the period of the Tibetan Buddhist kings, the Tibetan empire expanded and became powerful.

From around 877, there were frequent civil wars among different regions of Tibet, disrupting peace and causing famine in the country. For China, the period coincided with the end of the Tang Dynasty in 907 and the foundation of the Song Dynasty, characterized by political turmoil in the country. China was therefore not in a position to pose a threat to Tibet.

In around 978, during the suppression of Buddhism by Langdar, 10 educated men from U-Tsang fled to Dome, where they took ordination from a monk named

Lachen Gongpa Rabsel. Then they came back and founded many monasteries in U-Tsang, resulting in the emergence of four major monasteries founded by Lumey, Barag, Rag and Dring. As these monasteries expanded in size and the population of monks increased, rivalry and hostility developed between them. They frequently engaged in conflicts through the 11th and 12th centuries. In 1106, a bitter conflict broke out between the two communities of Lumey and Barag, during which many of Samye Monastery's temples were destroyed by fire and its walls were demolished. The temples were later renovated by Ra Lotsawa Dorje Drak.

In around 1160, the four major monasteries were plunged into the civil wars affecting Lhasa, Yarlung, Phanpo and other parts of Tibet, and the conflicts continued for many years. Ramoche, Rasa Trulnang and Tradruk temples were damaged by arson. Dagom Tsultrim Nyingpo brought reconciliation among them through dialogue. He renovated and restored two temples in Lhasa and handed them over to Lama Shang of Gungthang. Details about these are found in the *History of Buddhism in Lhodrak*, the *Blue Annals* and the *Religious History of Lhorong*.

Civil wars caused tremendous suffering and loss to the people in terms of both lives and property, and temples created in the traditional Tibetan architectural style suffered great damage.

In 1040, about 30 years after the foundation of the four big monasteries mentioned above, Lha Lama Jangchup Woe, the king of Ngari Guge, invited the great Indian Buddhist scholar Atisha to come to Tibet. Atisha rejuvenated Buddhism in Tibet and therefore Tibetans feel very grateful to him. His disciple Drom Tonpa Gyalwe Jungne founded the Kadampa School of Buddhism. Khon Konchok Gyalpo founded the Sakya School in 1073. After that, Marpa Lotsawa, Jetsun Milarepa and Dakpo Lhaje established the Kagyu School, which branched out into four primary and eight secondary sub schools[1]. Each school established its monastic seat. Gradually, many monasteries mushroomed in different parts of Tibet, and each school preserved, maintained and promoted its own doctrines and practices. From Tibet, Buddhism spread itself further towards the north. We should be grateful to them and commemorate the great services they have done for all sentient beings. However, on the other hand, those monasteries became embroiled in bitter sectarianism and rivalry.

---

[1] The four primary sub schools of Kagyue are 1) the Karmapa school founded by Düsum Khyenpa, 2) the Barompa school founded by Darma Wangchuk, 3) the Tsalpa school founded by Zhang Tsalpa Tsöndrü Drakpa, and 4) the Phagmo Dru school founded by Phagmo Drupa. These are called Primary Schools of Kagyue because they are directly originated from Dakpo Lhaje, the founder of the Kagyu School.

The eight secondary sub schools of Kagyue are 1) Drigung Kagyue, 2) Taklung kagyue, 3) Trophu kagyue, 4) Drukpa kagyue, 5) Marwa kagyue, 6) Yerpa kagyue, 7) Yasang kagyu and 8) Shugseb kagyue. These are called the Secondary Sub Schools of Kagyue because they were developed by the eight disciples of Dakpo Lhaje.

In short, after the fall of the Tibetan empire in 846 and for the following 393 years, Tibet lacked a central administration to rule over the whole of the country. In those times, not only Tibet, but even China and India had no central rulers, and they were divided into many small kingdoms that often engaged in civil wars. However, as for Tibet, the Tibetan people themselves had been ruling their own country until Genghis Khan, who, after becoming the king of all the tribes of Mongolia, invaded Tibet and embarked upon a campaign to expand his power into central and western Asia and eastern Europe. This will be discussed in later chapters.

Chapter Seven

Regional Conflicts during the Periods of Sakya, Phagdru, Rinpung and Tsangpa

❖

As briefly discussed in the previous chapter, during the period of political disintegration of Tibet, the high lamas, regional rulers and landlords maintained their own armies to rule their territories, secure their power and increase their influence. These petty rulers often waged war with each other. Around the year 1200, Genghis Khan led a military expedition into Tibet from the northeastern border. Tibet was not able to make a unified resistance against the Mongols; each regional leader tried to avoid confrontation in their own sphere of influence, by greeting the Mongols with gifts and promising to pay tribute on time.

In 1206, a large Mongol force arrived in U-Tsang. Sakya Pandita and Genghis Khan established a relationship between them that we could call "priest-patron" relationship. Following this, the Mongol army diverted its military campaign into China, central Asia and Eastern Europe, conquering them one by one. Accounts of these campaigns are found in many sources.

Nowadays, China claims that Genghis Khan destroyed all the external forces from China and unified the whole country of China militarily, implying that Mongolia is a part of China. According to many reliable sources, the truth is that the Mongols invaded China only to extend the Mongol empire, not to help China.

Tibetan high lamas, regional rulers and landlords gave annual tribute to the Mongols in order to avoid any conflict, and at the same time they sent emissaries to the chiefs of the different Mongol tribes to gain their support.

In 1207, when Genghis Khan's troops came to Tibet, the Tibetan regional rulers Desi Joga and Tsalpa received them with a grand banquet and surrendered themselves to them. Genghis Khan sent a letter to Sakya Pandita, expressing his desire to invite him to Mongolia in the future to become his spiritual teacher. He excused the Tibetans from paying tax to the Mongols and became a devout and powerful patron of Buddhism.

In 1227, Genghis Khan died, and was succeeded as Great Khan by Prince Godan. Taking advantage of this, Tibetans stopped paying tribute to the Mongols for several years. Godan Khan got angry and sent an army of about 30,000 troops under the command of his minister Dorta Darkhan (Dorta Nagpo) to Tibet on a punitive mission in 1240. They burned Reting Monastery and Gyal Temple, among others, and killed around 500 monks, including Soton. After that, they went on to attack Drigung, but they spared it at the request of Chenga Rinpoche. Godan was looking for the most educated religious master of Tibet, and he was informed that Sakya Pandita was the one. He therefore invited Sakya Pandita to Mongolia. He ordered Tibetans to continue paying tribute to the Mongols and left unchanged the status quo of a decentralised Tibet. The regional rulers were required to entertain and host Mongol emissaries and imperial messengers whenever they came to Tibet. However, no Mongol rulers remained in Tibet.

Following this, a detachment of the Mongol army arrived in Tibet to conduct a census. They divided Tibet into 13 myriarchies, each with a fixed number of households. Soon after that they returned to Mongolia.

Later, on the invitation of the Mongol emperor, the Karmapa went to the Mongol's court and established "priest-patron relations with the Emperor. In 1244, Godan Khan invited Sakya Pandita and his nephews (Phakpa Lodro Gyaltsen and Chagna Dorje) to Mongolia, where the lama gave religious speeches to the Emperor, his ministers and the people. The lama also performed many other religious activities there. From Mongolia, Sakya Pandita sent letters to Tibet, advising all the people, lay and ordained, of the three provinces of Tibet to pay tribute to the Mongols and telling them how to deal with the Mongols in order to avoid conflict. Entrusting his spiritual lineage to his nephew Phakpa Lodro Gyaltsen, Sakya Pandita passed away at the age of 70 in 1251. Not long after that Godan Khan also died.

In 1253, Kublai Khan, called King Sechen by the Tibetans, who had been appointed as the Khan of Western Realm of Ningxia and Kansu, became the undisputed Great Khan of Mongolia. He invited Phakpa Lodro Gyaltsen to his court and received the empowerment of the Secret Vajrayana from him for the first time. In reward for this, Kublai Khan granted him authority over the 13 myriarchies of Tibet.

In 1260, Kublai Khan was enthroned as the Great Khan, the emperor of Mongolia. Phagpa performed auspicious prayers at the investiture. Kublai Khan again received the empowerment of the Secret Vajrayana from Phagpa, and in return, the Khan offered him ownership over three provinces of Tibet and the title of Tishri, or the Imperial Predecessor. When the Khan received the empowerment from Phagpa for the third time, he granted the lama a large area of land in Chinese territory, but the lama refused. Instead, the Lama requested him to stop the practice of drowning thousands of young Chinese, who were killed as a means of both population and political control. The lama also advised the Mongols to stop torturing and looting the people of China and other countries. This shows that Drogon Phagpa was very kind.

Phagpa appointed his close attendant Shakya Sangpo as the Ponchen, or Viceroy, and Kunga Sangpo as the manager, and proclaimed an edict to this effect throughout the country. He declared that Tibetans did not have to pay any more tribute to the Mongols. He appointed one tongpon, a leader of 1,000 families, to each of the 13 myriarchies created during the time of Godan Khan. He created an administrative body, comprising both civil and military officials.

From the time that they established the relationship of "priest and patron" the Mongol emperors served Phagpa, their spiritual teacher, without deviating from the lama's wishes, but they never interfered in the governance of Tibet. Tibet's independence was reestablished and its governmental system of combining religion and policy was restored. In 1264, Kublai Khan moved his capital to China, and in 1265 Phagpa returned to Tibet.

In 1268, Lama Phagpa, accompanied by a retinue, returned to Mongolia. He met Kublai Khan, the queen and ministers, and was received with great honour. He improved the system of Mongolian writing which he had previously invented. He bestowed the empowerment of the Secret Tantra on the Emperor, the queen and ministers for the fourth time, and received a seal of authority and rich gifts in return. In 1276, Phagpa returned to Tibet for the second time.

In China, due to the Mongol's continuous military campaigns, the emperor of the Song Kingdom was forced to move his capital to southern China. In 1279, the Mongols conquered the whole of China and dethroned and imprisoned Emperor Zhao Weiwang. Kublai Khan declared himself Emperor of China and established the Yuan Dynasty. This is a fact accepted by all the historians in the world.

At present, Chinese have exhausted all their attempts to integrate Tibet into China, so they are now trying to manipulate Mongol history, saying that the Yuan Dynasty of China having the right to grant or withdraw Sakya authority over the three provinces of Tibet is a proof that Tibet had been incorporated into China by the Mongols. This is just like "using the example of a hat for a shoe." This attempt by the Chinese to distort history and to say irrelevant things to further their own advantage has clearly demonstrated their real face of greedy colonialism.

As we have seen above, both Tibet and China were equal victims of the Mongol invasion and exploitation during the time of the successive Mongol emperors Genghis Khan, Godan Khan and Kublai Khan in the 10th (sic) century. However, the Mongol emperors became patrons of the Sakya School and offered the three provinces of Tibet, with authority to rule them, to the Sakya lamas. To the Tibetans, the Mongol's invasion was a blessing in disguise because the Mongols helped Tibet in accordance with the wishes of the Tibetan lamas and preserved the independence of Tibet. As for China, it remained under Mongol rule for almost a century, and it managed to overthrow the Yuan Dynasty only in 1368 during the time of the last Yuan emperor, Toghun Temur. China then became independent and the Ming Dynasty was established, with Taizu (Hongwu Emperor) as its first emperor. In 1950, when Outer Mongolia gained independence from the USSR, China put its signature in recognition of Mongolia's independence. In this way, China has regarded Mongolia as a foreign nation throughout its history.

As noted above, before Kublai Khan became emperor of Mongolia, the three provinces of Tibet had been already offered to the Sakya lama. Prior to the Mongol invasion, Tibet was ruled by successive Tibetan Buddhist kings during the Tibetan imperial period, and after the Tibetan empire collapsed, the country was ruled by independent regional leaders. During the period of political disintegration of Tibet, there was no central administration in the country, but the Tibetans themselves ruled the country and no foreign powers, including China, had a role in Tibet. Hence, from a historical perspective, it is clear that Tibet, Mongolia and China existed as separate countries; this truth will come to light eventually. This is my personal opinion.

In 1280, Phagpa passed away, and was succeeded by Chagna's son Dharampala. The close attendants of Lama Phagpa poisoned the relations between Phagpa and Ponchen Kunga Sangpo by giving false reports to Phagpa that the Ponchen was not respectful to him. The Mongol army arrived in Tibet and executed Ponchen. At that time, Kublai Khan said that he wanted to go on military expeditions to India and Nepal by way of Tibet. However, on the advice of the Deputy Ponchen and Drubthob Ogyan, among others, he abandoned this idea.

Just before the above events unfolded, a dispute arose between Sakya and Drigung. The situation deteriorated, and eventually Drigung burned Jayul, a district of Sakya, killing several people, including Tsangton. In 1285, Drigung Gompa Kundor Rinchen brought Emperor Helegu's force of 9,000 troops to Tibet to attack Sakya. Ponchen Aglen of Sakya led his army to the Palmo Palthang area to fight the Drigung's force. The Sakyapas performed rituals to defeat the enemy, and the Mongol army left suddenly without fighting.

In 1290, with the escalation of bitterness between Sakya and Drigung, Ponchen Aglen launched a war on Drigung, using a large force that comprised Prince Temu Boga's troops as well as troops from Tsang. They burned the Great Temple of Drigung to ashes and killed thousands of people. Ponchen Aglen snatched Jara, Dakpo, Kongpo, E, Nyal, Loro, Lhoka, Drakgar, Yarkyab and Mon from Drigung. This war was called the "war against Drigung".

Since the time that Kublai Khan offered the three provinces of Tibet to Drogon Chogyal Phagpa, the successive throne holders of Sakya, with Ponchen Shakya Sangpo as the first Viceroy, had ruled the country for 105 years. After that, Phagdru's regime began, as discussed below.

The power struggle between Sakya and Phagdru

In around 1334, a disagreement arose among the four palaces of Sakya over rights and powers. Consequently, Sakya split into two rival groups, led by Ponchen Gyalwa Sangpo on one side and Wangchuk Tsondu on the other side. The two groups engaged in a bitter fight, involving killing, capturing or imprisoning each other's members. Moreover, the relationship between Ponchen Gyalwa Sangpo and Tripon Jangchup Gyaltsen, the regional leader of U, also became strained. In addition, Tripon Yasangwa, Tripon Thangpoche and Tripon Tsalpa on one side and Phagdru on the other side formed two opposing factions. They fought frequently, and there was no peace and stability in the country in those days.

The Sakya government several times sent delegates to have discussions and to try to resolve their disputes, but in vain. Ponchen Gyalwa Sangpo therefore decided to go to Yarlung, with a force, to investigate. He decided to execute Phagdru if he did not obey his judgment and to consolidate Yasang, Phagdru and Thangpoche under the direct control of the Sakya administration. Phagdru tightened security at Nedong Fortress and mobilized troops in preparation to fight in the event of a Sakya attack. He sent instructions to his district officers about what they should do in the event of war. He also sent a secret message to the leader of Yardog, his close ally, to give him military help in case of need.

Following this, Phagdru arranged for good accommodation near Nedong Fortress for the Sakya Ponchen and his soldiers, and sent a messenger to the Ponchen to tell him that he would respect the Ponchen's judgment if he decided to talk about the case honestly. When the Ponchen arrived at Gongkar, Phagdru himself went to receive him. He said to the Ponchen, "If you decide to talk about the case honestly, it will be a great honor to all the Sakya masters. If you kill me without any fault of mine, someone will come to take my dead body and the Sakya members will face difficulties in the long term." The Ponchen only nodded and said nothing in reply. This account is found in the The Rhinoceros, the Book of the Lang Family (Langyi Puti Seru).

On the day of the trial, which was to be held at Nedong, the Ponchen arrested both Yasang and Phagdru and put them in jail. He questioned Phagdru both gently and harshly, and asked him to sign a document saying that he was handing the Nedong district over to Sakya. Phagdru refused, saying that he had burned the seal. The Ponchen could do nothing. Phagdru made up his mind to take revenge against Sakya. In prison, he pretended to have fallen sick. He requested the Ponchen to send a messenger to Nedong to ask his official Shonu Sangpo to send someone to care for him. Someone came from Nedong to help him. At the time of the helper's departure, Phagdru gave him a verbal message to be given to Shonu Sangpo, stating "I burned the seal. So, even if you hear that I signed any papers or that I have died, you must never surrender Nedong Fortress."

After this, the Sakya leaders threatened to kill Phagdru if he did not hand over Nedong Fortress to Sakya. Led by Shonu Sangpo, Phagdru's men strengthened the fortifications around Nedong. Knowing that Phagdru had played a trick on him, the Sakya Ponchen gave him 135 lashes. Dressed in prison clothes and with a long animal tail, mounted backward on an ox and escorted by many troops, Phagdru was taken to Tsang, through lower Nedong. When Phagdru saw that the local people were upset, he said in a loud voice, "Do not feel sad, I will come soon. As I am mounted backward on this ox, it is a sign that I will be coming back." When they reached Tsang, people who were in favour of the Sakya leaders threw dust in his face. At this, he said, "This is an auspicious sign that Sakya itself will eat this dust." For several months, he suffered great physical torture, but he endured it very bravely.

In the meantime, the Ponchen removed the tripon leaders of Yasang and Thangpoche from their posts and proclaimed that Nedong, Yasang and Thangpoche had been united as one state under the direct administration of the Sakya government. However, Nedong had not capitulated, and Phagdru's supporters were still guarding it strongly. The Ponchen was in a hurry to return home. Before he left, he placed a large force at the Jasa bank near Nedong.

At Sakya, the hostility between Ponchen Gyalwa Sangpo and Wangtson worsened. The Mongol Emperor was planning to replace Ponchen Gyalwa Sangpo with Wangtson. Gyalwa Sangpo thought that there would be no more suitable supporter than the brave and determined Phagdru in case such a thing happened. With the help of Lama Nyemepa, he sought an alliance with Phagdru, and they agreed to help each other for their mutual benefit. In 1352, Phagdru was released from prison and a rumour was purposely spread that he had escaped. All the troops stationed at Jasa were gradually withdrawn.

Under unbelievable circumstances, as if it was a dream, Phagdru returned to Nedong. His officials and supporters were very happy to see him back and he was received with much joy and honour. At a large gathering of his ministers, officials and others, he praised his ministers, especially Shonu Sangpo and his main supporters for guarding the Nedong district during his absence. He said, "As Sakya is in disunity, we should take the opportunity; we must strike the iron while it is hot. We must stand united."

Phagdru seized the monastery of Yasang and Thangpoche through military force. In 1354, when the Sakya lama Kunpangpa Chenpo visited Gongkar, he was accompanied by Ponchen Gyalwa Sangpo. Phagdru invited the Ponchen to Gongkar and apologized to him for his past actions. In The Rhinoceros, the Book of the Lang Family, Phagdru says, "At that time I treated the Ponchen with a false respect." This means that he did not give genuine respect to the Ponchen at that time.

When Ponchen Gyalwa Sangpo returned to Sakya from U, Wangtson suddenly arrested and imprisoned him. Then, leading the armies of the 13 myriarchies, Wangtson headed to Yarlung to attack Phagdru. Acting as the commander, Shonu Sanpgo led Phagdru's army along the main road. At Mon Dokhar, they encountered and crushed the Sakya army, which had around 10,000 troops. At another battlefield, Tronpa Lhatsun, with a group of troops, fought and defeated another Sakya force. The two forces of Phagdru returned to Nedong, carrying the good news of their victory and some of the enemy's heads and banners as a symbol of their victory.

Phagdru himself, leading his troops, went to Gongkar, Drapchi and other places, where his troops fought against the Sakya forces for many days, causing high casualties. Many Sakya soldiers were killed or captured alive; many committed suicide by jumping into the river. Many great lamas and important figures came to mediate and bring reconciliation between the two sides. Gyalwa Sanpgo was released from the prison. Phagdru invaded the Tsang region as far as Jomo Khareg.

Shonu Sangpo was the man who helped Phagdru defeat the Sakya and achieve political success. *The Rhinoceros: Book of the Lang Family* says:

> He [Shonu Sangpo] is very helpful to me, as he protected Nedong Fortress and saved my life. Because of him, this state has suffered no destruction. In life and death situations, he is the one in whom I have great confidence.

In the meantime, although Tselpa, Drigung and Yasang made minor attacks on Phagdru, his forces counterattacked them from different directions, defeating the opponents with high casualties and taking all their states. After that, the senior lamas and important figures from U, Doto and Dome congratulated Phagdru and offered him their submission, granting him the seal of authority over selection, appointment and removal of officials in their areas.

Following this, the assassination of Lama Kungpangpa led to a civil conflict in Sakya between Ponchen Wangtson, who was backed by Lhatsewa, and the Sakya manager Nangchen Namkha Tenpa, supported by Jangpa. Seizing his opportunity, Phagdru launched a war on Sakya. On the way, he commissioned the construction of a new Rinpung residence. Many important monks and lay figures from upper Tsang came to plead him for reconciliation, but he turned a deaf ear to them and headed onward.

Without having to fight, he took Sakya through his charismatic power. He dethroned Taben Lodro Gyaltsen the throne-holder of Sakya Monastery, and arrested the Ponchen. He punished more than 400 important Sakya officials and removed them from their jobs, and appointed new officials. He sent delegates to northern and southern Lato to examine the situation. He attained victory, partly due to the internal disunity in the Sakya, mainly due to the extreme injustice and ill treatment meted to him by Ponchen Wangtson (Shakya Sangpo?). The Rhinoceros, the Book of the Lang Family says:

In past, the glorious Sakya

> Was at the height of its power and
> Had abundance wealth;
> Ponchen Namkha Tenpa
> Made mistakes due to his immaturity.

As it has been said, whether because of the wrong actions of the Sakya manager Nangchen Namkha Tenpa or because of something else, Phagdru Tai Situ Jangchup Gyaltsen seized power from Sakya and established his rule over the whole of Tibet in 1358.

Having seized power, Phagdru created 13 large districts in Tsang and a system of appointing district officers for them. He created a 15-code law based on the legal system of the Buddhist kings of Tibet, replacing the old law which had been based on the Mongol legal system. The first code was entitled the "Code of the Heroic Tiger" and the second was entitled the "Code of the Timid Fox.' These codes of law were devoted to military theories, regarding how to design and apply military strategies and tactics to defeat ones enemies as well as for self defence. I will not discuss these in detail here to avoid taking up too much space.

In 1363, at the age of 62, Phagdru Jangchup Gyaltsen died, and Jamyang Shakya Gyaltsen succeeded him as the Nedong king. After that there were several successive Nedong kings, during which time there was great political stability in general and peace and happiness in particular in the country, as if "a roll of soft silk was spread over something."

In 1368, the founder of the Yellow Hat School, Jamgon Lama Lobsang Drakpa, arrived in U-Tsang from Tsongkha in Dome. In around 1385, the great adept Drubthob Chagsampa Thangtong Gyalpo built many iron chain bridges in Tibet from the iron he collected by begging throughout the country. Around that time, Bodong Chogle Namgyal visited Tsethang Monastery. Emperor Yungle, the second Ming emperor, sent his imperial emissary to present an invitation to the Nedong king Drakpa Gyaltsen to visit China, but the king declined. So, the fifth Karmapa Deshin Shegpa was invited to China in 1406. Later, the Ming emperor sent delegations to Tibet several times to invite Lobsang Drakpa to China, but the lama sent Jamchen Choje Shakya Yeshi in his place. From 1434, the year nicknamed "Conflict of the Tiger Year," or the "Year of Decline of the Phagdru Dynasty," Rinpung increased his political power while the Phagdru's authority continued to decrease.

During the reign of the Nedong king Kunga Legpa, his minister Rinpung Norbu Sangpo was not happy with the king's behaviour. The Phagdru dynasty split into two rival groups, with Rinpung and his partisans on one side and the king's supporters on the other side.

Rinpung seized some estates and districts in Nedong. After Kunga Legpa died, his ministers jointly enthroned Rinpoche Ngawang Tashi as the Nedong king. After that, when Minister Rinpung Tsogkye Dorje's son Ngawang Namgyal led military attacks on E Nyal, Shamar Chokyi Drakpa pleaded with him not to attack, and so peace was restored. However, shortly after that, Rinpung Dhonyo Dorje and his minister Yungpa Tsewang led a large force into Yarlung in 1480. In those times, each local ruler had his own army and there were frequent conflicts among different monasteries or among different religious schools. In 1485, Rinpung sent a force to upper Tsang. In response, the Nedong army under the command of Chongye Rinchen Gyalchok attacked Nyangto Gyantse, while the Ganden army leader Sonam Gyalpo led Kyiphan's troops up to Shang. They captured Yungpa (a minister of Rinpung) and imprisoned him, and took back the areas of Gyaltsepa and Panam that they had previously lost to Rinpung. The year is known as "the year of the failure of Gyangro's strategy."

In 1499, Minister Rinpung (Tsokey Dorje) and other regional leaders assembled at Nedong, and installed the 12-year-old Ngawang Tashi on the throne. Rinpung offered him one of his sisters as a wife. Rinpung proclaimed his rule over Tsangrong and other areas. A few years later, the regional leader of Tsang led a peasant's revolt against the Rinpung's rule and took control of the upper Tsang. Sectarian violence between Tsang and Rinpung caused much disturbance in Central Tibet. At that time, there was a dispute between the Karmapa and his disciples on one hand and Drukpa Kunkhen on the other. The Karmapa was backed by Rinpung, the Kongpo king Sarkhangpa, the Kyenpa king Palsang, Yudruk who defeated Singpo, and Kongpo Karsipa. Drukpa Kunkhen Pekar was supported by Japawa, Chongyepa, Kurapa and others. There were frequent armed conflicts between the two sectarian factions in Tasri, Dakpo and Kongpo. The district officers were taken as hostages.

The Nedong kings ruled Tibet for more than 100 years. During that period, delegations from China and Mongolia arrived in Tibet occasionally, carrying gifts, to extend the hand of friendship to the successive Nedong kings. In return, the Nedong kings sent letters of praise and gifts. There were however no political connections between Tibet and these two countries.

Rinpung loses power

Rinpungpa Norbu Sangpo served under the Nedong king. He first served as a district officer, then as the leader of a myriarchy and finally as a senior minister of Nedong. Later, because of his matrimonial relations with Phagru, he gained great authority and extended his powers in Tsangrong, upper Tibet and central Tibet. This led to rivalry among the ministers of Nedong, resulting in frequent conflicts in Yarlung. With the support of the Kamtsang School of Kagyu, Rinpungpa launched military attacks in the Nedong region and seized some estates.

Rinpung Norbu had two sons; the younger son, Dhonyo Dorje, held the administrative responsibility for 12 major districts. In 1480, Dhonyo Dorje and Yungpa Tsewang led a large force up to the end of Yarlung. They dismissed Kashipa from the post of Sharnub's treasurer. They snatched Drakarpa, Chushur Lhunpotse's district and other areas from Nedong. They also attacked Jangdakpa Namkha Dorje's territory in northern Lato and Chogyal Norbu's villages in southern Lato (Dzongka). Then, they went to attack Kyishopa, but retreated when Kunkhyen Monlam Palpa performed a ritual to avert the attack. In 1497, after the death of Kunkhyen, Dhonyo Dorje sent a large Tsang force to U on a punitive mission to avenge the murder of Nangtse and his nephew in Kyisho. Depa Ganden Namkha Gyalpo surrendered. The Karmapa, Taklungpa, Olkhawa and others approached them for reconciliation. According to the agreement, Sakyong Miwang Lhunpo and his brother moved to Kyormolung with their belongings. Neudong was seized.

Dhonyo Dorje also took control over Lhasa and the Potala. His power greatly increased. He banned Sera and Drepung monks from attending the Great Prayer Festival in Lhasa. In 1512, just before his death, Dhonyo left a last testament, instructing that Depa Silnon of Nakartse should be appointed the commander of his army. Accordingly, Silnon was invited to be the commander; he continued the king's political activities.

In 1510, Tsokye Dorje's son Ngawang Namgyal, a great traditional Tibetan scholar, offended the Neudong King by his military expedition to E Nyal and did not apologize to the King. As a result, he lost some districts and estates in U, including Neudong, but he managed to take control of Senge and Lato in Tsang by force.

Ngawang Namgyal had three sons, of whom Pema Karpo was murdered in an internal feud, and Dhondup Tseten Dorje became the king of Neudong. He conquered the district of Panam Lhunduptse, which had not been done in his father's time. The youngest son, Ngawang Jigten, was an accomplished scholar; he was brilliant in both religious and secular fields. He composed a large number of treatises on poetry. When Sakya and Jang Dakpa went into a dispute, Rinpungpa sent his army to attack Yeru Jangpa in support of Sakya. Depa Ngawang Jigdrak himself, with a force, went to Shika Samdruptse, by way of Panam Gadong, to command his troops. On the way, he assaulted and caused many casualties among the monks of Jago Shongpa.

In the same year, Shingshagpa Tseten Dorje, a stable-manager of Rinpung and district officer of Shika Samdruptse, murdered Ngawang Namgyal's son Pema Karpo. From that time on Shingshakpa was opposed to Rinpung. An armed conflict ensued in Tsangrong. Rinpungpa attacked Gyantse, Drongtse, Narthang and so forth, and Shingshakpa came to their assistance. Since Rinpungpa had so many enemies, the leaders and subjects under him lost their patience completely, just like "an old bird, whose feathers have worn out." He did many things in transgression of both religious principles and secular etiquette. This resulted in bitter friction between him and his ministers, and many bad omens and events started to appear. The Rinpung Dynasty lasted for about 80 years, after which the power was lost to the governor of Tsang.

The end of Rinpung's rule and the beginning of Depa Tsangpa's rule

The first Depa or regional leader of upper Tsang was Shingshakpa Tseten Dorje. He had only one field as a source of his livelihood and one residential house. He thus got the name Shingshag, meaning "one field and one house." Since he was a relative of Rinpung, he worked as an official at Nedong as well as under Rinpung, having a foot in both houses. He first served as the chief stable manager of Rinpung house under Desi Ngawang Namgyal. Following this he became an officer and served as tax collector for Shang and Gyantse Nyang for many years. In 1548, he became the district officer of Shika Samduptse district. During the reign of Desi Ngawang Jigdrak, he assassinated Pema Karpo, the elder brother of Desi Ngawang Jigdrak. Although Desi Ngawang tried to take revenge on him, he did not succeed. Shingshakpa revolted and became independent from the Rinpung's authority. In 1557, Rinpungpa and Samdruptse nearly went to war over the issue of the territory of Shang Dhonrapa. Drukpa Kunkhen Pema Karpo initiated a dialogue and saved Dhonrapa's life. He entrusted Dhonrapa to Shingshakpa; after that Shingshakpa came to be known as Kundun Shing.

In 1565, with himself as the commander, Kundun Shing (Shingshakpa) took Panam Lhundup Kyungtse and Dzongsar Phakmori by military means. Lhunduptse was likely to be seized eventually and it was uncertain about which side the Nyangto people would support. Rinpungpa was on the verge of defeat, when Drukpa Kunkhen Pema Karpo initiated a dialogue and brought reconciliation between them.

In 1566, just after the Tibetan New Year, forces from Tsang and Rinpung fought at Nyang. Once again Drukpa Pema Karpo came and mediated between the two. Kundun Shing demanded the areas above Jomo Khareg, but did not get them. Rinpung however had to give him the whole region of Panam. Around that time, the two sons of Jangdak got into a dispute. Kundun Shing expelled the younger son, Tashi Topgyal, to U, and said,

> You powerless wanderer called "Powerful,"
> I am expelling you to the realm of hungry ghosts!

This infuriated Tashi Topgyal. When he was at Chongye, he performed the wrathful tantric rites, such as those of the Vishnu and sword bearing Rahula. Not long after that, Kundun Shing died, suffering a sharp pain caused by Vishnu. Then Tashi Topgyal remarked,

> You, who are called Shing (zhing)
> and endowed with the "ten objects of destruction (zhing bcu)",
> I have placed you into the Rahula's mouth.

Following this, in 1611, Tenzin Wangpo's son Phuntsok Namgyal assumed political responsibility at the age of 14. In 1612 and 1623, he waged wars against Ngari, Lhopa and Jangpa, and brought them under his rule. In 1618, he raided U with a large Tsang army. In the battle on the hill behind Drepung, hundreds of monks and U soldiers were killed. The monks of Sera and Drepung monasteries fled to northern Tibet. Ponsa Taklung appealed to Phuntsok Namgyal and the monks were allowed to return. Phuntsok Namgyal subjugated almost the whole of U and Tsang.

While relations between Jetsun Taranatha (Kunga Nyingpo) and Depa Phuntsok Namgyal were hostile, Bhutanese campers (nomads?) and campers from Lhodrak got into a fight at Tagdrukha ferry crossing over the ownership of the ferry resulting in the death of several Tibetans, either in the fight or due to the influence of oracles. Depa Phuntsok, the king of Tsang, demanded high compensation for the lost people. Shabdrung Ngawang Namgyal fled to Bhutan, while Depa, with his troops, went to attack Bhutan, but had to return as his men were unable to fight because of the tough terrain of Bhutan.

In 1631, Depa Phuntsok Namgyal led a military campaign into U. He died while fighting against the Kurapa army. He was succeeded by his son Karma Tenkyong Wangpo as the ruler of Tibet. He was very educated in both the secular and religious fields. However, as it is said, "If one is driven by the force of karma, even a wise man can follow the wrong path," and his religious sectarianism caused frequent conflicts between U and Tsang. As the maxim goes, "When you have two enemies, you should take one of them as your friend," so his younger brother Kunga Rabten proposed a peaceful reconciliation with Drukpa Ngawang Namgyal. In this way they forgot their past misunderstandings and became friends.

Depa Phuntsok Namgyal often harassed Tashi Lhunpo Monastery and the Three Monastic Seats, and he even imprisoned the Great Fifth's father, Hor Dodul Rabten, who died in prison. Depa Taktsewa of Kyisho and his son, who were patrons of the Geluk School, had to flee to Mongolia. Phuntsok allied himself with the Choktu Mongol leader and the king of Beri.

Desi Sonam Choephel and others in the lower chamber of Drigung consulted the Lama Tsangpa oracle. Following the words of the deity, they sought help from the four tribes of the Oro Mongolians. In 1642, Gushri Khan led a large Mongol force into U and Tsang, destroying the Tsang dynasty, which had lasted for more than 70 years. Gushri Khan consolidated all the depas or independent regions of Tibet under the direct control of the central government, called Depa Shung or the Ganden Phodrang Government. The whole of Tibet was put under one law and one ruler. There were no conflicts based on sectarianism after that, and all the religious traditions, including Sakya, Nyingma, Kagyu, Geluk and Bon enjoyed complete freedom to practise their own doctrines. All the people, high and low, ordained and lay, lived happily from that time on.

The fall of the Tsangpa dynasty and foundation of the Ganden Phodrang Government

I will narrate a brief history of Tibet before the Ganden Phodrang Government was founded so that it will be easier to understand the sequence of historical events. In 1617, the Fifth Dalai Lama was born at Chingwa Taktse in Chongye, coinciding with the time when Tsangpa King Phuntsok Namgyal was active in sectarianism and often harassed Tashi Lhunpo Monastery.

In 1618, many Mongol Chokur pilgrims who had come to Tibet looted the Karmapa's herds of cattle. Following this, Phuntsok Namgyal and Kurab Namgyal, leading many troops from Dakpo and Kongpo, headed to Lhasa on a punitive mission. In response, Tume Taiji's two princes, royal descendants of Halha, the local leader of Kyisho Sonam Gyaltsen and the Three Monastic Seats prepared for war. A deadly conflict was impending, but the Ganden Phodrang mediated and tried hard to bring a peaceful reconciliation between the two sides. However, the Tsangpa king Karma Tenkyong Wangpo turned a deaf ear and remained stubborn. The joint forces of the Mongol and Kyishopa's troops fought the Tsang forces in Lhasa. The battle lasted for several days, resulting in high casualties on both sides.

Many strong and well equipped front line soldiers of the Tsang army occupied the hilltop behind Drepung Monastery with the aim of seizing the monastery. Daiching, leading his troops, went to the hilltop and fought the Tsang troops, killing or wounding most of them. The next day, the Tsangpa army set up a very large army camp, bigger than before, on the banks of the Kyichu River, and they mobilized more troops and were ready to attack. The Mongol force was too small to overcome the Tsang army, so they retreated. As a result, the monk troops and Depa Kyisho's army lost ground and fled to northern Taklung via Phanpo. The Tsang army, with the help of local militias of Dakpo and Kongpo, attacked Sera and Drepung, killing countless numbers of monks and lay people. They seized all the estates of Depa Kyisho, who fled to Kokonor along with his family. Depa Karma Tenkyong Wangpo declared his rule over Tibet. He and his son were very hostile towards the Geluk School and its followers. They killed many Geluk monks and imprisoned many others. They converted many Geluk monasteries into Kagyu monasteries. The members of the Geluk School were the main target of their hostility.

Later, when the Tsangpa king Phuntsok Namgyal launched extensive military campaigns in southern Tibet, he and his wife both died from smallpox, allegedly due to black magic conducted by Shabdrung Ngawang Namgyal of Bhutan.

At that time, Choje Taklungpa mediated and brought about a peaceful reconciliation. The Tsang King allowed all the exiled monks to return to their monasteries on the condition that Ganden Phodrang's administrator Chagdzo Sonam Chophel came to Shigatse with 300 zho coins as ransom money for the monasteries. Chagdzo informed him that the monasteries had no way of producing such a large amount and that he would pay it from the former Dalai Lama's treasury at Chokhor Gyal. Chagdzo and his servants went with the representatives of Tsangpa King, pretending to go to Chokhor Gyal. On the way, Chagdzo and his servants suddenly fled to Mongolia, by way of Kongpo and Nagsho, and there they approached Prince Lobsang Tenzin, a descent of Genghis Khan, and sought his military assistance.

In 1621, Lhatsun Lobsang Tenzin and Gungru Hong Taiji, leading more than 2,000 cavalry, travelled speedily to U, where they were joined by the army of Depa Kyisho. They camped north of Lhasa and prepared to fight. A few days later, they encountered the Tsang army in a battle, which lasted several days. The casualty rate among the Tsang army was more than 1,000 soldiers killed, excluding the number of wounded soldiers. Several Mongol troops were also killed or wounded. Foreseeing their defeat, the Tsang army pulled back to the hilltop of Chakpori. The Mongol and U troops surrounded Chakpori from four sides and cut the food and water supply to the Tsang army, causing them tremendous problems. The Tsang army was about to surrender, when the 4th Panchen Rinpoche Chokyi Gyaltsen, the Throne-Holder of Ganden and Taklung Shabdrung Ngawang Namgyal, among others, mediated and arranged a meeting of reconciliation between them. In this way the problem was solved. Otherwise they would have been attacked by the second division of the Mongol cavalry.

The Tsangpa King was made to return all the lands he had seized from the monasteries. The Guluk monasteries which had been converted into Kagyu institutions were restored to their previous status. Chagdzo Sonam Rabten was allowed to remain permanently at Ganden Phodrang at Drepung Monastery. The Tsangpa King reluctantly had to accept these terms of agreement.

The Tsangpa King could not bear this defeat. He secretly made an alliance with Ligden Khan of Chakhar, the chief of 49 Mongol tribes, and the king of Beri, who was a patron of the Bon religion. He also swore to destroy the Gelugpas in Tibet and establish his rule over the whole country. Ligden Khan destroyed monasteries in Kokonor and killed or imprisoned many lamas and monks.

He then headed towards Central Tibet. Hearing the news, in 1634, Desi Sonam Chophel and Depa Kyisho urgently sent a Drepung monk named Garu Lotsawa Nechen with Semnyi Khenchen to Gushri Khan in Mongolia to seek his military help. In the fall of 1635, Ligden Khan sent his son Arsalang, with a large cavalry of more than 10,000 men, to Tibet. Hearing about this, Gushri Khan, with some servants, went to meet Arsalang on the way, and pleaded him not to attack the Geluk followers. As a result of this meeting Arsalang changed his mind. He sought an audience with the Dalai Lama and attacked the Tsang army in support of the Gelukpas against his father's orders. He did this because due to his father's overbearing and harsh rule, his subjects were rising against him, while Gushri Khan's power was increasing.

Karmapa Shamar secretly sent a letter to Ligden Khan, informing him about his son's actions in defiance of his father's instructions. In 1636, a cavalry, pretending to be relatives of Ligden Khan, arrived in Tibet. They murdered Arsalang and his two confidants. Ligden himself, leading a large force, headed towards U to help the Tsangpa King. However, he became suddenly ill and died at Sharatala (Sira Tala in modern Gansu) on the way. His troops returned to Mongolia.

In 1637, the combined force of more than 10,000 troops of Gushri Khan and Hong Taiji entered Kokonor and battled with 30,000 troops of Ligden Khan of Chakhar over several days. The battlefield was reported to be covered with blood. Eventually, army was defeated. He fled and hid in a cave, but was caught and executed by the enemy. His remaining troops surrendered. Gushri Khan conquered all the Tibetan areas in Kokonor. In the same year, he moved his army from Kokonor. Disguised as a trader, he went to U-Tsang and met with the Fifth Dalai Lama and the 5th Panchen Rinpoche. The Dalai Lama conferred him the name Gushri Tenzin Choegyal. Soon after this he returned to Kokonor..

In 1639, a large force made up of more than 10,000 troops of Gushri Khan and Batur Hong Taiji raided Kandze, Dengko, Markham, Chamdo, Riwoche and the six areas of Nagsho which were under the jurisdiction of King Dhonyo Dorje of Beri. They fought the Beri army in a series of battles, eventually defeating the Beri force. The king was captured alive on the 25th day of the 11th Tibetan month of the same year. He was taken to Chamdo and imprisoned. The whole of Kham was conquered. All the lamas and monks of the different Buddhist schools such as Sakya, Geluk, Kagyu and others who had been imprisoned by the Beri King were released. The King and all the other major offenders were executed. Gushri Khan consolidated the whole of Kham from Dartsedo in the east to the kingdom of Jang Satam , under his rule, and brought peace to the region. Kachu Dhondup, Sechen Epa and Shichan were sent to Lhasa to deliver the good news. In Lhasa, the people were overjoyed to hear the news. They evoked and praised the protector deities, flew new prayer flags, blew conch-shells and installed large flags. Gushri Khan appointed new local leaders in Kham and created a tax system for the region.

Soon after that, Gushri Khan deliberately spread a rumour to U and Tsang that he was returning to Kokonor from Kham. The Tsangpa King took the rumour to be true. Gushri Khan and his army went up to the Drichu, pretending that they were going to Kokonor, but turned back and galloped to U. Though the Tsang forces put up resistance at each garrison, they were defeated, just as "the sunlight dispels the darkness." Some Tsang troops surrendered or returned to their homes, while the majority of them fled to Shigatse. The Tsangpa King collected many strong troops and deployed them at the Fortress, Chode, Pangchal, Luding and other fortified sites. The Mongol troops arrived and on the same day, started attacking the positions of the Tsang army. However, they were not able to seize them as the fortifications were so strong. They occupied nearby strategic areas and villages, and remained there.

At the same time, on the 25th day of the 5th month, young monks of Drepung Monastery and the militia of Drepung's ancient monastic estate Shun planned to attack Shun Dongkar. They guessed that the battle would last for several days. However, they managed to take the upper and lower compound of the Fortress by that evening after a minor fight. Overwhelmed by the enemy, the Tsang forces in Dechen and Neu lost courage to fight and fled. The district officer of Dechen approached the Panchen Rinpoche and his manager, and offered his submission. After that, the regional leaders of Neu, Olka, On Draka, Chongye, Lhagyari and Gongkar also surrendered.

Revolts then broke out in Jayul and Kunrab. Neudong and Chogyal Phodrang were expelled. Shokhapa and Kongpo Karsi led their troops to fight on the plain of Gyal Metog. The left wing of Oro Mongolian's army and the militias of Nyerpa Ngodup and Choje Tsepa went there to fight. Before they arrived at E, the Kongpo troops fled from the battlefield to Kongpo. Shalngo and his servants, leading the troops of Lhajawa and southern Tibet, went to Nyangto Gyantse. Tardongne assisted Shalngo in the fight. Sepo Rabten agreed to collect firewood, food and other provisions. Drongme took the responsibility of supplying catapults and occupying the hilltops.

On the 25th day of the 2nd month of 1642, Mongol troops entered Chode Sarpa in Shigatse. In the beginning of the 3rd month, they attacked the main positions of the Tsang army. Many Tsang troops were killed, arrested or dispersed. Gradually, as the Tsang army lost ground, the Mongols besieged the Shigatse Fortress. The Tsangpa King, with his officials, fled, and his troops capitulated. The Sakya and Karmapa lamas mediated and an agreement was arranged between the two sides. The Tsangpa King was given resources and allowed to reside peacefully at his own place. However, he was later arrested and executed. In some accounts, it is said that he was put into a leather bag and thrown into the Tsangchu River in Shigatse. Whatever the case, the Tsangpa King and his partisans were destroyed—killed or captured. Their ancestral estates and properties were confiscated.

The main cause of all these civil conflicts can be attributed to religious sectarianism and the political ambition of those who held power. With the end of the Tibetan royal dynasty, the Tibetan empire had disintegrated into many small principalities. Since that time, there had been endless civil strife among the regional rulers who contended with one another for territory, often resulting in armed conflicts and killing. There was no peace and happiness in the country in those times. Those who suffered losses sought help from outside and brought external powers into Tibet. Fortunately, the main foreign powers from whom they sought help were the Mongols, who happened to be devout followers of Buddhism. The Mongols destroyed the Tsangpa regime and suppressed all the local leaders of Tibet. They appointed the Fifth Dalai Lama as the supreme leader of the whole Tibet—stretching from Dartsedo in the east to Ladakh in the west—and founded the Ganden Phodrang Government, a dual religious and political system, whose authority prevailed over the entire country of Tibet.

Not long after that, with the support of some regional leaders on his side, the Tsangpa King (before he was killed) captured Namling and Rinpung. His army besieged Panam and the siege of Gyantse Fortress and Shigatse was impending. War again broke out in Tsang, and the regions which were under the control of the Tsangpa King were in an uncertain situation. Shokhawa's army burned Singchi Monastery. The situation was very tense. Gushri Khan's army, with Tibetan troops, went to take Dakpo and Kongpo. Shokha and Kongpo's troops, numbering around 6,000, fled in disorder, just as "a heap of hay was put on fire." They also crushed, without much difficulty, the local militias of Olka and Dakpo, numbering around 8,000. After that, Gushri's army, including both Tibetan and Mongol troops, marched to Tsang to suppress the Tsangpa forces. Without much difficulty, they defeated the Tsang forces, whose troops either fled or surrendered.

Among Dakpo Karsipa's soldiers who were captured by Gushri Khan's army, one named Jama Choying was found in possession of a secret document hidden in his amulet. Written in the Karmapa's hand, it contained a plan of how to overthrow the Ganden Phodrang Government. The document fell into the hands of Gushri Khan. Karsipa burned the Geluk monasteries in Kongpo and killed or arrested many Geluk monks. Gushri Khan, leading a force of more than 10,000 troops, went to Kongpo and crushed the Karsipa's force. Karma Choying Dorje fled to Lhodrak, from where he travelled to Kham by way of Kongpo, and finally to Jang Satam. This was the only violence that occurred in the country after the Ganden Phodrang Government was established.

Following this, all the local administrations were amalgamated under the central government of Ganden Phodrang, eliminating the bitter power struggles among various local rulers in the name of religion and the people. By establishing a centralized administration over the whole Tibet, Gushri Khan brought peace and happiness to the people of Tibet and ended their sufferings, as if "a soft piece of brocade is spread over something".

Gushri Khan wanted to convert all the Buddhist monasteries in Tibet into Gelukpa monasteries and monks, but the Dalai Lama advised him that all the Buddhist schools in Tibet were the same in the sense that they were the followers of the Buddha, and it would therefore be better for themselves and others if they were allowed to practise and promote their own doctrines. The Dalai Lama explained this by giving examples from the life history of Drogon Chogyal Phakpa. Gushri Khan, his hands folded in devotion, promised to follow his advice. As a result Tibet gained a strong integral power and its political and religious affairs improved.

After its foundation, the Ganden Phodrang Government created 13 different grades of official rank, such as minister (bka' blon), regimental commander (mda' dpon), judge, head of the craft department (bzo rigs do dam pa), finance minister (rtsis dpon), district officer (rdzong dpon), settlement leaders (gzhis sdod), etc. Likewise, the Kashag, or the Cabinet, Shol Office, Audit Office, Magistrate Office at Nangtseshag, Tse Office, Sho Office and so forth were created. A survey and census was conducted throughout Tibet and a tax system was created. Envoys from different neighbouring countries, including India and Nepal, arrived to offer congratulations and ceremonial gifts to the Dalai Lama on his enthronement as the new ruler of Tibet. This marked the beginning of a new, strong government in the country.

Chapter Eight

Series of Wars Fought by Tibet

❖

The first Tibet-Bhutan war

In 1644, a disagreement arose between the five ecclesiastical states of Mon and Bhutan, and Tibet sent a combined force of Tibetan and Mongolian troops to Bhutan from Lhodrak. However, because of the tough terrain in Bhutan, the Tibetan force suffered losses and some of the military leaders, including Ngodup, Drongtsewa and Dujungne, were captured and imprisoned by the Bhutanese. For these reasons, the Tibetan military strategy was a failure.

On the 28th day of the 3rd month of 1645, on the site of the Palace built by King Songtsen Gampo, the construction of the Potala Palace, which has no match in the world, was begun.

Because some Tibetan troops had been captured by the Bhutanese during the previous year and kept as hostages, Panchen Lobsang Chogyen[1] and Sakya Dagtri Rinpoche acted as mediators, and an agreement was signed by Mon and Bhutan that they would not fight again and would remain peaceful. Bhutan agreed to give rice to the Tibetan government, as they had formerly done to the Tsangpa kings, and to free all the Tibetans who had been captured during the war.

However, not long after that, some regional leaders of Tibet, such as Depa Norbu, driven by selfish and imprudent motives, led military attacks on Bhutan from three sides. After three months of fighting, one division of the Tibetan army arrived at a one-day journey from Puna Kha. The Tsang troops seized Sindo Castle, and undertook a long journey around the Humrel-la pass. A report was sent to the Desi by the leaders of Saga, Dromo and Tsete, saying that they were progressing well. However, panicked by a rumour, the Tibetan troops led by Depa Norbu, who were on expedition to Padro, suddenly fled to Phari during the night, leaving behind all their tents and equipment to the Bhutanese. They had to sleep in the open as they had no tents. Because of this, the other Tibetan troops who had arrived in Bhutan faced uncertainty and had difficulty withdrawing. Moreover, Bhutan had tough terrain and thick forests, and the castles were strongly fortified. Therefore, the Tibetan military expedition failed, and the troops returned to Tibet.

---

1   Lobsang Chokyi Gyaltsen (1570-1662), the Fourth Panchen Lama, (1st to hold the title).

Around the same year, the Tibetan government conducted a census in all regions in Doto to the east of the Drichu River, registered all the families, created a tax system and fixed the rate of tax on all the farmers and nomads. A register to record the tax was made. A rule was made that the entire surplus of revenues left after spending for religious offerings and the renovation of monasteries, development of the country and army salary, was to be sent to the government's treasury.

Soon after that, in 1652, in order to bring an end to the ongoing conflicts between the Chinese and Mongols at the Sino-Tibetan borders and the north-eastern region of Tibet, the Shunzhi Emperor[2] sent his emissary several times with a letter and gifts to the Fifth Dalai Lama, requesting him to visit [Peking] to bring an end to the violence. In view of the priest-patron relationship between China and Tibet, the Dalai Lama travelled to China.

The Emperor accorded the Dalai Lama an excellent reception, both on the way and in China itself, for the first time in history. The Emperor himself arrived at Khotor, one day's journey from Peking, to meet the Dalai Lama. He constructed a new palace called the Yellow Palace, enclosed by a garden, for the Dalai Lama's use. At their every meeting, they conversed freely and at length on religious and secular topics. The Emperor presented gifts of gold, silver, brocade and other valuable articles to the Dalai Lama. At the request of the Emperor, the Dalai Lama issued an edict, impressed with his seal, addressed to all the Chinese and Mongols, advising them to act according to the principles of the Dharma, and gave advice in person to them several times. The Dalai Lama in this way benefited both the Chinese and Mongol peoples. The Emperor treated the Dalai Lama with great respect whenever they met and whenever a reception was arranged for the Dalai Lama, in recognition of the two countries' equality. They also exchanged emissaries and gifts, on the basis of equal status.

On the 20th day of the 2nd month of 1654, after being seen on his way by the Emperor's senior civil and military officials, the Dalai Lama left China for Tibet, by way of Domé. On the 5th day of the 10th month he arrived in Lhasa, where he was greeted with a grand traditional official reception organized by the Tibetan government.

On the 17th day of the 12th month, Gushri Tenzin Chogyal died at the age of 73. The most important achievement of his life was that he militarily conquered the three provinces of Tibet and, because of his great faith in the Fifth Dalai Lama, offered them to him, and pledged that his descendants would serve the Dalai Lama with great sincerity. After that, during his stay in Tibet, he held the title of Great Khan but did not interfere in the political affairs of Tibet. He remained as the protector of

---

2   The Shunzhi Emperor (1638-1661) was the third emperor of the Manchu-led Qing dynasty, and the first Qing emperor to rule over China, which he did from 1644 to 1661.

the Tibetan government. He used to spend the winter and summer alternatively in Lhasa and Dhamshung, and occupied himself with religious activities.

Gushri Khan's death was followed by friction between his lineage and the senior officials of the Tibetan government. By virtue of his charismatic power and the fame of his leadership qualities, the Fifth Dalai Lama prevented any serious disturbances. However, at that period, the Mongols dominated the military affairs of Tibet.

The second Tibet-Bhutan war

In 1657, suspecting that Choje Namkha Rinchen was conspiring with Tibet, Desi Tenzin Drugdak led an internal feud against him, and around 20 people were killed in the violence. Choje approached the Tibetan government, which sent Tibetan and Mongol troops to help him. By way of Phari, the Tibetan and Mongol troopstogether entered Bhutan and travelled as far as Bumthang. Hearing that a large number of Tibetan and Mongol troops were arriving, the Bhutanese forces planned to leave their embankments and fortified garrisons. A disagreement arose between the Tibetan commander Depa Norbu and the Mongol commander Dale Batur over leadership, and the Tibetan and Mongol troops became separated. As a result, all the troops had to return from the Bhutan border to Phari, where they stayed for more than one year. After that, they abandoned their military mission to Bhutan.

The first Tibet-Gurkha war

In 1658, after Desi Sonam Chophel died, Drongmepa Trinle Gyatso became the Regent. The main political and religious responsibilities of the country continued to be handled by the Fifth Dalai Lama.

In 1661, without any warning or reason, Gurkha troops suddenly entered Tibet and attacked Langbu Khar. The Tibetan government appointed Tashi Tsepa, Gyang Drongne and Me Chagne as commanders and dispatched them, along with the Tsang army, to eject the Gurkhas from the country. With great force, the Tibetans fought the Gurkha invaders for several days, ultimately pushing them beyond the border. However, this event did not damage the relations between Tibet and Nepal—the representatives from the three kingdoms of Nepal attended the Tibetan New Year in Lhasa that year.

In 1668, Desi Trinle Gyatso died. In the same year, Tenzin Dale Khan also died and Konchok Dale Khan succeeded him. In the following year, Chopon Lobsang Thutop was appointed the Regent. However, not long after his appointment,

Chopon was removed from the post of Regent on the grounds of having an affair with a woman from a Sakya family. He was retired to Gongkar, and in his place, Lobsang Jinpa was appointed to the office of Regent.

The third Tibetan and Bhutanese war

Just before the above events, a Bhutanese force attacked and carried out looting in the village of Monpa Ajok, which asked the Tibetan government for help. Accordingly, three columns of Tibetan forces attacked Bhutan from three sides— one led by Mechagpa, Drumpane and Migpane attacked Bumthang; the second led by Tardong Lobsang Tsewang went to Tsona and the third under the command of Tagruwa Namgang marched to the capital of Bhutan. After a long period of fighting, the Tibetan forces were on the point of winning, but the Bhutanese side proposed a ceasefire and the signing of a peace treaty. Representatives of the two sides met and signed a treaty of peace.

Reinstating Gyaltang in Kham under the Tibetan government's control

In 1674, under the evil influence of China or Jang, Gyaltang refused to obey the orders of the Tibetan government. Prompted by this, the Tibetan government sent UljoTaiji with Kagya Norbu Mechagpa as his assistant, along with a force, to Gyaltang to deal with the matter. Through both heavy fighting and diplomatic means, they were able to suppress the riot in the first month of the year. They arrested about 20 of the main offenders and took them to Lhasa. The Dalai Lama pardoned them from being executed, and they were sent to different remote districts for imprisonment.

The fourth Tibet-Bhutan war

In 1675, when it was heard that Bhutan had once again attacked Mon Ajok's territory, disregarding the existing agreement between them, Lag Ngog set fire to Tengdung Fort, and there were many violent incidents in the first month of the year. In 1676, Bhutan turned towards the west and sent a secret expedition to Sikkim. Ajok was killed on the field of Daling Amdrok of Mon. The Bhutanese army caused great destruction in both the eastern and western border areas. The Tibetan government ordered its troops who were already on the mission to launch a war on Bhutan. After engaging in continuous combat, the Tibetans were able to retake some of the territories seized by the Bhutanese and ejected the Bhutanese troops from Mon and Sikkim. During the following year, 1678, the Tibetan representatives Kyishopa and Tsagurshagpa and the Bhutanese representatives Gendun Choephel from Puna district as well as Lama Chodrak met at Phari to sign a peace treaty. During the negotiations, the Bhutanese claimed that Monpa Ajokwas a part of Bhutan and that Sikkim should be governed jointly by Bhutan and Sikkim, and made many other wild claims. The two sides did not reach any agreement. Tibet closed the trade route between Shelkar and Tsona and stationed guards along the border. This caused great problems to both Bhutan and Tibet.

In 1679, with the resignation of Desi Lobsang Jinpa, Drongmepa Sangye Gyatso assumed the office of Regent. Friction developed between the descendants of Gushri Khan and the senior officials of the Ganden Phodrang Government. Around that time, China was in a great state of turmoil caused by a revolt against Emperor Kangxi. The Emperor requested the Dalai Lama to send a force to help him suppress the revolt. The Dalai Lama rejected the request, stating that the climate of China was hot and the pox disease had spread there, and that the Mongol troops were very destructive and difficult to control, and therefore his troops would not be helpful. He advised him that instead of resorting to violence, which would cause losses on both sides, it would be best to solve the revolt through peaceful reconciliation. He sent this message to both the Emperor and the rebel leader Fing Siwang. This was of great benefit in settling the turmoil. It is therefore clear from this that not only the Tibetans but also the Mongol armies were under the control of the Dalai Lama.

Desi Sangye Gyatso created a new permanent army called the Simpa Guard, or the "outer and interior guards of the Dalai Lama." Their duties were to preserve the ancient Tibetan army system, serve as external and internal guards at the Dalai Lama's palaces and perform the traditional Tibetan military parade during the Monlam Festival every year. Sources of recruitment and income were created for the new army.

After that, the Dalai Lama entrusted the sole governmental responsibility to Desi Sangye Gyatso. Tenzin Dale and his supporters felt jealous of him and created many kinds of rumours against the Desi, causing internal hostility among officials of the Tibetan government.

Tibetan army invades Ladakh

Ladkah in the past had been a patron of the Geluk School and had enjoyed good relations with Tibet. However, later on, the Ladakh king Deden Namgyal started harassing the monasteries and communities belong to the Gelukpa School. His ministers Nono Shakya, Jora Nono and Bita Jogi, leading a large force, penetrated into Tibet from Ngari, harassing the villages and monasteries. They also attacked Saga and Drosho. The Tibetan government appointed Khong Taiji's son Ganden Tsewang Palsang, a military leader and proctor of Tashi Lhunpo Monastery, and sent him to repel the Ladakhi troops. Along with him went Ganden Tenzin Boshog Tuji Nong's son Lhawang Palbar and Taiching Kholoche Erdi Taiji, as well as about 20 soldiers from Jesang. They hurried to Ngari. Upon arrival at Khangmar, they encountered Ladakhi troops. The fighting went on for several days. The Ladakhis were finally defeated and retreated to their previous positions at Purang Takla Castle, Tsareng Tashigang and others. The Tibetan forces faced some difficulty in pushing them further. Lhasa ordered Ngamruwa, Kongpo Apho Tashi, Pholha Pema Gyalpo Taktse Jedrung and others, with a large force, to go to Ngari to help the Tibetan forces already there. Since it would be time consuming and physically gruelling for them to go to Ngari and then fight the Ladakhi troops who had occupied highly fortified castles and strongholds, they decided to march straight into Ladakh and attack the capital. They divided themselves into separate divisions and planned to enter Ladakh from three sides—Chushul, Lhenle and Dechok. As they did so, the Ladakhi forces left their positions and attempted to confront them in valleys and narrow ravines. The Tibetan troops arrived at Leh, the capital of Ladakh, where they fought the Ladakhis for several days. Thereafter, the Ladakh king and ministers fled to Timur Gang in Kachul, and the Tibetans captured Leh. At the request of the Ladakhis, the Khachul king Nebo sent troops to Leh. They destroyed the camp of the Tibetan army, captured many soldiers and took them to Kashmir for imprisonment.

The Tibetan army again, in a well-planned move, attacked the Ladakhi and Kashmiri forces. After suffering a heavy defeat, the Ladakhi and Kashmiri troops fled, leaving behind all their belongings. Because of this the Kashmiri king could not give effective support to Ladakh. Kunkhen Mipham Wangpo of Bhutan mediated and arranged a peace negotiation between Tibet and Ladakh. King Senge Namgyal and Deden Namgyal as well as their relatives surrendered to Gaden Tsewang. In consideration of their future relationship, Leh, Pitub, Trikse and other monastic estates, along with their dominions, were returned to them. It was agreed that they would look after the Buddhist schools in general and the Yellow Hat School in particular with equal care, without feelings of hatred and discrimination. According to the agreement, the Ladakhi king was to send representatives to Tibet every three years to pay tribute. The agreement also said that the two sides would not fight again. After that, the Tibetan troops returned to Tibet. Ganden Tsewang Palsang, with his troops, was posted in Ngari as acting governor.

By this time, the Fifth Dalai Lama's authority extended from Dartsedo in the east to Ladakh in the west, as if "a white scarf has been spread over an object". The Tibetan government appointed district officers and assigned duties, as well as sending edicts and guidelines from time to time to all the regions of Tibet, and this marked the beginning of progress in the country.

Gushri Khan's son Tenzin Dale was proud of his military power. He often meddled in the governance of Tibet and caused internal hostilities among the officials.

On the 25th day of the 3rd month of 1682, at the age of 66, the Fifth Dalai Lama passed away in the Potala Palace. With his death, the political and religious status of the country declined. In accordance with the Dalai Lama's final will, the Desi (Sangye Gyatso) kept his death secret and continued ruling the country. At the same time, he searched secretly for the reincarnation of the Dalai Lama. In 1683, the true reincarnation of the Dalai Lama was found in Mon, and with great secrecy, he was recognized and kept at Tsona for some time.

Friction between Desi Sangye Gyatso and Lhasang Khan

In 1696, Desi Sangye Gyatso announced the death of the Fifth Dalai Lama throughout the country. In 1697, the sixth Dalai Lama, Tsangyang Gyatso, was enthroned in the Potala Palace. In that year, Tenzin Dale Khan died, and Gushri Khan's grandson Lhasang Khan was appointed as his successor. Lhasang Khan was very arrogant, cunning and oppressive, and criticized the Desi to whom he showed great disrespect. He spread various unpleasant rumours regarding the behaviour of the Sixth Dalai Lama, and interfered in the government's affairs in an attempt to seize power. The Desi tried his best, using peaceful and diplomatic means, to deal with the various internal troubles. In 1703, Lhasang Khan arrested and executed some Tibetan officials who were on the side of the Desi. The Desi ordered the Tibetan army to attack Lhasang Khan and his troops. This led to intensive battles between the two sides in Lhasa and Central Tibet. Lhasang Khan and his forces remained at Dhamshung, where they reinforced their army and marched into Lhasa in 1705. The Sixth Dalai Lama, the Three Monastic Seats, Jamyang Shepa and others mediated and restored peace. Finally, the representatives of the two sides met in the assembly hall in the Potala Palace and made an agreement that the Desi would retire to Gongkar and his son would hold his post, and that Lhasang Khan would return to his native land.

Pretending that he was returning to Mongolia, Lhasang Khan stayed at Dhamshung, where he mobilized his troops and made preparations for war. Leading a combined force from Phanpo and Tolung, he attacked Lhasa. The Tibetans put up a strong resistance, but due to the overwhelming size of the Lhasang's army, they were defeated. Desi Sangye Gyatso went to Nangkartse to request help from Lhasang's wife Tsering Tashi, with whom he had good relations. Shockingly, she arrested and beheaded him on the spot. This was a terrible tragedy for the country and everyone was overcome with great sadness. On the site where he was murdered was constructed a small stupa, which can still be found today. Desi Ngagrin (Ngawang Rinchen), along with his wives, children and servants, was banished to China.

Lhasang Khan seized control of the Tibetan government and caused tremendous suffering to the people, who could do nothing against him. He criticized the Sixth Dalai Lama as a false reincarnation of the Fifth Dalai Lama, and took him to China and Mongolia by force. The people of Tibet, including the Three Monastic Seats, appealed strongly against his action, but in vain. When they arrived at Kokonor, Tsangyang Gyatso suddenly disappeared. He bought a corpse of a Mongol who had just died, and pretended that he himself had died. He then went with a group of Arig pilgrims to Mongolia and later returned to Tibet in the guise of a yogi. He travelled around Tibet, and served as abbot of Serkhog and Jarung monasteries in Domé. In 1739, he passed away at the age of 56. Details about these aspects of the Sixth Dalai Lama's life are found in his secret autobiography.

In 1706, Lhasang Khan installed a boy from Chakpori who was said to be his son as the Sixth Dalai Lama in the Potala Palace, and named him the Pekarchangwa Ngawang Yeshi Gyatso. In 1708, when the news spread to U-Tsang that the reincarnation of the Sixth Dalai Lama had been found in Lithang, Lhasang Khan made plans to remove him. In 1710, when he was at Dhamshung, he heard a rumour that Daiching Boshuchi had dispatched a large force from Qinghai to U-Tsang. Concerned with this, Lhasang Kan sent his older son, with about 1,000 troops, to Nagchu to confront them.

Fearing that Lhsang Khan would harm the Dalai Lama as he had done to the former Dalai Lama, the patrons of the Geluk School in Kokonor invited the young boy to Kokonor from Derge for safety. In addition, the Tibetan government and people in general and those in Kokonor presented him with a letter of recognition, confirming him as the true and real reincarnation of the Sixth Dalai Lama, as well as presents and offerings. Emperor Kangxi, following the footsteps of his father, who treated the Fifth Dalai Lama with great respect, when the latter visited Peking, sent his minister Patung Gingjang and assistants to receive the Seventh Dalai Lama. The Tibetan and Mongol patrons invited the Dalai Lama to Kumbum. At that time, it came to light that Lhasang Khan had harassed the former Dalai Lama in the name of the Manchu emperor.

The fifth Tibet-Bhutan war

In 1714, in Mon Tawang two lama states and Ganden Namgyal Tse plunged into a factional conflict. Bhutan attacked monasteries in Mon Tawang, nearly leading to war. When the news reached Lhasa, Lhasang Khan sent a message to the ruler of Bhutan, to the effect:

> If you control your own territory, there will be no jealousy or rivalry from the Tibetan side. If you harass the villages and monasteries in the Tibetan district of Mon under the influence of others, the small cause will lead to a big war, and this will bring much suffering to many people, the result of which will have to be borne by both of us. Therefore, it is better if you adhere to the agreement made with the Tibetan ruler Sangye Gyatso in the past and live peacefully. Otherwise, Tibet will send four columns of Tibetan and Mongol forces to destroy your country.

Being an arrogant man, the ruler of Bhutan, Drugye Gyau, responded harshly, saying, "Even if you attack us, you cannot move even the hairs on our bodies." Lhasang Khan was further angered and he ordered the Tibetan and Mongol forces to attack Bhutan. He himself led a large force and arrived at Padro. Pholawa and Bumthang led their forces from Pungthang via Mon Lakar pass. Baring Taiji, Dokharwa, Surkhang and Lhari governors and others, leading a force, raided Bhutan from the eastern side. The Tibetan and the Bhutanese forces fought continually for several days, and finally the Bhutanese were defeated, as if "a cloud was scattered by a strong wind". Severely defeated, the Bhutanese troops fled in disarray and hid in castles, forests, mountains and other fortifications, as if "marmots had runaway and hid in their holes". After a long period of continuous fighting, the Tibetan and Mongol forces had killed or wounded many soldiers of the enemy. They emerged victorious. However, the Panchen Rinpoche, Sakya Dagchen and some senior lamas of the Kagyu School mediated and arranged a peaceful settlement of the issue. Because Bhutan was densely forested and the climate in the valleys was hot, Lhasang Khan found it risky to stay there for a long time. He thus ordered all the troops to return to Padro. Pholawa Sonam Topgyal and his troops, numbering several hundred, concluded the mission. These accounts are in the biography of Pholawa Sonam Topgyal.

The Dzungars murder Lhasang Khan

The Oro Dzungars (Kalmyk) enjoyed friendly relations with Tibet. They were patrons of the Fifth Dalai Lama and very close to Desi Sangye Gyatso. In order to take revenge on Lhasang Khan, some Tibetan government officials who were close to the Desi fled to Dzungar country and sought their help. Dzungar Hong Taiji's son Ganden Tsewang Gyalchok had taken ordination from the Fifth Dalai Lama. He had helped Tibet during the wars between Tibet and Ladakh. He thereafter became the governor of Ngari and then returned to his native land where he became the Dzungar Khan. He lost his life in a battle with Manchu forces.

After that, Tsewang Rapten became the Dzungar king and constantly opposed the Manchus. At that time, Lhasang Khan's son Ganden Tenzin sent his men to the Dzungar king, requesting him to send his daughter to Tibet to become his wife. The Dzungar king accepted, but Lhasang Khan, being suspicious of the Dzungars, wanted to wait for the time being to assess the situation. His son pressed him hard, even threatening to commit suicide if he did not allow him to bring the girl to him. Lhasang Khan, therefore, sent him, along with several troops and rich gifts, through Ngari to fetch the girl.

In 1717, the Dzungar king appointed his younger brother the leader of his army and sent a military expedition into Tibet with more than 6,000 cavalry troops. On the way, they met Lhasang Khan's son. They arrested and murdered him on the spot. The governor of Ngari, Khangchenpa, found out that the Dzungar army was coming, and immediately sent a message to Lhasang Khan. However, Lhasang Khan remained unprepared, unable to judge whether the Dzungars were his enemy or friend.

At that time, Lhasang's younger son Surya, having brought a bride from a royal family in Kokonor, was celebrating his wedding party. Although he received several messages that Dzungar troops were coming from Nagtsang, he sent only a few cavalry soldiers to checkpoints to see if they actually were coming. They encountered a spy unit of the Dzungar army near Namtso Lake, and fighting broke out between them. Seeing a large unit of cavalry coming, Surya's cavalry galloped back to Dhamshung and told Surya about the arrival of the Dzungar army. Surya's doubts vanished and he instantly took precautions. They made fortifications at important locations in Dhamshung and remained there.

In the seventh month of 1717, the Dzungar troops arrived near the hills of the Dham Khudu. They were dressed in animal skins and conical hats, and equipped with long spears, fire guns, swords and other weapons, and their horses had plaited tails. Lhasang Khan instructed his army to prepare their defences as quickly as possible, since they would be crushed if they remained unprepared. Accordingly, Pao Khushochi, Kheturkhe and Pholawa made their military strategies, held different positions and remained in wait. When the Dzungars arrived, Lhasang Khan's troops immediately came out from different embankments and charged at the Dzungar troops, holding arrows, swords and spears, waving military flags and shouting. The Dzungar troops came forward and chased the Lhasang's troops, as if "a pack of wolves chased a flock of sheep". Lhasang Khan shouted, "Attack! attack! attack!", but none of his soldiers advanced. Just then, Pholawa charged at the Dzungars, killing some of their bravest soldiers. This was a setback for the Dzungar army. However, it gained Pholawa the confidence of Lhasang Khan and he was named the leader of the Tibetan army.

Following this, on the 29th day of the 8th month, Dapon Orongpa of U, a brave and skilled commander, leading a Rongpa force, attempted to occupy from the rear the hilltop of Dhamshung Khudu, where the Dzungars had camped. Seeing this, the Dzungars immediately ordered their cavalry to attack them. Many Tibetan soldiers, including Orongpa, were killed or wounded. The Tibetan force, composed of the U-ru and Yonru regiments of U, and the Yeru and Rulag regiments of Tsang, with others, confronted the Dzungars, with great determination. However, the Dzungar army was well organized, well trained and skilled in war strategy, and the Tibetans could not defeat them. In the fight, Pholawa injured his leg. The military leader Bumthangpa lost his life when he was hit by a shell. Kyelpoche Sonam Drak was killed during hand to hand fighting with the Dzungar troops. Rabten Shar was wounded. Many other Tibetan soldiers were killed. In that battle, the Tibetan troops performed better than the Mongol troops and received praise from Lhasang Khan.

The teachers of the Three Monastic Seats and the Panchen Rinpoche himself from Tashi Lhunpo came and tried to mediate in the conflict, but failed. The Dzungars claimed that they had not come to attack Lhasang Khan, but were on an important mission—to protect the Buddhadharma and the Tibetan people, and to escort the seventh Dalai Lama from Domé to Tibet (Lhasa) in accordance with the wishes of the people of Tibet. They suggested that everyone should be happy with them and advised the Tibetan soldiers to withdraw. As they spoke persuasively and cunningly, the Tibetan forces withdrew. In this way, the Dzungars accomplished their missions.

The Dzungar army in Tibet became more and more powerful with each passing day, while Lhasang Khan's army (Tibetan and Oro Mongol's soldiers) dwindled in strength. The unopposed Dzungar soldiers moved further towards Lhasa from Dhamshung. Lhasang Khan immediately occupied the major important strong fortresses in U and Tsang and at the same time decided to seek military help from the Manchu Emperor and Kokonor. The Dzungar troops soon arrived in Lhasa. Pholawa, Orongpa, Bumthangpa, Samdup Lingpa, Tashi Tsepa and others, with their forces, confronted the Dzungars with great determination. However since the majority of the Tibetan and Mongol soldiers were not happy with Lhasang Khan, they did not fight with much enthusiasm.

Pholawa suggested to Lhasang Khan that he should go to Kokonor, taking with him a small force, to seek military assistance. Lhasang Khan ignored his advice. The Dzungar troops camped near the western areas of Lhasa, at Drapchi and on the plain of Kumbum Thang. Lhasang Khan's troops struggled hard for many days to drive them out, but they were defeated and fled. The Dzungar troops chased and assaulted them severely. In great fear, Lhasang Khan, with some of his troops, ran into the Potala Palace. The Dzungar troops surrounded the Potala. Khan decided that he would rather die while killing some troops of the enemy than sit helplessly under the enemy's attack. Accompanied by two servants, he ran out of the palace and charged the Dzungar troops. After killing six or seven soldiers in hand to hand fighting, the three lost their lives.

With Lhasang Khan's death, the role of Gushri Khan's descendants in the Ganden Phodrang Government came to an end. Gushri Chogyal had promised, when he offered three provinces of Tibet to the Fifth Dalai Lama (in 1642), that his descendants would serve the Dalai Lama's government and his lineage protected the government for more than 60 years. However, Lhasang Khan was arrogant and harsh and had little respect for Desi Sangye Gyatso, and problems arose between them. This was an internal struggle for power, rather than interference by foreign powers, as is clear from the historical records.

Following the attack on Lhasa, the Dzungars removed Lhasang Khan's son Yeshi Gyatso from the Potala Palace, and executed some of the main supporters of Lhasang Khan. The Dzungars took control of the Tibetan government. They appointed Depa Taktse Lhagyal Rapten as Regent. He was 75 years old, with hair as white as a conch shell. He had no teeth and his voice was inaudible. He walked like an old bird. He was very kind-hearted and loving to his subjects. The Dzungars demolished Dorje Drak and Mindroling monasteries, and killed many high lamas of the Nyingma School. They stole many valuable religious articles from ancient monasteries and took them to their country. When they were about to ransack the sepulchre of Lord Tsongkhapa and the golden sepulchres at the Potala Palace, Desi Taktse pleaded with them not to do so, and they were spared. Many government officials who had sided with Lhasang Khan were killed or arrested. When they arrested Pholawa and was about to execute him, Desi Taktse pleaded for his life. Pholawa was permitted to live at his estate in dignity. Later, at his own request, he was appointed the governor of Ngari.

During their stay in Tibet, the Dzungars were immoral, very oppressive and rude to the monasteries, officials and people. They engaged in many unlawful activities, such as raping women. Tibetan history books written by modern Tibetan writers and published by the Chinese government maintain that Emperor Kangxi's son Yindi went to Tibet to expel the Dzungar forces from Tibet, that the Tibetans and Manchus jointly expelled the Dzungar forces, that the Tibetan people appreciated the Manchu army for doing the good job of stabilizing the border of China, and many other irrelevant things. I believe that the Tibetan scholars who wrote such an untrue history of Tibet were under the duress of the Chinese government. The actual history of Tibet has been illustrated above, but I request readers to study the old records and conduct further research themselves.

Chapter Nine

Wars Fought by Tibet during the Reign of the Seventh Dalai Lama

···

The first intrusion of the Manchu army into Tibet

In 1718, Manchu troops entered Tibet to eliminate the Dzungar army. They fought the Dzungars not far from Nagchu. Badly defeated, the Manchu troops returned to China. Fighting was also taking place between the Dzungars and Manchus in the Oro region of Mongolia. The Dzungars caused frequent problems for China.

The Dzungar troops, led by General Tsering Dhondup, remained in Tibet for four years, on the pretext of having come with a very important mission, to protect the Dharma and the people of Tibet. During their stay in Tibet, they were very hostile to the Nyingma School. They repeatedly announced that they would bring the Seventh Dalai Lama to U, but they did nothing about it. However, the Mongol patrons of the Geluk School and the Manchu emperor, by virtue of their priest-patron relationship with the Dalai Lamas, were trying hard to move the young Seventh Dalai Lama to Lhasa from Kokonor.

In Oro, as mentioned before, a Dzungar force under the command of Taiji Tsewang Rapten was battling against the Manchu forces. From Lhasa, Tsipon Lumpane and other government officials as well as representatives of the Three Monastic Seats were making continuous contact with Kumbum to bring the Dalai Lama to Lhasa. In 1719, the Geluk School's main patrons Tenzin Chingwang and Ganden Junang,and leaders of Kokonor Mongols, assembled and unanimously decided to move the Dalai Lama to Lhasa as soon as possible. When Chang Xun Yinti, the 14th prince of Kangxi Emperor, went with some troops to Oro from Siling to reinforce the Manchu force there, he paid a visit while en route to the Dalai Lama at Kumbum. On the 22nd day of the 4th Tibetan month of 1720, the Dalai Lama, along with his retinue, left Kumbum for Lhasa. On the way, he was again met by Prince Yinti at Gayag Thang. With his troops, he escorted the Dalai Lama up to the bank of the Drichu and returned. The Dalai Lama's travelling party consisted of his Mongol patrons, his patrons from Kokonor, his disciples and many dignitaries, and a large number of Mongol and Chinese soldiers as his bodyguards. Many high lamas and regional leaders from Kham and the four regions of northern Tibet came to greet him. According to Situ Tenpai Nyinje's autobiography, the king of Derge, accompanied by a large retinue, as well as the Situ Rinpoche, went to greet the Dalai Lama on the way.

From upper Tsang, Khangchene mobilized many militia troops from Saga, Drosho, Shelkar, Lhangam Phunsum and Sakya, and obstructed the Dzungars from crossing the Gampa-la pass. Pholawa Sonam Topgyal was serving as the governor of Nyanang, and he was outwardly a supporter of the Dzungars, but in fact he was a secret ally of Khangchene. He and Khangchene jointly prepared a war against the Dzungars. In U, Depa Ngabo and others mobilized their troops.

The Dalai Lama was on his way to Lhasa from Dome, escorted by a large force consisting of Mongol, Tibetan and Chinese troops. Out of fear the Dzungar troops left Tibet hurriedly in two groups: one group returned to Dzungar by way of Nagtsang, the same road that they followed when they entered Tibet, and the other followed the main road via Nagchu. Khangchene, leading the army of the upper Tsang, pursued the Dzungars who fled via Nagtsang. He attacked the Dzungar army camp near Nagtsang under cover of night, killing many Dzungar army leaders and troops, and took back all the religious objects, including the three representations of Avalokitesvara, as well as ornaments and many other valuable goods stolen by them. They also managed to release the servants of Lhasang Khan, who had been kidnapped by the Dzungars. The Dzungar troops who followed the main road and the Dalai Lama's party came within view of each other on the way, and fighting nearly broke out between them. The Dzungars hurriedly turned away towards the north.

On the 20th day of the 9th Tibetan month of 1720, amidst various levels of receptions arranged by the government and joyful greetings from monks and lay people, the Dalai Lama arrived and was ushered to the Potala Palace, where he was installed on the golden throne. This was followed by a gift-offering ceremony, as was the custom, and people from the three provinces of Tibet and delegates from neighbouring countries presented their investiture gifts to the Dalai Lama.

Thereafter, a seven-member Tibetan-Mongol joint committee was set up to investigate the Dzungars and their partisans. Theseven members included Ngabo, Lumba, Manchu Baisi Chang Jun, Gung Tsewang Norbu and Mongol Dhondup Wang. The committee questioned the Dzungar partisans, including Desi Taktse, and it came to light that all of them were working under pressure from the Dzungars. Desi Taktse was found guilty of handing Lhasang Khan's younger son, Surya, over to the Dzungar army, when Surya, along with his force, tried to flee through Phanpo after he failed to escape by way of Chagla. Taktse, along with Gunglon Tashi Tsepa (a relative of the Panchen Rinpoche) and Acho as well as some others were subjected to extreme torture and then taken to the bank of the Kichu River where they were executed. Desi Taktse's wife and his sons were expelled to China. Desi Taktse was very old and had been honest and kind to his subjects. He had also saved the life of Pholawa from the Dzungar army. On these grounds, people appealed to the Manchus to spare his life, but in vain.

By the order of the Manchu Emperor, Chang Jun and Tsewang Norbu, with about 4,000 Chinese troops, were stationed in Lhasa, claiming that they were representatives of the Manchu government to serve the Dalai Lama on the grounds of the priest-patron relationship, and the rest of the troops were withdrawn. The Manchus in Lhasa however did not have any political role in Tibet, and they were regarded by Tibetans as foreigners stationed there only to maintain peace and security in the country.

In 1724, the Mongols and Amdo people in Kokonor were planning to attack the Manchus. Therefore, in the first year of his reign, Emperor Yuangzheng called back all the Manchu officials and troops from Tibet. Led by Chingwang Tenzin, a descendant of Gushri Khan of the Oro Mongols, the Tibetan and Mongol troops attacked the Manchus, and there was no peace in the country. The Dalai Lama sent Trichen Palden Drakpa of Ganden and his steward Dronyer Lobsang Konchok, with a message, to end the conflict. Many Chinese troops led by the commanders Shinkaya, Suutsang, Nigung and Yaoto arrived in Kokonor, where they destroyed and looted thousands of monasteries and villages in Serkhog, Kumbum, Juyag Semnyi and other areas, and murdered many monks and lay people, including Tripa Chusang Rinpoche. Through Dugan Ngawang Chokyi Gyatso, the Dalai Lama appealed directly to the Manchu Emperor to stop the violence, and the fighting was thus stopped. The Chinese and Tibetan governments jointly provided resources and sent many expert artisans to renovate the damaged monasteries.

This was the first infiltration by the Manchus into Dome; since the fall of the Tibetan empire, China had never before succeeded in penetrating into Tibet. Later, many Chinese belonging to Chinese rebel groups fled into Dome and settled there. Gradually, the rebel group leader Mapu Feng based in Sining became a powerful and semi-independent ruler under the nominal rule of the Kuomintang government of China. He established his rule in Dome. He reinforced his army by recruiting many men from the regions under his rule by force and often carried out raids in Dome, causing frequent problems for the Tibetan government. This will be discussed below.

Civil war between U and Tsang, and the reinstatement of the four Hor states under the direct control of the Ganden Phodrang Government

In 1721, the Seventh Dalai Lama instituted an office called Kashag, or Cabinet, with Taiching Batur Sonam Gyalpo, Ngabo Dorje Gyalpo, Lumpa Tashi Gyalpo and Jarawa Lodro Gyalpo as the ministers. Taiching Sonam Gyalpo was appointed their leader. The ministers were granted the seal of Prime Minister (ching sang). Pholawa Sonam Topgyal was granted the title of Taiji. The Dalai Lama then gave them advice regarding their responsibilities for the preservation and further improvement of the political and religious affairs of Tibet. He had a farsighted vision for the country. However, soon internal jealousy and political rivalry divided the ministers into two rival factions—Ngabo, Jara and Lumpa of U on one side and Taiching Batur and Pholawa of Tsang on the other side. The two groups engaged in bitter conflicts, seriously affecting the governance of the country. Rumour had it that the Dalai Lama's father, Sonam Dhargye, was cooperating with the U faction. When Pholawa and some senior and loyal officials of Daiching Batur came to know that the other three ministers were planning to kill Daiching Batur, they told him about this. Daiching however did not take it seriously and rashly left for Ngari on an official trip. Pholawa went to Nagtsang on the pretext of having an important task to do there, but in fact went hunting and did military practice. In the meantime, in Lhasa, Ngabo, Lumpa and Jara made a plan and prepared to destroy Daiching and his supporters.

At that time, hearing that the Mongol Chingwang Lobsang Tenzin had assaulted Erdine Ereke and the emissary of the Manchu Emperor, Pholawa sent messengers, one after another, to Daiching Batur, asking him to return to Lhasa immediately. Daiching returned. China sent the Amban, with 2,000 troops, to Lhasa to take revenge on Chingwang Lobsang Tenzin and his troops. All the Tibetan Cabinet Ministers discussed among themselves about how to defeat Chingwang Lobsang Tenzin. Pholawa, with his forces, was sent to Tolung. General Lobsang Dargye, with his forces, was sent to Phanpo. The two columns of troops travelled along the Nyenchen Thangla. On the way, they met Kalon Lumpa and his forces at Yakto Khaleb. All of them joined up at Nagchu, where they made their war plans. The leaders of the six districts of Nagsho, including their people, surrendered to them. Thereafter, the leaders and people of the four Hor tribes surrendered to Pholawa. Among them were Erdine Jinong, Noyon Nangso and Me Daichi, who had previously attacked the emissary of the Manchu Emperor, and they were sent to Lhasa. Through negotiation without using force, they subjugated Sogde, Khyungpo Karnagsersum, Droshul, Yushul, Dronga and others and put them under the jurisdiction of the Tibetan government. An order was issued to the people, "Though you are no doubt the subjects of the heavenly appointed Ganden Phodrang Government, recently you were forced to turn towards Chingwang Lobsang Tenzin of Kokonor to escape from the extremely oppressive rule of your local leader. However, now Chingwang has been defeated by the Chinese army, and he has fled to the Dzungar country. Henceforth, you are again the subjects of the Ganden Phodrang Government and you are on the path of the noble tradition of your ancestors." The people agreed willingly and pledged to live under the rule of the Ganden Phodrang Government. The Tibetan forces then returned to Lhasa. The large amount of property, horses, cattle, weapons, etc., seized from the Mongol camp (sog sde) was handed over to the government. After that, those who had performed well on the mission were granted valuable rewards in accordance with their performance. However, Kalon Lumpa was not satisfied with the difference in rewards given to him and Pholawa, and his antagonism against Pholawa grew stronger.

The Manchu Amban, with his troops, returned to China by way of Dome. The hostility between the two factions of ministers increased after that. Pholawa was a man endowed with three good qualities—capability, intelligence and energy. Using his wife's illness as a pretext, he returned to Tsang, taking with him a small elite party of his officials, including army commander Lobsang Dhargye, Trimpon Borig Ngawang Dechen, Phodrang Gampa and Dokhar Tsering Wangyal. From Namgyalgang, Dokhar Tsering Wangyal returned to Lhasa. On arrival at his home estate, Pholawa stationed three circles of guards around his residence and remained alert all the time.

On the 18th day of the 6th Tibetan month of 1727, as preplanned, Ngabo, Lumpa and Jarawa convened a cabinet meeting in the Khamsum Chamber of Labrang Teng at the Tsuglakhang temple. When Daiching Batur entered the hall, Dronyer Lobsang Dhonyo, who was hiding behind a curtain, grasped Daiching by his hair, and the three ministers immediately pounced upon him with knives, stabbing him all over his body until he was dead. They also killed Daiching's treasurer Sithar and secretary Dongnawa, who were waiting outside the door, and arrested and imprisoned his other servants. A group of soldiers was sent to kill Daiching's two wives. When the troops arrived at Daiching's house, they were overwhelmed by the beauty of the two women, so they hesitated and dared not kill them. The commander Tashi Palrab commanded them loudly to kill the women. As the soldiers raised their swords, the two women folded their hands in prayer, kneeled down, cried and pleaded with the soldiers to spare their lives. Despite this, they were murdered.

Kyipathang, Tashi Palrab and Kyakhangpa, with their forces, were sent to Tsang to kill Pholawa. Pholawa's servants in Lhasa were arrested and imprisoned. The three ministers collected local troops from U, Dakpo and Kongpo, and sent them to northern Tibet to expel the last of the Mongols. Ngabo, Lumpa and Jarawa's plans were so far going well.

Pholawa defeats his enemies and the Manchu army begins a period of oppression in Tibet

Pholawa remained in Tsang guarded by tight security. When Kyipug Wangdu arrived at his home from Lhasa, he sent his servant Penpa, with instructions to travel day and night to Pholawa to inform him about the murder of Daiching Batur in Lhasa and the impending arrival of troops to kill Pholawa. On the pretext of going to Northern Tibet to expel the Mongol troops, Pholawa went to Gyantse Latsel. There, he collected his horses, and consulted and made war plans with his officials. They decided to collect troops from Tsang and Ngari and to go on a punitive mission to Lhasa. Pholawa instructed his officials and the guards at his estate as to how to make defensive preparations, such as the construction of fortifications around the estate and the mobilization of local militias. He kept his ailing wife and daughters at a secret place. He and his two sons, with a small elite force, rode off to Tsang, and the Nagari troops hurriedly headed to upper Tibet to back him.

Pholawa sent messengers to the military leaders of Tsang Changlochen and Samdupling at Shelkar, Numa at Ngamring and Taiching Batur's elder brother Ngari governor Gashiwa (Doring) to give details about the Lhasa incident and to request their support. Gashiwa refused, saying that he had to go to Shang at that time. Numa did not take it seriously. The Lhatse district officer Sadru Sharpa and Tsenyul consulted Numa, and did not give a clear reply. Except for these people, all the others agreed to support Pholawa and pledged to take revenge for Daiching Batur. They immediately started mobilizing troops. The leader of Porong Ajo, although highly advanced in age, took a solemn vow to take revenge for Daiching's murder. With a cavalry of about 100 soldiers, he joined Pholawa.

Saga's leader Uching Noyon was doubtful at first about Pholawa's connection with the Dzungars, because Pholawa alone was spared when the Dzungars murdered, tortured or imprisoned all other partisans of Lhasang Khan. Pholawa did not get full support from them initially. Being capable and intelligent, Pholawa once again sent convincing letters to the above regional leaders, telling them about the selfishness and evil plans of the three ministers who had murdered Daiching Batur, an honest, dedicated and valuable official. In the letters, he asked them why they should not confront the rebels for the benefit of the government. Gashiwa, once he was convinced, quickly collected around 2,000 mounted militias from Garthog and Ruthog, and joined Pholawa. Changlochen and Saga's leader Uching Noyon, with their own troops, bringing along with them various kinds of weapons and many saddled riding horses, joined Pholawa. After this, Pholawa's fame gradually spread throughout U and Tsang.

Kyipathang and Tashi Palrab, leading about 300 cavalry, arrived from U at Pholawa's hometown on the 17th of the seventh month of 1727 to attack Pholawa. They tried to overcome Pholawa's forces for over five days, but Pholawa was guarded by sixty strong men. Unable to overcome his guards, they quickly proceeded to Gyantse and occupied the Fortress. The army of Tsang surrounded the Fortress from four sides and made several attacks upon it. The Fortress was very high and heavily fortified; it took a long time to seize it. In the meantime, Lumpa and Jarwa, leading a large force, comprising the troops from U, Kongpo and Dakpo, and Mongol soldiers, were advancing towards Tsang. Hearing the news of their arrival, the leaders of Tsang alliance such as Drongkar Tsepa Tenzin Noyon, Nangkarwa, Galowa, Nyenkharwa, Ching Batur, Kyongapa Khunu and Thangmepa quickly mobilized troops, constructed fortifications and made other defensive preparations.

Soon after that Ngabo, Lumpa and Jara, with their forces, arrived in Tsang and fought the Tsang army for many days. Both sides suffered some casualties, but there was no decisive victory on either side. Having exhausted their ammunition, the U troops returned to their homes. Hearing this from one of his secret informers, Pholawa quickly led a large force from Lhatse and crushed the army of U.

Numa, a leader of the Tsang army, despite being a relative and protégé of Daiching Batur, sent a confidential letter to the Dalai Lama's father Sonam Dhargye and the three ministers. The letter fell into the hands of Pholawa, who sent 40 soldiers led by his servant Tenzin Gokye to arrest Numa. They arrested him at Ngamring and took him to Pholawa. Numa was stripped naked and his tongue was cut off. With his hands and legs tied with ropes, he was then thrown off the cliff at Samduptse Palace. The news spread throughout Tsang and instilled fear among the people. After that, many people came to offer submission and support to Pholawa, and his supporters increased in number.

Dapon Changlochen, leading his forces, went to the south of the Nyangchu River. Pholawa, with his army, left by the northern route. On arrival at Drongtse and Drakhu, he was confronted by the forces of Lumpa and Jara. Changlochen climbed the mountain from behind and fired rapidly on the enemy. They also occupied many houses in the villages and used them for hiding places. The fighting between the two sides was intense. The troops of the U faction had been almost cornered and had no way to escape. Pholawa's younger brother Tenzin, Uchi Noyon, Palshiwa, Nangkarwa and others who belonged to the Tsang party arrived to support Pholawa. Kalon Lumpa and his troops fled in disorder, and they even lost their military flag. Both sides suffered some casualties, but there was no decisive victory on either side.

The civil strife between U and Tsang lasted for several months, without a major victory on either side. The war caused tremendous hardship to the people of the country, due to robbery, plundering and extortion carried out by the troops. Pholawa therefore proposed a cease fire and pulled his forces back to Saga. The troops of U pursued them as far as Ngamring and returned. The leaders of Ngari suggested to Pholawa that they should take a rest for a few days so that they could collect more military supplies and food. After a month, Pholawa heard that the U troops were harassing the people of Tashi Lhunpo and Narthang. He immediately went to Tsang, taking with him a detachment of the Tsang army, by way of Ngamring, and circulated pamphlets everywhere.

Uching Batur, with an elite force, travelled day and night to take the Gyantse Fortress. Two days after they gained control of the Fortress, a large force of U arrived and camped around Gyakhar, close to and to the east of the Fortress. It was reinforced by more troops. Pholawa, with his troops, arrived in Gyantse on the 25th day of the 10th month. Fighting started between the U and Tsang armies soon after his arrival. They fought every day. Gashiwa was killed in the battle. Both sides suffered high casualties. The U force had, with great effort, brought with them four locally made muskets from Lhasa, and they tried to bombard the Fortress but could not cause any damage to it, so after a few hours, they stopped shelling the Fortress.

The Panchen Rinpche's representative Dronyer Sakyupa and the Sakya Dagtri Rinpoche's representative Dronyer Ngawang came to mediate in the conflict and made great efforts for many days to bring reconciliation between the two factions. From Lhasa, the Seventh Dalai Lama sent a message, advising the two groups to stop fighting and restore peace. Thus, the U and Tsang parties signed an agreement on the 3rd day of the 3rd month of 1728 in the presence of witnesses. Both sides released all the prisoners of war and withdrew their troops from the battlefield. Ngabo, Lumpa and Jara returned to Lhasa, claiming widely that they had won the war. The U and Dakpo troops also returned hurriedly, as if they had been released from prison.

Pholawa stationed 3,000 troops at Thongchag Dzong to help Sumgyapon and Shabpa Sangye Tenzin, and 2,000 troops under Changlochen and Noyon at Gyantse Fortress. At Rinpung, he kept 1,000 troops under the leadership of Dayan Hong Taiji and 500 troops at Lingar Dzongunder the command of Lhatsewa. Pholawa himself went to Panam and resided there. Around that time, Mergen Taiji, who belonged to the U party, unaware of the peace agreement signed by the U and Tsang parties, attacked some members who belonged to the Tsang alliance in Nagtsang. Provoked by this, Pholawa exclaimed with anger, "Those evil people do not know how to live properly!" He decided to go on a punitive mission. Once again the representatives of the Panchen Rinpoche, Sakya Lama and others tried to stop him, but in vain. He called his older son Gyurme Tseten from Shelkar and summoned the Tsang army. He instructed his son and Changlochen to lead military campaign to Lhasa by way of Yamdrok and the Nyasab-la pass. He himself, leading an elite cavalry of 300 troops by way of the northern road, headed to Yangpachen, where he executed the Hor tribal leader Lama Kyab, and put all his troops under his own command. Taking 3,000 troops of northern Tibet, he headed to Lhasa, via Phodo and Phanpo.

Gyurme Tseten and Changlochen, with their forces, traveling via Nyasab, crossed the Tsangchu River from Dau ferry using coracles and plank boats. There they faced a minor resistance from a small U force. After a brief skirmish, the U troops fled in disorder.

The Panchen Rinpoche, Sakya Dagtri Rinpoche, Ganden Tripa, the Three Monastic Seats and the Upper and Lower Tantric Colleges sent their delegates to intervene in the ongoing violence. When they arrived, Pholawa said to them, "When the U army came to destroy me, and thereafter when the troops of U, Dakpo and Kongpo engaged in oppression and brutality in Tsang, did you come to mediate? Now when I am doing something for the sake of the Yellow Hat School and to take revenge for Daiching Batur, you have come to mediate. This is not fair!" Having said this, he set off on his military mission. Traveling through Phanpo, he camped at Garpa. Kalon Lumpa's force encountered the Tsang's force at Gamo Trang passage, but was badly defeated by the Tsang army in a night attack made from the Jomo Silsil Mountain peak. Pholawa, leading his force, fearlessly marched along the main road. When he was about to attack the U troops face-to-face, the opponents fled in disorder. Pholawa and his army pursued them, killing or wounding several of them.

Ngabo, Lumpa, Jarawa and some other leaders from U fled to Lhasa, taking any roads they found. They hid in the Potala Palace and appealed to the Dalai Lama to save their lives. They closed the main gate of the Palace. Pholawa besieged Gashi Trulnang Tsuglakhang and the whole of Lhasa. Two days later, Dhokhar Tsering Wangyal, General Lobsang Dhargye and Bonrig Ngawang Dechen, who were partisans of Nga-Lum-Jar's party, offered their submission to Pholawa. He pardoned them. To prevent the three ministers escaping from the Potala Palace, he placed 3,000 cavalry and 9,000 infantry soldiers around the Potala, Lhasa and Shol. The Tsang troops who came from southern Tibet also arrived and camped in the northern area of Lhasa. Pholawa circulated an edict saying that he had established his rule over the whole of the three provinces of Tibet and proclaimed a law demanding that everyone should maintain peace and stability in the country.

Tsenpo Nomihan, On Gyalse Rinpoche, Tri Rinpoche, teachers and officials of the Three Monastic Seats, approached Pholawa and declared their non-involvement in the U-Tsang conflicts, from beginning to end. They pleaded with him to pardon the great Seventh Dalai Lama and his noble father, saying that the two had no role in the murder of Daiching Batur and the civil war between U and Tsang. Pholawa responded, "I said many times, both in writing and verbally, that I have the profound faith in the All-Knowing Dalai Lama, who is the protector of all sentient beings. However, his kindness is prejudiced, because he had ordered the three ministers to destroy Daiching Batur and me. He is hence not even an ordinary good human being, far from being a protector of the world. Now the Dalai Lama and his noble father should not stay with those ministers; they should reside either at Sera, Drepung or Ganden Monastery. If not, they must send out the three ministers from the Potala, along with their soldiers. Whatever the Dalai Lama and his father tell me, I will accept it."

Tsenpo Nomihen went to the Potala Palace and reported these words to the Dalai Lama, who said, "I and my father always had good feelings towards Daiching Batur; we had no connection with his murder. Now if Taiji (Pholawa) does not harm us, my father and I will go to Drepung and stay there for the time being." Accordingly, it was decided that the Dalai Lama and his father would move to Drepung Monastery, guarded by thousands of monks. At that time, Lelung Jedrung went to the Potala Palace and again appealed to the Dalai Lama to save the lives of the three ministers. Out of great compassion, the Dalai Lama decided to save them and their dependents. The Dalai Lama requested Pholawa not to harm the ministers and their relatives. Pholawa agreed, saying "I will not kill the ministers— instead I will allow them live peacefully at their homes, with bodyguards, and their relatives and servants, properties and houses will not be harmed. However, they must be subjected to investigation in front of the public to know who among them committed wrongdoings. The Manchu Emperor will send an investigation team, and when they arrive, the investigation will be conducted." The three ministers were sent home safely, escorted by 300 troops. The Dalai Lama remained at the Potala Palace.

Losempa, Lelung Jedrung, Tsenpo Nomihen, Baso Trulku, Tri Rinpoche and Pholawawent to the Potala Palace and were given an audience with the Dalai Lama at his residence, called the Sunlight Chamber. Pholawa explained the past mistrust between the Dalai Lama and himself, and apologized to the Dalai Lama for his past actions. After that, Pholawa took an oath of allegiance to the Dalai Lama, while Lelung Jedrung Trulku placed on Pholawa's head an image of the deity Palden Lhamo and an image of Padmasambhava called Tashi Dokhama, which had been discovered in a secret place.

Shortly after that Dokhar Shabdrung Tsering Wangyal, a scholar, who was involved in the U-Tsang strife, came to Pholawa's Ganden Khangsar residence to confess his guilt. He after that became an important official of Pholawa's.

The above-mentioned so-called "Manchu investigation team" arrived in Tibet at the request of Pholawa. He had requested the Manchu Emperor to give him military assistance in the case of a war breaking out between U and Tsang. This is evident from the coordination between his statement and the arrival of the Manchu troops. Otherwise, the Manchu Emperor would never have interfered in the internal affairs of Tibet. Likewise, some lamas and leaders of Tibet allied with Chinese for their personal political gain. This serious mistake led to the present tragedy of Tibet.

The Manchu General Tra Liang and Lu Chun, leading around 8,000 troops, arrived in Tibet from Siling. The Chinese minister Chao Eng, with around 4,000 troops, arrived from Kandze. From Yunan, the Chinese general Nantien brought about 3,000 troops to Tibet. In total more than 15,000 Chinese troops arrived in

Lhasa, following three different routes. Immediately after their arrival, they had discussions with the Manchu minister Shaochou, the Manchu emissary Mala and others. They bound Ngabo, Lumpa and Jara with iron chains and questioned them harshly for several days in front of the Chinese army leaders. Finally, the three were executed by slicing method (cutting their bodies). They strangled Kyorlung Lama and the manager of Namgyal Monastery. Some partisans of the three ministers were beheaded. On the same day, 22 people were executed. Their wives and children, though innocent, were banished to China.

Though Pholawa knew that the Dalai Lama's father Sonam Dhargye was a close associate of the three ministers and was actively involved in the U-Tsang violence, he dared not include him among the culprits. Pholawa requested the Dalai Lama to go to Lithang in Kham to meet the Manchu Emperor, who was on visit to Tibet's border areas, urging that his meeting with the Emperor was very important. All the people of Tibet, lay and monks, appealed for the Dalai Lama's trip to be cancelled. Pholawa assured them that the Dalai Lama would return to Lhasa within one year. In 1729, the Dalai Lama, with a retinue of about 200 people, lay and monks, including his father, set off for Doto.

The Manchu officials and troops who had arrived in Lhasa returned to China in the same year. Pholawa kept two Manchu officials named Meta Xin and Sengta Xin, with 2,000 troops, in Lhasa for his personal security, on the pretext that they were bodyguards of the Dalai Lama. This paved the way for the evil custom of stationing the so-called Ambans in Lhasa. After Pholawa's son Gyurme Namgyal was murdered by the Manchus, the Tibetan army annihilated all the Manchu officials and soldiers residing in Lhasa, by killing or capturing them. Once again an Amban was posted in Lhasa after that incident. He was killed in 1912, when the Tibetans expelled all the Chinese from Tibet. Later, after the Chinese revolution, the Kuomintang's representatives were kept in Lhasa. The Kuomintang's spies created rumours among the people and hostility among the government officials. In 1948, they were expelled from Lhasa. Later, the Chinese communist government forced Tibetan writers to write in their books that Tibetans who were supportive of foreign colonialists expelled the Chinese officials from Tibet. The fact however is that both the Tibetan government and Tibetan people rose against China whenever it attempted to invade Tibet, as is evident from the Tibetan historical records.

The sixth Tibet-Bhutan war

In 1734, in Bhutan, due to the emergence of two candidates for the reincarnation of Pal Narotapa, a dispute arose between the supporters of the two candidates, one side led by the 9th Desi Ngawang Gyatso the secular ruler of Bhutan, and the other side led by the 8th Desi's minister Kape Dhondup Gyalpo and Mipham Wangpo. Desi Ngawang Gyatso aka Wang Phajo was expelled from Tashi Chodzong Fortress, the seat of the Bhutanese government. He sent his men to Tibet to appeal to the Tibetan government for military assistance. In the meantime, he occupied a small fortress called Lhuntse Fortress. His enemy made strong attacks on the Fortress, forcing him to flee towards Tibet. However, he was caught and killed on the way. Wang Phajo was the one who fought against the Lhasang Khan's force during the fifth Tibet-Bhutan war.

There was another intense clash between the two rulers of Bhutan, with the ecclesiastical and secular rulers on the one side and Lama Dhondup Kape on the other. Kape's party had a narrow victory. He sought military help from Pholawa, who mobilized border troops and sent them to Bhutan. The Tibetan troops and Kape's troops jointly fought the enemy's forces, but they were not able to achieve victory. Pholawa sent the army leaders of U and Tsang Dhokar Shabdrung Tsering Wangyal, Nyanto Drongkar Tsepa Tenzin Noyon, Manthangpa, Paldong Darhen Drakpa, with a large number of troops from U and Tsang and a Mongol army, to reinforce the Tibetan force in Bhutan. Together they attacked the enemy, both causing and suffering heavy casualties. They ultimately crushed the enemy's forces.

Out of great concern over the chaotic situation in Bhutan, the Panchen Rinpoche, Sakya Dakchen and Mipham Karmapa, including their disciples, appealed to Pholawa to allow them to mediate in the civil war in Bhutan. Having obtained permission, theysent their representatives to Bhutan. The lamas and leaders of Bhutan accepted their mediation and stopped fighting. They determined their territorial areas and agreed to live in peace forever, without fighting each other, and that they would send envoys to Tibet annually to present ceremonial gifts to the Tibetan ruler on the occasion of Tibetan New Year. They took vows with the Three Jewels and Dharma Protector deities as witnesses. The agreement was recorded and under their names, the mediators put their seals moistened with their own saliva. Desi Rinchen Trinley Rabgye sent his own uncle Tsering Wangyal to Tibet as guarantor. Gangteng Lama and Kape Dhondup, with a large retinue, including their ministers, arrived in Tibet to pay tribute to the Tibetan ruler. They presented a letter of praise and offered their submission to the Tibetan ruler, pledging that they, including their subjects, would live under his rule and that all the wealth in Bhutan belonged to him. After that, Tibet and Bhutan ceased fighting and continued their religious, political and trade relations. This marked the beginning of the Bhutanese annual visit toLhasa to pay tribute to the Tibetan government. Details about this are in the biography of Pholawa.

Tibetan ruler Gyurme Namgyal's political policy and the creation of a government army

In 1735, the Seventh Dalai Lama, with his retinue, accompanied by local leaders from Kham, including the king of Derge and monastic officials, left Kham for Lhasa. Amidst a grand reception organized by the government, aristocrats and monastic officials, particularly by Pholawa, and greeted by a large crowd of devotees, the Dalai Lama arrived in Lhasa.

During his twenty year rule, Pholawa maintained peace and happiness in the country. He improved the economy of farmers and nomads, promoted Buddhism, founded the Narthang Printing House, produced new woodblocks for scriptures and improved the government and military system, besides introducing some social reforms. He died on the 2nd day of the 2nd Tibetan month of 1747, after an illness.

Pholawa had two sons. Gung Gyurme Tseten, the elder, was appointed governor of Ngari, and Gung Gyurme Namgyal, the younger, was made his father's successor, and granted the title Dale Daiching Batur and the seal by the Seventh Dalai Lama.

Dale Daching Batur maintained superficially amicable relations with the Dalai Lama, but in reality, they were lacking in mutual trust and respect. Unlike his father, he regarded the Manchus as his main enemy. In 1748, he told the Manchu emperor and two Ambans stationed in Lhasa:

> The Manchu Ambans who have been posted in Lhasa on the pretext of being assistants to the Dalai Lama, and the Manchu officers and troops who have been left in Lhasa as a security force against the Dzungars are causing great suffering to the people. They give their riding and pack animals to the people to feed and look after them. If an animal dies, is lost or becomes weak, people are forced to produce a substitute or compensation. They harass and rape women. They force people to supply free transportation, corve service, firewood and accommodation beyond the limit sanctioned to them by the Tibetan government. They often try to interfere in the governance of Tibet. They are hence very harmful to the political and religious affairs of Tibet, at present as well as in future. Therefore all the Manchu officials and troops in Tibet must be withdrawn. Tibet has its own army to safeguard itself against the Dzungars. Tibet has again recruited 6,000 new troops. Tibet can protect its own territory.

The Emperor replied that he would keep only 100 Manchu troops in Lhasa as bodyguards of the Amban and would withdraw the rest. The Emperor further assured him that the Amban would never interfere in the governance of Tibet and that the Manchu government would send sufficient salaries to the Amban and his assistants, Chinese officers and troops to discourage them from exploiting people.

In that year, Dale Batur, accompanied by a large retinue, went to Shigatse to meet Palden Yeshi, reincarnation of the fifth Panchen Rinpoche. He sent Tsedron Lotsawa Kachen Yeshi Chophel to Nepal, with a letter and gifts, to advise the three kingdoms of Nepal and the Gurkhas to live in peace, in order to improve trade relations between Tibet and Nepal and to allow pilgrims and artists to travel freely in both countries. Later, caused by a rumour circulated by the Manchu Amban in Lhasa, a dispute arose between the two sons of Pholawa, followed by military conflicts. The Seventh Dalai Lama advised them to stop fighting and to agree to a peaceful reconciliation. The two sides turned a deaf ear and kept fighting. Dale Batur asked the Ganden Tripa, the throne-holder of Ganden, to conduct a ritual to destroy the governor of Ngari, just as "dust is blown away", but the Ganden Tripa refused.

Dale Batur summoned Gashi Pandita and Dokhar Shabdrung Tsering Wangyal, and said, "You two, with Phurchok Ngawang Jampa and my elder sister Deden Dolma, told the Ngari Governor to launch a war on me. Why did you ask him that?" The two explained that they had never said such a thing to the governor of Ngari. Later it came to light that some evil-minded people who were connected to the Manchus had created the rumour under the influence of the Manchu Amban in Lhasa. Since Dale Batur was hostile to those Tibetan officials who were close to the Manchus, Gashi Pandita and Dokhar Shabdrung, among others, also became the targets of his hostility. Soon news spread that Gung Gyurme Tseten had died from an illness, but many people believed that he was killed in a battle.

Gyurme Namgyal arrested the partisans of Gyurme Tseten and executed or imprisoned them. After that he demanded that all the Manchu officers and soldiers in Tibet must return to China, saying that they were an extra burden on the people, and that the two Ambans were trying to destroy the unity of the people. He also proclaimed that the religious practices and traditions in the Buddhist monasteries in China and Mongolia had declined, and that the Tibetan government should control them, as had been done during the reign of the Fifth Dalai Lama.

As discussed in the fourth chapter, Dale Batur not only instituted a permanent national army to safeguard the country's borders, but also sent delegates to the Dzungars to improve relations with them. The Manchu Amban Fuxin and his assistant Labadunin Lhasa sent secret reports to Peking. Before they received a reply, on the 13th day of the 10th month of 1750, with the collusion of some Tibetan officials who associated themselves with the Manchus, Dale Batur was summoned to Tromsigkhang, with the excuse that the Manchu Emperor had sent an honorary title and gifts to him. Dale Batur, with some servants, incautiously went to Tromsikhang. He entered the room with two servants, leaving the rest at the door. As soon as he entered, Chinese soldiers who were lying in wait leapt upon him and his two servants, killing all three on the spot with knives. Dale Batur's servants, who were waiting outside the gate, ran to Ganden Khangsar and reported the incident to Dronyer Lobsang Tashi, Sangpukpa, Paldrong Sharpa, Dingkhang Chodze and two army leaders. They immediately ordered the Tibetan army in Lhasa to attack the Manchus.

Elimination of the Manchu Ambans, officers and soldiers who killed Sikyong Dale Batur

Under the command of Dronyer Lobsang Tashi and others, the Tibetan army surrounded the residence of the Manchu Ambans and Tromsigkhang, where their bodyguards resided. After several hours of fighting, the Ambans and several hundred Chinese troops were killed near Tromsikhang. The place where the Chinese were killed later on became known as Gyabumgang, meaning "the ground of 100,000 Chinese." The Tibetan troops also attacked every Chinese they saw, including civil and military officers, traders, restaurant owners and beggars. In short, all the Manchus in Lhasa, including the two Ambans, civil and military officials and traders were eliminated. About 247 Chinese, including the two Ambans' wives, Bichechi, the salary officer, traders, restaurant owners and the remaining Manchu troops put on Tibetan dresses and went to the Potala Palace to seek protection from the Dalai Lama. Immediately the Tibetan troops and people went to the Potala Palace and requested the Dalai Lama to send back all the Manchus who had come to him to seek his protection. The Dalai Lama asked his people to calm down and act peacefully. He ordered an edict to be pasted on the walls at Lhasa and Shol, asking the people to refrain from violence. The Dalai Lama's tutor Yongzin Trichen Nomihen went down to advise the people to restrain from violence. Some people hurled abuse at him and tore down the posters. However, eventually, the people obeyed the Dalai Lama's order and peace was restored. The Dalai Lama appointed Gashi (Doring) Gung Pandita Ngodup Rabten as the Regent in place of Dale Batur.

Dronyer Lobsang Tashi, sensing a threat to his life, went to the Dzungar country. The new regent Doring Pandita, a partisan of the Manchus, proclaimed an edict throughout the country that everyone must maintain peace in the country, and issued an order to arrest Dronyer Lobsang Tashi, Paldrong Sharpa and Sangbugpa wherever they arrived. The three were finally arrested as they tried to escape.

In the 12th month, a Manchu force led by the Sichuan ruler Tsering arrived in Lhasa and put the supporters of Dale Batur under harsh investigation in the courtyard of Changlo residence in Lhasa. They executed six people, including Dronyer Lobsang Tashi, by striking hot iron on their bodies and six other men by cutting their throats, and imprisoned the rest. Dale Batur's son Dargye Tsering and two wives were banished and their properties were seized. The Manchu troops indulged in extreme militarism.

Dale Batur was a very courageous, wise and virtuous man who sacrificed his life for the welfare of the religion and beings of the country. Partly due to hasty actions and partly due to the obstruction created by the people who were born out of evil prayers and who conspired with the Manchus, he did not live long enough to accomplish his visions. During his four years of rule, he was generally strict towards high officials and wild by nature, but he was kind to poor and needy people. He reformed the tax system for the benefit of the common people, and investigated from time to time whenever there was anything improper and dishonest in the implementation of law and taxation. He not only looked after all the Buddhist schools in Tibet, but also made great efforts towards the preservation and promotion of Buddhism in China and Mongolia. In an important achievement, he was able to drive out from Tibet all the Chinese officers and troops who had arrived in Tibet during the time of his father, and he obtained a signed warranty from the Manchu Emperor, guaranteeing that the small number of Manchus in Tibet would not meddle in Tibetan internal affairs. He even tried hard to expel these remnants of the Manchus as soon as possible. He created a permanent army with sufficient numbers of troops to protect the country, and had a plan to improve the army system. In short, he did much for the country during his reign. However, some Chinese and Tibetan officials with vested interests poisoned the relationship between him and his bother. He earned a bad reputation for the murder of his brother. In addition, some Tibetans who favoured the Manchus did not cooperate with him. He was doubtlessly a hero of Tibet who was able to sacrifice his life for the sake of the country and religion, and we should therefore commemorate him.

Pacification of the violence in Sangen in Doto

After the Seventh Dalai Lama passed away, the Eighth Dalai Lama was enthroned at the Potala Palace in 1762. After thatthere was total peace in Tibet for more than a decade.

In 1779, the people of Sangen in Kham robbed the governor of Dartsedo, who transported tea to the Lhasa government, and looted travellers, pilgrims, traders and others travelling through the area, so that people stopped travelling on that road, and there was no peace in the area. Many cases of robbery and raids were also taking place in Lithang, Gojo, Markham and Drakyab. The local leaders and village and monastic people appealed to the Tibetan government for protection. The Tibetan government sent Kalon Gashi Gung Pandita as the Commander-in-Chief, Dapon Changlochen Tashi Phuntsok of the U army, Dapon Phajo Lhagangpa Tenzin Namgyal of the Tsang army, accompanied by Drash Taiji and Taiji Lhabu Langchenpa from Markham as their assistants, with large forces from U and Tsang, to control the criminals. In the 9th month of the same year, they arrived in Sangen. They besieged Sangen from three sides, and set fire to the Sangen Fortress, with all its wealth. Sangen had a strong army, but its leaders and soldiers surrendered after a brief period of fighting. Derong Atsok and other ringleaders, as well as Rushe Tago Jampa and his son, were killed in the fight. Some offenders were captured and banished to the districts of Rima Changra and Dartsedo in Sangen and Powo in Derge. Peace was restored in all areas of Kham and all the government's troops gradually returned to Lhasa

The Second Gurkha-Tibet war

Nepal in the 13th century was composed of several small kingdoms, with Kathmandu, Patan and Bhaktapur being the three largest ones. Since that time these kingdoms had shared longstanding trade and cultural relations with Tibet. In 1751, due to political turmoil in the country caused by civil wars within the kingdoms adulterated Nepalese coins were minted and circulated in Tibet. The Tibetan government sent a delegation, with a letter, to ask Nepal to control the adulteration of its currency.

Not long after that Prithvi Narayan Shah (r. 1768–1775)[1] unified the whole of Nepal and established his rule over the country. Tibet sent a delegation, with a letter and gifts, to congratulate him and to ask him to continue the existing friendly relations between Tibet and Nepal. In return, Prithvi sent a delegation of about 30 members to deliver some of the first new-minted coins, with a letter and gifts, to Tibet. The delegation met the Dalai Lama and the cabinet ministers. The two countries appeared to be enjoying friendly relations with each other during that time. However, a few years later, in 1775, a war broke out between the two neighbours. Regarding the real causes of the war, at the instigation of Bhutan, Nepal invaded Tibet from its border area of Sikkim up to Walung. The king of Sikkim fled from Gangtok to Dromo. Tibet sent Dapon Kipug of the Tsang army, with a force, to push back the Nepalese troops. The Nepalese troops retreated without fighting. The Kashag sent a delegation, whose members included the abbot of Shalu Monastery and Dapon Petsel of Tsang army, to Walung to make a peace treaty with Nepal. Nepal was not satisfied with the terms of the agreement.

---

1 Prithvi Narayan Shah, King of Nepal (1723–1775) was the first king of the House of Shahs to rule Nepal. He is credited with starting the campaign for a unified Nepal, which had been divided and weakened under the Malla confederacy. He was the ninth generation descendant of Dravya Shah (1559–1570), the founder of the ruling house of Gurkha. Prithvi Narayan Shah succeeded his father King Nara Bhupal Shah to the throne of Gurkha in 1743.

Another cause of the war was connected to the dispute over the properties of the late Panchen Rinpoche, between his relative Chagdzo Drungpa Lobsang Yesh Jinpa and the 6th Shamar Choedup Gyatso. Shamar went to Nepal on the pretext of going on a pilgrimage and requested the Nepali king to attack Tashi Lhunpo. Another cause of the war could be attributed to the issues of taxation on Tibetan and Nepal traders, the exchange rate, the price of goods and Nepalese counterfeit coins[2]. During the time of the Malla king of Nepal, the Nepalese government minted lower quality coins. After that, the new Nepal king [Prithvi Narayan Shah] issued pure silver coins. The Tibetan government treated the two coins as equal in value. Nepal complained to Tibet against the equal treatment to the two coins, and banned the circulation of the adulterated coins. It also sent a letter to the Tibetan government saying that Nyanang, Rongshar and Kyirong should be handed over to Nepal, since they had been previously invaded by the former Nepali king Yombu, and or else Nepal would launch a war on Tibet. Before the Tibetan government sent a reply, Gurkhas kidnapped two Tibetan idol makers in Nepal as guarantors. Later, Shamar Rinpoche cunningly sent the two image makers to Tibet to ask the government to send a reply, and he and Decho Trulku stayed in Nepal in their place. The Tibetan government replied that it did not send Shamar Rinpoche and Decho Trulku to Nepal as the representatives of the Tibetan government and that the two were in Nepal for private purposes. An order was sent to the Tibetan border areas to guard the borders. At the same time troops were secretly mustered and war preparations were made, in the event of any offensive move from the enemy. Monasteries of different sects were asked to perform rituals to avert wars. The government sent a polite letter to the Shamar Rinpoche, saying that there was no other issue between Nepal and Tibet apart from the problem of the value of the Nepalese currency. The edict said that the Shamar Rinpoche should try to solve only that problem. However, I have not found any letters sent to the Gurkha king.

In July 1787, brought by Shamar Rinpoche's servant Karma Chogjin, a large Gurkha force suddenly attacked Nyanang, Rongshar and Kyirong. The local Tibetan troops opposed them as well as they could, but they were too small in size to push them back. The Kyirong district officer Rambu Lungpa and others died in the defensive fight. The Gurkha troops who arrived at Nyanang and Rongshar headed to Shelkar. The government sent Dapon Changlochen of the Tsang army with forces to Dzongkha and Kyirong, with instructions to gallop day and night to oppose the

---

2 Tibet had been using Nepali coins since the time of the Malla kings. Jaya Prakash Malla of Kathmandu faced an economic crisis, so he minted a lower quality of coins mixed with copper. Again, when Prithvi Narayan Shah conquered the Kathmandu Valley and firmly established the rule of the Shah Dynasty in Nepal, he minted coins with pure silver. So, the two types of coins were found in the Tibetan market. The Lhasa government complained to the Nepal government to control the fake coins. The countries decided to settle the issue through negotiation.

Gurkha troops. Many local troops were urgently mobilized from U, Lhoka and Dakpo and Kongpo. Commander-in-Chief Kalon Yuthog Tashi Dhondup, accompanied by some government officials from the Tse and Sho offices as his assistants, with the above local troops, was sent to Kyirong to help the Tibetan force there. When they arrived at Shelkar, Kalon Yuthog sent a report to Lhasa, saying:

> The Gurkha troops tried to seize Saga and Shelkar districts, which are under the jurisdiction of the governor of Upper Tibet. Our troops opposed them with great force, causing heavy casualties. Now the Gurkhas have retreated to Shol and Luding, and we are continuing to fight them.

The Manchu Ambans in Lhasa might have sent a report to the Manchu Emperor about the Gurkha-Tibet war. However, the Tibetan government decided to defend itself against the Gurkhas and did not request the Manchu Emperor for military help. In view of the priest-patron relationship between China and Tibet, the Emperor sent a large number of Chinese troops from Sichuan, led by Ngao Changjun, Chin Taitu, ChangdaLui and Mu Darinto help Tibet.

In that year, the Panchen Rinpoche was invited to Lhasa. From Kyirong, an Avalokitesvara image was brought to Phagpa Lhakang temple at the Potala Palace. A small group of Chinese troops led by Chin Taitu arrived in Lhasa. Soon after that, a large force comprising Tibetan and Chinese troops was sent to confront the Gurkhas. On the ground of his capability and experience, Kalon Doring Tenzin Paljor was requested to lead the expedition. With him were sent Tsipon Dongna Tsadiwa Sonam Tashi as his assistant, the cabinet secretary Dekharwa as staff and Dolpo Donga as their guide. The Chinese troops caused a lot of trouble for the village people on the way by making them provide free riding and pack animals, fodder, firewood and labours, and forcing woman to sleep with them.

The Tibetan government received a report from the battlefield stating that the Gurkha forces had retreated from Shelkar in different groups and had camped at Nyanang, Rongshar, Kyirong and Dzonga.

At that time, the remaining Manchu troops led by Ngao Chanjun and the Manchu minister Chintripa Darin arrived in Lhasa. Chin Taitu stayed in Shigatse for five days. He suggested that they should initiate a peaceful negotiation with the Gurkhas until the remaining Chinese arrived, and that they should send a petition to the Dalai Lama in Lhasa for his advice. Kalon Doring told him that it was not possible to send a letter to the Dalai Lama before they fought the enemy. Chin Taitu became angry but he could not find any excuse to offend Kalon Doring, so he tortured the leaders of the district and villages along the way by tying iron chains or cangues on their necks, accusing them of not providing riding and pack animals and lodgings to them properly.

When they arrived at Shelkar, the Tibetan and Chinese armies camped separately at Dingri. The Tibetans had no plans to hold a negotiation. The Chinese however sent letters to the father of the Panchen Rinpoche and Sakya Lama's chamberlain asking them to mediate. The two arrived at Shelkar to witness the negotiations. However they could not proceed to Nepal since the Thong-la pass of Nyanang had been covered with thick snow. The Shamar Trulku sent a private proposal to the Tibetan government, stating that Tibet should sign a treaty with the Gurkhas, and if Tibet paid 300 coins to Nepal annually, Nepal would return Nyanang, Kyirong and Dzonga to Tibet. The Kashag rejected his suggestion.

In the 4th month of 1789, the remaining Chinese troops arrived at Shelkar. Instead of supporting the Tibetans they asked them to send an envoy to the Chinese Emperor to request him to arrange an agreement with the Gurkhas. The Tibetan government did not listen. When the mediators had crossed half way over the Thong-la pass, they felt unsure about whether they should return or go ahead. They sent messengers and letters to Nepal several times, requesting Nepal to return the Tibetan areas, but the Nepalese turned a deaf ear. The Chinese officials stressed peaceful reconciliation with Nepal, giving the impression that they were not willing to fight. Lhasa sent a delegation led by Tsipon Depugpa and Tsedron Dhondup Phuntsok, to join Kalon Doring and Tsang Dapon. They met the representatives of Sakya and Tashilhunpo at Dzonga, and together they arrived at Shelkar.

In the meantime, the Gurkha troops were engaged in looting the monasteries and villages in Dzongka. They plucked all the valuable ornaments from the sacred statues and removed precious materials from many sepultures and large statues. They also took the mummy of Lha Lama Jangchup Woe, the robes of Padmasambhava, a handwritten letter by Tsogyal and Milarepa's text Damcho Konchok Tsegpa, among other valuable articles. One of Tashilhunpo's servants named Ladakhi Oma Chigpa brought them back with great hardship and handed over them to the negotiation team. The sacred articles were later taken to Lhasa.

Thereafter, through correspondences and messengers, the two sides decided to conduct negotiations at Kyidrong, where the negotiation teams of both sides met. Nepal was represented by Lama Shamar, Bhim Sahib, Achia Sukbidar, Hasing Dzamindar, Brhamin Takshar Hari and Kaji Shing Tharpa.

A large tent was pitched on a field in Kyidrong village, and mats and other things were arranged inside it. All the negotiators assembled in the tent and discussed the issues for whole day. Finally the Gurkha members drafted a treaty with the terms that Nepal would return Nyanang, Kyirong and Dzonga to Tibet while the Tibetan government would pay 300 Chinese tamigma (rta rmig ma)[3] coins to Nepal annually. The Tibetan side had no option but to accept the terms. To make sure of the validity of the treaty they decided to ask the Chinese representatives to put their signatures on it. A messenger was sent to Shelkar to call the Chinese officials, and

---

3   A unit of silver coin in the shape of a horse-hoof.

Amban Mu, Amban Tang and their assistant Nuen Chonge arrived and signed the agreement.

Amban Mu asked the negotiators to send an envoy immediately with presents to China to express their gratitude to the Emperor for the fact that the Chinese had acted as witnesses in the smooth signing of the Tibetan-Gurkha agreement. The Gurkha team sent a report to their king about this, and the reply said that due to the long distance, it was not possible for the Gurkha members to go to China, but the Ambans and assistant were invited to Nepal. The Ambans' assistant, with some officials, was sent to Nepal, with the help of Shamar's chamberlain master Yeshi Gyaltsen. Meanwhile, the three Tibetan areas were handed over to the Tibetan government, and the Tibetans promised to pay the ransom to the Gurkhas.

Manchu's internal minister Thapa Darin, Chinese troops led by Ngao Chanjun and the Tibetan troops were withdrawn from the battle site. The Chinese officials who came to witness the Tibetan-Gurkha treaty were not satisfied with it, and said that Ambans had made a mistake by acting as witnesses. They borrowed the treaty and appendix, and returned them after cutting the last part of the papers which bore the Ambans' names. These accounts are found in the biography of Doring Pandita.

Soon after, led by Captain Bhim Sahi Hasa Dharma Sahib and Sri Kasah Upagya, about 40 delegates from the Gurkha court arrived in Lhasa to offer congratulations to the Dalai Lama. When they returned, the Tibetan government sent Tsedron Dhondup Phuntsok and Shodrung Dalpor Dongpa, among others, to deliver gifts to the Gurkha king and to request him to decrease the ransom amount.

The Gurkha king did not reduce the ransom amount. The Tibetan again sent a delegation to Nepal at different times for the same purpose, but each time the Nepal government rejected their request. After that, the Gurkha court sent Bhim Sahib and Lama Shamar, with their retinues, to the trade center in Nyanang to discuss the issues related to Lama Shamarwa and the ransom for the Tibetan areas, and asked the Tibetan government to send Kalon Doring and assistants there immediately. The Regent Tri Rinpoche Nomihen considered that the Tibetans and Chinese were excessively submissive to the Gurkhas. He said, "If the Gurkhas wanted to collect the ransom, there is no need to please them. In the event that they come to demand the ransom, we must stop them at the borders. If they still come, we must conscript troops from all the three regions of Tibet and fight them. Even if I, the Throne-holder of Ganden, have to go to the war, I will go and attack them. For the time being, no Tibetan official should go to Nepal." The Regent passed away in the third month of 1791, as a manifestation of obstruction to the Dharma and political affairs of Tibet. His assistant Nominhen Ngawang Tsultrim was appointed the Regent.

Lama Shamarwa sent several letters to Lhasa urging the Tibetan government to come to terms with Nepal. Lhasa sent a delegation of seven monk and lay officials headed by Kalon Doring and Yuthog, with a force. From Nepal, Bhim Sahib, Lama Shamar, Kaji Kalopata, with a force, arrived at Nyanang.

At that time, by the miraculous powers of the deity Palden Lhamo, lightning struck the roof of the royal palace of Nepal, killing several people.

The Gurkha-Tibet war brought huge losses to both the government and people of Tibet. Since one cause of the conflict was the issue of the old and new Nepalese coins, the Tibetan government established a new mint at Shol and started producing silver coins in the denomination of 5 kar. The coins bore the letter "46th year of the 13th Rabjung cycle," with the chain of lotus on its edge, the pinwheel of joy (dga' 'khyil) at the centre and a full lotus (pad ma tshang 'khor) on the reverse side. The coins were issued throughout the country for circulation, with an edict that the coins were equal in value to the old and new real Nepal coins in 1792.

In that year, the Manchu Emperor sent some 20,000 Chinese troops led by his minister Fusi Gungda Trungthang and Hegu, the leader of Solong Bhadur, out of consideration for the Sino-Tibetan's priest and patron relations. From Dome, by way of Nagchu, they headed to U-Tsang and joined the Tibetan army at Shelkar. From another direction, by way of Kham, Manchu Batur's leader Ngao Darin and Tritu Chanjun, with 10,000 troops, arrived in Lhasa. They were given an audience with the Dalai Lama and went to Shelkar, via Shigatse, to join the Tibetan army there.

The Tibetan and Chinese forces jointly combated the Gurkha forces in Nyanang, Kyirong and Rong, inflicting heavy casualties. The Gurkha troops retreated, and the Tibetan and Chinese forces pursued them continuously, even crossing into Nepal and marching through the country. A rumor spread widely that they were going to destroy the three kingdoms of Nepal. The Gurkhas immediately improved the food and living conditions of Kalon Doring and Yuthok, who had been captured in Nepal. They sent a request to Lord Cornwallis (1738–1805) for military assistance against Tibet, but in vain. The Gurkha king therefore fled on the pretext of going hunting. Lama Shamar committed suicide by consuming poison, unable to face the dire consequences.

The Nepali ruler Bhadur Shah sent a trader named Machi Dara, a close acquaintance of Kalon Doring, with an elephant, to bring him from prison. He told Doring that they had not disregarded Tibet-Nepal relations, and they had acted at the repeated request of Lama Shamar who had been keen to attack Shigatse, as he wanted to take revenge for not getting a share of the late Panchen Rinpoche's wealth from his brother. Bhadur told Doring that he would return all the properties seized from Shigatse and other areas, and requested him do something to prevent the Tibetan and Chinese armies from entering Nepal. Kalon Doring replied that he would try his best in this regard regardless whether he would be successful or not. He left Kathmandu to meet the Tibetan army wherever they had arrived. He was accompanied by the Gurkha officials including ministers Kazi Ratna Pata, Taksar Narismar and Sri Krishna, as well as the Tibetan ministers and Tibetan army leaders. Tibetan general Changlochen had already died in prison.

At that time, the road from Nepal to Tibet was congested because many wounded Gurkha soldiers were returning from the battlefield and many new Gurkha soldiers were going to the battlefield as reinforcements .The Tibetan and Chinese troops marched down the road, beating drums, shouting "ki hi hi" and sounding bugles. When they arrived at a distance of 40 km from the Nepali capital, Kalon Gashi, Yuthok and the Gurkha representatives met them. Dapon Phajo of the U army and Lhagangpa Tenzin Namgyal and Salong Batur's leader Hegu asked the Tibetan and Gurkha officials where they were going. They replied that they were going to meet the Chinese and Tibetan army leaders. Dapon Phajo told them that Chinese army leader Fusi Trungtang and Tibetan minister Shadra Kunga Paljor, who had been sent in place of late Dzasak Horkhang Rongtse, would be arriving at the Dopung slope, across the river. In the evening of the 27th day of the 6th month of 1792, the Tibetan ministers and Gurkha representatives met the Chinese and Tibetan military leaders, and told them in detail what had happened and about the message sent by the Gurkha ruler Aku Bhadur Shah. The Chinese and Tibetan army leaders told them, "If the Gurkha king really wants to negotiate, the Gurkha king himself should come or send a plenipotentiary to negotiate. Shamar Trulku's servants and his wife Bomola, and other confederates, as well as all the properties and wealth stolen by them from Tibetans in Shigatse and other places should be handed back to us. If this happens, we will withdraw all the Chinese and Tibetan troops, otherwise we will invade Nepal by sending a large military expedition. Until we receive a clear reply, the Gurkha ministers Kaji Ratna Pata and Tasarnr Singh should stay with us." At that time, the Tibetan troops who had left Nyanang had already entered Nepal and camped at Nawa Koti, some distance away from Nepal's capital.

The Gurkha king and ministers held an urgent meeting to discuss the issue. After much deliberation, they sent a delegation, comprising the Gurkha's senior most figures Bhim Sahib, Kulla Bhadur and Juta Bhadur. By that time, Shamar's bone relics and Gagpa Gelek had already arrived in Tibet. Shamar's attendant Jedrung killed himself on the way to Tibet by taking poison. Shamar's chamberlain Yeshi and his wife Bumola, with about twenty monks, came and handed over the Tibetan soldiers captured by the Gurkha army and the goods robbed from Tashi Lhunpo and others, carried by 300 coolies, to the Tibetan and Chinese army leaders. They apologized and pledged to obey the government.

Thereafter, because the Tibetan and Chinese army leaders recognised the importance of friendly relations between Tibet and Nepal, the Tibetans and Chinese jointly signed treaties with Nepal at different times. It was resolved that Tibet did not have to pay a ransom to Nepal for the Tibetan areas returned by the Gurkhas. The borders were delineated and both sides promised not to offend each other. The issue of the old and new Nepali coins was resolved. The two countries agreed to continue with their old friendly relations. I have not inserted here the contents of these treaties. The Tibetan and Chinese armies were withdrawn from Nepal. At the end of 1792, Kalon Shadra and other Tibetan delegates, as well as the Chinese officials including Fusi Trungtang arrived in Lhasa.

Thereafter, the Tibetan government confiscated the monastic estate, properties and monastic land Yangpachen of Lama Shamar, on the grounds of his misdeeds. The government also banned the discovery and recognition of his reincarnation. The people of U-Tsang and Kham had to bear great burdens during this war, as they had to provide free labour and food. The Tibetan government gave them grain compensation from its store. The chief military officials Doring Pandita and Yuthog were stripped of their official power on the grounds of their bad performance during the war. Those who had given valuable service were rewarded. The government sent orders throughout the country that they should organize grand parties to welcome home their soldiers. The Tibetans emerged victorious in the above war for the protection of their country, but on the other hand a negative result of the war was that Fusi Trungtang installed a tablet inscribed with Manchu and Chinese letters, listing his so-called "ten achievements", near the outer stone pillar at Shol, below the Potala Palace. Moreover, he indulged in extreme militarism in Tibet and frequently harassed the Tibetan government.

Therefore, the Tibetan clergy and laypeople petitioned the government, insisting that the Manchu troops had come to Tibet uninvited, on the pretext of having come to reinforce the Tibetan army out of consideration for the priest-patron tradition, and their presence in the country posed a great danger to the country, both at the present time and in the future. They must be withdrawn immediately. Fusi Trungtang, in order to appease the people, blamed the Amban Fozhiin Lhasa for all the mistakes. He was demoted and kept in the Lhasa streets with a cangue around his neck for three months. The Amban's assistants Shau and Pau, with cangues around their necks, were expelled to China. After carrying out these audacious deeds, Pu Trungtang and the Manchu troops had to return to China on 25 March 1793.

During this Gurkha-Tibetan war, though not requested, the Manchu troops came to help Tibet out of consideration for the priest-patron relationship. This incident was later misinterpreted and used by China to claim Tibet as part of China. They published a corpus of literature on Tibetan secular and military history, containing many distorted facts. So it is very important that everyone should be careful to seek the true version of events.

In 1804, the Eighth Dalai Lama died after a prolonged illness. In 1808, the Ninth Dalai Lama Lungtok Gyatso was enthroned in the Potala Palace.

Suppression of Jonangpas in Gulok and Tsonong

In 1808, the Tibetan government sent a team headed by Kalon Shadra Dhondup Dorje, with the U army led by Dapon Phalhawa, to investigate Gulok Khangsar and Khangan, who had been engaged in unlawful activities. They collected the local militia from northern Chushur in Derge. When they arrived in Gulok, the ringleaders of the Gulok bandits fled and others surrendered and took an oath to obey the government's order. The Gulok bandits were suppressed without using force.

In 1815, the Ninth Dalai Lama died at the age of 11, and the Tenth Dalai Lama Tsultrim Gyatso was enthroned in the Potala Palace in 1822.

In 1931 and 1932, Jonang Dzasakand his gang raided and looted Dranag villages. To investigate the matter, a delegation led by the Dalai Lama's special attendant Kuchar Khenche Lobsang Gyaltsen was sent. They were given authority to summon local militia from Tsaidam Buyan Dzasak if they needed to. When the team conducted their investigation, Jonang Dzasak, instead of cooperating, threatened the investigation team. Therefore, Khenche Lobsang summoned local troops from 25 Dhimchi states, Ragshul and Yulshul. Dapon Sarjungpa and Rupon Rampa, with the U army, were already there. More troops were called from Derge. From Lhasa, Kalon Thonpa as the Commander-in-Chief, with assistant staff Tsipon Posho, payroll officer Gyatso, cabinet secretary Sarjungpa, Tsedrung Treshong Thogme Chojor and others were sent to help the investigation team. When they reached Nagchu, they met a mounted messenger, who informed them that Jonang Dzasak had surrendered. They therefore returned. Jonang Dzasak, his son and other leaders of Jonang arrived at Lhasa and confessed their mistakes to the Dalai Lama, and the incident was closed. This short account is found in Shakabpa's Tibet: A Political History. I have not found any other sources about this event.

Tibet-Ladakh war

A decade earlier, Sikh soldiers sent by the Dogra King raided the Ladakh borders, forcing the Ladakh king, who hailed from the Tibetan royal lineage, to take asylum in Tibet. In 1834, the Kashmiri king Maharaja Gulab Singh sent troops led by the commander Wazir Zorawa Singh to help the Sikh army, and invaded Ladakh from its western side. The Ladakh army, which was small, attempted to obstruct them at the borders, but was easily overpowered. The Singh's troops arrived in Ladakh's capital Leh. The Ladakhi minister Ngodup Tenzin surrendered to Zorawar Singh. In return, Singh declared the dethronement of the Ladakh king and appointed Ngodup Tenzin as the new king. He was made to pay an annual tribute of 5,000 rupees to Kashmir. After this the Sikh troops returned home. Ladakh paid the tribute for six years. After that, whether because Ladakh did not pay the tribute or for some other reason, Zorawar Singh once again led a force of about 6,000 troops to Ladakh and removed Tenzin Ngodup from the throne and enthroned the former king.

In 1837, the Tenth Dalai Lama passed away, and in 1842, the Eleventh Dalai Lama Khedup Gyatso was enthroned in the Potala Palace.

In the past, Tibetan traders exported tea, fabrics, wool, etc., to Ladakh, and imported from Ladakh dry fruits, lena (goat's hair), clothes, and other items required by the Tibetan government. Ladakh used to provide loaders, lodging, food, firewood, horses, pack animals, servants, etc, to the Tibetan traders. In 1841, as if Ladakh and Kashmir had made a secret agreement, Ladakh stopped providing these facilities to the Tibetan traders. Moreover, a large force, comprising the troops of Ladakh, Dogra and Sikh penetrated into Tibet as far as Ngari from the western side.

The Governor of Ngari sent a report to Lhasa about the coming of the invaders from the Ladakh side. The government immediately sent Dapon Pal Shiwa of the Tsang army and Dapon Surkhangpa Tseten of the U army, with their forces, to Ngari to eject the invaders. The Tibetans had only a few Mongol and locally made guns, and their main weapons were bows and arrows, swords and spears, while the Sikh soldiers had automatic guns and cannons. Due to lack of good weapons, the Tibetan forces lost the battles, ceding Pureng Takal Koata and Saga Drosho to the enemy.

Thereafter, the Kashag quickly sent the Commander-in-Chief Kalon Palhun and Dapon Shadra Wangchuk Gyalpo of the U army, with many local militias from U and Tsang, to reinforce the Tibetan defense force there. The enemy's troops had occupied Ruthog, Tashi Gang and Rubshu. The Tibetan force attacked the invaders wherever they were. In 1842, the Tibetan vanguard force led by Kalon Palhun, with some selected troops, taking advantage of the chilly weather of the 11th Tibetan month, attacked the enemy's positions from all sides. After three days, there was a heavy fall of snow and rain in Ngari. The Sikh troops at Kota lost their vigor because of the extremely cold weather. The Tibetans continuously attacked the Sikhs in hand-to-hand fighting. While Zowar Singh was riding here and there around the battlefield, the Tibetan commander named Yasor Migmar recognized him and threw a spear at him. Zowar Singh fell off his horse. Migmar immediately took out a sword and beheaded him on the spot. He took the head to the Tibetan army camp. Seeing this, the Sikh troops lost courage and fled in all directions. The

Tibetans pursued them, killing about 300 and capturing about 700 Sikh soldiers. Among the captured were two ministers from Ladakh who were sent to U-Tsang, escorted by some troops.

The Tibetan armies pursued the Sikh troops from the various battle sites. They entered Ladakh, marching up to Dumra, close to the mountain behind Leh, where they stayed for one year. After that, in the early summer of 1842, Maharaja Gulab Singh of Kashmir sent Diwan Harish Chandra and Wazir Ratun, with 8,000 troops plus some Dogra troops, to drive away the Tibetan forces. They attacked the Tibetan army camp at Dumra under the cover of night, causing severe casualties. Dapon Surkhang and Dapon Palshi, along with 60 Tibetan soldiers, were captured and taken to Leh. According to Ladakhi history, Dapon Ragshag, who was among the captured, committed suicide on the way by eating a piece of diamond, but Tibetan records say nothing about this.

Kalon Palhun sent a delegation to Leh to begin the negotiations. The delegation met Diwan Chandra and proposed that they should sign a lasting agreement. They signed an agreement on the terms that Tibet was to withdraw all its soldiers from Ladakh and both sides would release all the captured war prisoners, who would be provided with escorts, horses and pack animals. After that, Dapon Surkhang and Palshi, with their troops, returned. The two Ladakh ministers and two third of the Sikh troops returned, while one third of them settled in Lhoka, Yarlung, Chongye, Sangri and other areas of Tibet, with their Tibetan wives. They cultivated apricots, apples and grapes. Hence there are many people of Sikh descent in Lhoka.

Thereafter, Kalon Palhun, Dapon Surkhang and Dapon Palshiwa, among others, arrived back in Lhasa. Kalon Palhun was rewarded for his remarkable leadership in the war. Dapon Surkhang was promoted to the post of minister with the title Taiji. However, there is no mention in the record whether Dapon Palshiwa received any rewards. Soon after, Kalon Surkhang, with Tsang Dapon Palshiwa, Tsechag Sarjung and Nyithang Lama, was sent to Ladakh to finalize the agreement. When they arrived in Leh, Drikpa Sri, Halapji Apra Shri and Maharagan also arrived there as representatives of Ladakh. They signed an agreement that both Ladakh and Tibet would coexist in a friendly manner as in past, without feelings of revenge, and that they would never attack each other over their borders. The agreement also said that when the Ladakhi king, his queen and brother returned, they must be treated with due honor and their positions were to be restored. Trade relations between Ladakh and Tibet should be continued. After that, the Ladakhi king and his brother, queen and ministers took an oath that they would pay tribute to the government regularly and would protect their own territory.

After Ladakh and Tibet had signed the peace agreement, Dapon Shadra Wangchuk Gyalpo of the U regiment was promoted to the post of Kalon in honor of his performance in the conflicts. In 1742, on the Drapchi ground in Lhasa, the Tibetan government organized a grand ceremony in honor of the Tibetan war heroes, during which Yasor who had killed Zarowar Singh was granted a tax-free piece of land with permanent ownership over it. After that, Tibet and Ladakh lived harmoniously and peacefully.

The second Tibet-Nepal war

In 1855, the Eleventh Dalai Lama assumed the full responsibility of the government at the request of the people of Tibet. Nepal had been in turmoil and disunity for a long period as a result of violent conflicts between the royal family and the ministers. Later, Maharaja Rajendra Vikramsha had a capable young army general called Jang Bhadur, and the king appointed him his Prime Minister. Disregarding the previous Tibet-Nepal treaties, Jang Bhadur frequently harassed the Tibetan government, demanding that Nyanang, Kyirong and Rongpo be handed over to Nepal. This coincided with the period when revolts against the British were breaking out in many parts of India. Jang Bhadur sent Gurkha troops to help the British in suppressing the revolts. As a reward for this effective help, the British granted him triple shri rank and a large area of land lying on the border of India and Nepal. The Nepali king appointed Jang Bhadur the permanent administrator of the country. Jang therefore became powerful. Proud of his power and unconcerned about the consequences, he sent Gurkha troops to Nyanang, Kyrong, Dzonga, Rongshar and Pureng, where they looted and tortured the people. The Tibetan government sent Dapon Rangjonpa Dorje Dhondup of the U army and Dapon Patsel of the Tsang army, with their forces, to expel the Gurkha troops. The Tibetan forces combated the Gurkha forces as well as they could in several battles, but they failed to push back the Gurkha troops because the Gurkhas had better weapons.

The government sent Kalon Palhun, with assistants, to Derge, Dhimchi 25, Riwoche, Chamdo and Pasho, and Kalon Tashi Khangsar, with assistants, to Bah, Lithang, Gyalrong, Gyalthang, Chakla, Beri and other areas to collect troops. They collected many local militias. Many monks from the Three Great Monastic Seats volunteered to join the Tibetan forces. Back in Lhasa, Kalon Tashi Khangsar was appointed the Commander-in-Chief and sent to Lato, with a contingent of troops and several thousand members of local militias. After good preparations, they attacked and caused heavy casualties on the enemy's side. They retook Nyanang and besieged Dzonga. In Rongshar, both the Tibetan and Gurkha sides suffered casualties, but the Gurkhas suffered heavier casualties. The Gurkha force of around 7,000 troops converged on the Tibetan position at Nyanang and captured the area.

At that time, a wild rumour circulated in Nepal that an extremely large Tibetan force, comprising local militias from the three provinces of Tibet and volunteer monks, was on their way to join the Tibetan forces that were fighting against the Gurkha army. This appeared to have lessened the enemy's fighting spirit. In 1855, in the 9th Tibetan month, the Gurkhas proposed a ceasefire. Kalon Shadra, with his assistant staff and representatives of the Three Monastic Seats, was sent to Kathmandu to negotiate with the Gurkhas. Kalon Shadra and his assistant staff stayed at Shelkar and then at Nyanang, and sent a negotiation team to Nepal.

In that year, the Eleventh Dalai Lama died. The National Assembly appointed the Reting Rinpoche, former Regent, as the Regent on the grounds of his experience.

In Kathmandu, the Tibetan negotiation team met with the Gurkha plenipotentiaries and held a series of meetings. The Tibetan negotiation team comprised the Dalai Lama's Master Chamberlain Dronyer Ngawang Gyaltsen, cabinet steward Kadron Drumpa Se and representatives of the Kashag, the Three Great Monastic Seats, Sakya, Tashi Lhunpo and Tsechokling monasteries. Finally on 24 Dec 1856, the two sides reached a 10-point agreement. According to the agreement, the Tibetan government was to pay 1,000 Ale (Nepalese coins) to Nepal annually, Nepal was to send troops to help Tibet whenever a foreign power attacked Tibet, there would be no tax imposed on Nepali traders in Tibet, and Tibet would release all the Pathan and Nepali war prisoners caught during the Tibet-Ladakh war. It was also agreed that Gurkha troops would be withdrawn from Tibet and a Gurkha army officer was to be kept in Lhasa as an ambassador from Nepal to Tibet. The agreement also prescribed rules on how to handle a case if a dispute arose between a Gurkha and a Tibetan in future.

Thereafter, the Gurkha troops in Tibet were gradually withdrawn. The prisoners were released. However, since the treaty was signed while the Gurkha troops were in Tibet, the treaty was completely in favour of the Gurkhas, as it was not made on a footing of equality and mutual benefits. Therefore the treaty was a disaster for Tibet. The Tibetan government paid tribute to Nepal until 1950 when the Chinese invaded Tibet. Nevertheless, the treaty has proved that both Tibet and Nepal are not part of China in the eyes of the international law. It has proved wrong the Chinese government's wild claim, made in writing and verbally, that Tibet is their territory.

In 1792, disregarding the stone marks installed on the Tibet-Nepal border, the Gurkhas installed new stone border marks and raised disputes over grasses and fencing issues. The U Dapon Dorje Dhondup, along with his aide-de-camp, was sent to the border to deal with the matter. From the Nepali side, Captain S. Khadri, with his assistants, arrived to hold peace negotiations. The Tibetans and Gurkhas together examined the border. They demolished the new border marks and left the earlier ones. A peace treaty was signed, after which the two countries lived as friendly neighbours and remained peaceful.

I want to make a short comment here. During the second Tibetan-Gurkha war, though not requested, the Manchu Emperor sent troops to help Tibet on the pretext of doing so in consideration of the Sino-Tibetan's priest-patron relationship. During the Tibet-Ladakh wars and the third Tibetan-Gurkha war, the Manchu government did not help Tibet; it did not even send weapons, let alone troops. The Chinese government nowadays cunningly explains that China did not help Tibet since China was in turmoil at the time due to the Taipei revolt and the opium war, otherwise China would have sent troops to help Tibet. The fact is that all the Tibetans' struggles against foreign invaders were aimed at protecting their country's independence, and there is no history of Tibetans having fought for the sake of China, in contrast to what the Chinese argue.

Around that time the British started harassing Sikkim on trade matters. A skirmish took place between a British force and Sikkim's local troops at Rongpuk. The British frequently troubled Sikkim's leader Trokhang Dronyer Namgyal, making him unable to live there. He fled to Tibet and took asylum with the Tibetan government. The Tibetan government granted him the fourth rank position in the government and Dokha Tashiling estate, with servants, for his residence. His family later became known as Taring.

Revolt by Drepung Monastery

Senior cabinet minister Shadra Wangchuk Gyalpo told his colleagues that the Regent was using his seal without constraint and that it would be a great risk in future. After discussion, they all went to the Regent and suggested to him that it would be safer in future if the Regent's seal was kept by a seal keeper, as with the seal of the Dalai Lama. They proposed that Shadra should be appointed the seal keeper. The Regent agreed with them. That evening, the Regent, the Chief Abbot Official and others met and talked about the topic of the Regent's seal. Some of them told the Regent that it must be a plot to seize his power. The Regent asked Kalon Tashi Khangsar in a friendly manner whose idea that was, and he replied that it was Shadra's idea. The Regent therefore became suspicious of Shadra. Accusing Shadra of having conspired with the Gurkhas and not performing his official duties properly, he dismissed him from the post of cabinet minister and instructed him to remain at his own estate in Nyemo.

While Shadra was residing in Nyemo, he received a letter from the Nepali Prime Minister Jang Bhadur. In reply, Shadra sent him a gift of a wooden table with carved designs and a letter. Knowing this, the Regent sent the army officer Dapon Tonpa, with a force, to Nyemo, with instructions that he must make sure that Shadra would be unable to come back. Dapon Tonpa, taking several troops, went to Nyemo and ordered his soldiers to surround the Shadra's residence. He entered the house and showed the order to Shadra. From the very wording "...

make Shadra unable to return," Shadra understood that the officer was sent to kill him. He told the officer about his past achievements and the dedicated service that he had given to the government. He further told him that during his posting at Nyanang, he had had correspondence with the Nepali Prime Minister Jang Bhadur on official matters, and that he had no personal relationship with him. Dapon Tonpa thought that if he killed such a noble man who had given great service to the country it would give the Regent a bad name and that he himself would end up in trouble in the future. He said, "I will make you unable to return by imprisoning you in a small room on the upper floor of Neymo Monastery. Your head will be shaved and you will not be allowed to meet anyone. I will hand over you to the officials of Nyemo Monastery." Having done this, the army leader and his forces returned to Lhasa. He reported to the Regent and the Kashag that he had made Shadra unable to return. The Regent and the Kashag took no further action after that.

Shadra was a major patron of Ganden Monastery. After one year, hearing that Shadra was at Gyalje Tsel Monastery, Palden Dhondup sent a monk in the disguise of a trader to examine the situation. He put a letter in a package of snuff to be handed over to Shadra through the prison guard. In the letter, Palden Dhondup said that he would contact all the senior officials of Ganden Monastery to revolt against the Regent. Shadra sent a reply put in the same package of snuff, telling Palden Dhondup that the Ganden monks alone would not be sufficient and he should try to gain support from Drepung Monastery.

In 1862, incidentally, Drepung Monastery received a smaller cash amount than usual in return for their religious offerings, and on these grounds, Drepung complained to the Regent. Due to this event, the Great Prayer Festival and Tsog Offering Ceremony of that year could not happen.

Ganden and Drepung monasteries jointly sent monks to Nyemo Gyalje Tsal Monastery to release Shadra. Shadra was brought to Lhasa and given a grand reception. A large number of monks guarded him. The Regent consulted the Kashag, and summoned the national troops and the Sera monks for the protection of the Regent. Shadra sent a notice to the government with instructions that all the officials must report to the Labrang Teng for a meeting the next day. He also informed the Ganden and Drepung supporters to remain on the alert. The government officials were not sure whether it was an official order and faced a dilemma as to whether to attend the meeting or not. Some of them attended the meeting.

At the meeting Shadra explained that he had been wrongly accused of wrongdoing even though he had not done anything wrong. He further said that if the Regent did not resign, he would revolt against him for the sake of the government and people, and asked the people to judge what was right and wrong and decide whether to give him support or not. He then set up a Joint Committee of Ganden and Drepung, comprising some officials who were on the side of Shadra. They criticized the Regent and posted guards at the Potala Palace and the Tsuglakhang Temple. A violent clash broke out in the compound of Shide Labrangof Reting. The government officials and the national troops remained neutral, giving support to neither side. The Regent was supported by Sera Monastery only. Therefore, the Regent, with some of his partisans, including Chief Abbot Official and Kalon Tashi Khangsar, taking along the Regent's seal, fled to Sera Monastery. But they could not stay there and fled to China through the northern route.

In that year, on the request of the Joint Committee of Ganden and Drepung and all the people of Tibet, the Twelfth Dalai Lama, though only 7 years old, assumed the leadership of the country. Kalon Shadra was appointed the Regent with the title of Nomihen to assist the Dalai Lama in governance.

Regent Reting and his party, via the northern route, went to Peking and tried to gain support from the Manchu Emperor. But they were disappointed and journeyed back. On the way, Reting passed away. Desi Shadra did a major staff reshuffle in the government and appointed Abbot Palden Dhondup of Ganden Shartseto the government. Palden Dhondup, thereafter, climbed up in the ranks—first he was lachak khenchung, and then became a cabinet minister and finally Chief Abbot Official. He was dominating, boastful and arrogant. He was feared and censured by all other civil and military officials. His thirst for power led to an internal feud in the government.

In 1864, Desi Shadra died after serving as Regent for three years, and Dedruk Khenrab Wangchuk was appointed as his successor. Chief Abbot Official Palden Dhondup criticized the new Regent as incapable. Palden Dhondup completely dominated the ministers. He threw Kalon Tsogo, Tsipon Changlochen and some other senior officials into a river. He was very autocratic and very ambitious to become the ruler of Tibet. Dedruk Khenrab prepared to arrest him and Shadra's son Tsewang. Palden Dhondup heard this while he was on his way to the Potala Palace from Lhasa. He immediately changed his way and headed to Drepung. As soon as he reached Jerag sandy bank, he met a messenger who informed him that two treasurers of Drepung Monastery had been arrested by the Drepung Governing Council and it was not safe to go there. He quickly went to Ganden and hid there. He planned to flee to his home (in Kham). The Ganden Governing Council granted him asylum and persuaded him to stay, telling him that they would appeal to the government for reconciliation, and that if the government did not respond positively, they would resort to force.

The Regent discussed the matter with the Kashag. The Kashag ordered the dissolution of the general-secretary committee of Ganden and Drepung monasteries and instructed the Tibetan army to seize Ganden Monastery. At that time, Sera monks volunteered to support the Tibetan army. Since Ganden was in a difficult location, the troops could not seize it easily. They surrounded the monastery and stopped the water and food supply to it. A rumour spread that the troops would soon take the monastery, so Palden Dhondup and his relative Dronyer Gonpo made their escape through Nyangre house at night. The troops pursued and caught them at Maldro. Palden Dhondup asked Dronyer to kill him, and Dronyer stabbed Palden Dhondup with a spear, killing him on the spot. Dronyer himself was injured in the leg by a gunshot, and was arrested and taken to Lhasa.

Thereafter, after a small fight at Ganden, the Ganden Governing Council surrendered. Most of the main culprits were arrested and taken to Lhasa. Palden Dhondup's corpse was tied on a wooden cross and paraded through the streets of Lhasa on horseback. Shadra's son and other offenders were severely punished. The riot led by Ganden and Drepung was finally suppressed.

1. Suppression of Nyarong bandits

A few years before the Ganden and Drepung riots broke out, a bandit group led by Rinang Palgon's descendent Gonpo Namgyal and his son Gonpo Tseten raided many regions in Kham, and engaged in looting, killing and vandalism. Unable to bear their harassment and ruthless activities, the Drago leader Wangchen Dradul, Ponmo Norbu, Jingsang and Lakho, with about 500 serf families, and Khangsar Ngodup Phuntsok, Masur Nyerpa and Shugu Tashi, with their 300 serf families, fled to Lhasa to take refuge with the Tibetan government. They were offered aid and temporary residences were provided in Chushur, Gongkar and Tonlung until they were able to return to their homeland. Thereafter, the Nyarong bandits again attacked Lithang, Chatreng, Dzakog, Minyag and Gyaltang, where they indulged in robbery and other crimes. They also looted the tea-stores of the Tibetan government and the Three Monastic Seats that were under the care of the Governor-General of Kham. They even blocked the trade routes between Tibet and China. They seized Derge Gonchen, the capital of Derge, and captured the king, along with his family and Kathog Bontrul as hostages. They put many villages and nomadic communities under their control.

The Tibetan government frequently received reports on these events from Kham. The Regent and the Kashag discussed how to deal with the matter. Kalon Phulungwa Tsewang Dorje was appointed Commander-in-Chief and went with troops from U and Tsang under the command of U army leaders Dapon Trimonpa Chime Dorje and Dapon Dokharwa Tsewang Norbu, as well as payroll officers and other staff, to suppress the Nyarong bandits led by Gonpo Namgyal and his son. The team left Lhasa on the 9th day of the 2nd Tibetan month of 1863. En route, they collected a large number of militias from Shotarlhosum and Richabpasum. They travelled on forced march.

Reaching Nyarong in the 9th Tibetan month, they immediately made their battle preparations. The Nyarong bandits had great confidence in themselves due to their success in military campaigns in Kham in the past several years and the tough terrain of their region. The Tibetan forces faced great difficulty in defeating the Nyarong troops and the fighting lasted for several months. The Nyarong invaders had been blinded by their irreligious attitude and had indulged themselves in the habit of robbing and killing; they used to set fire on the houses, hay and forests if they did not succeed in capturing them. They were ruthlessly oppressive in such ways.

In those days, the people of Kham used to call the Tibetan army "God's Army" and they gave full support to them in their fight against the enemy. Donkong Trulku himself arrived on the battlefield, leading the local militias of Markham, Drago and Gojo (Mardragsum). Lamas and trulkus of the area, such as Kongtrul Gyatso, performed meditations and prayers for the Tibetan army. Dapon Trimonpa and his force made strong attacks and captured Do Dzong, Jago Dzong and Ngyagchu Kha Fortress one by one. In the 7th Tibetan month of 1865, the Tibetan army besieged the Rinang Dzong from four sides and torched it, burning Gonpo Namgyal and his son alive, along with their 30 family members and forty senior ministers, who were inside the fortress, on the 1st day of the 8th Tibetan month. The remaining leaders and members of the Nyarong bandit force surrendered. The victory of the Tibetan army was proclaimed.

Commander-in-Chief Kalon Phulungpa went to Nyarong. He appointed the Payroll Officer Phunrab Tsering as the governor of Nyarong, with the title of Taiji, and assigned him assistant staff, bodyguards and others as required. In the presence of the leaders of all the local regions of Kham, including the 25 states of Dhimchi, Derge, Lingtsang, Lhatog, Gulug, Beri, Marukhangsar, Drago, Tongkor, Geshe, Chakla, Gokyab, Lithang, Bah and Chatreng, people were allowed to take back their belongings that had been stolen by the Nyarong invaders. All the prisoners kept by the Nyarong bandits were released. All the local leaders were restored to their previous positions, with their rights and powers. They were instructed to pay taxes and obey the Tibetan government's law. They were also instructed to keep troops and send them to serve in wars whenever the government sent orders. The governor of Nyarong was invested with powers to decide disputes among local rulers or principalities and he was instructed that in the event of his inability to handle any cases, he should consult the Lhasa government. The local people, both monks and lay, pledged to obey the orders of the Tibetan government and live in peace. Jamgon Kongtrul Rinpoche conducted a special ceremony when the Derge king, queen and princes, as well as the Bontrul Rinpoche returned from prison, and praised Kalon Phulungwa, the army leaders and the payroll officers for restoring peace and happiness in the area.

Thereafter, some of the fugitives belonging to the Nyarong bandits sent a petition to Lhasa against Kalon Phulungwa, complaining that he was not giving justice to the people. Phulungwa was a man of great wisdom and dignity and became popular after he successfully suppressed the revolt in Kham. He was a partisan of Palden Dhondup. However, fearing that he would not able to put Phulungwa under his control, Palden Dhondup sent a fake edict, with the seal of the Dalai Lama, to the district officer of Palbar to kill Phulungwa, when he was returning to Lhasa from Kham. When Phulungwa and his assistants arrived at Shabye Bridge, the district officer met him, but dared not kill him right away due to Phulungwa's charismatic power. The officer showed him the edict. Phulungwa lamented, "Now, there is nothing to do, so I will kill myself by jumping into the river." After reciting a long prayer, he jumped from the Shabye Bridge into the river, holding his son's hands.

In 1875, the Twelfth Dalai Lama passed away, and in 1879, the Thirteenth Dalai Lama was installed on the golden throne in the Potala Palace.

During the time of Khenchung Yeshi Thupten as the governor of Nyarong and Dapon Dudul Dorje, a census was conducted in Nyarong, including Dampa Rangdol Monastery and villages of Dranagshogsum, and a tax system was created. At that time, under the bad influence of the chief of Chakla, the local communities protested to the Nyarong governor, complaining that the census was not done in a fair manner. The Sichuan governor sent an officer named Tangli, with a force, to back the chief of Chakla. A war broke out between the Sichuan troops and the Tibetan army. The Sichuan troops kidnapped the king of Derge, along with his queen and two princes, took them to Chengdu and imprisoned them there. The two princes were rescued by the Tibetan army and the elder brother, Akya, was given his father's title and powers and married to Rampa's daughter. It was agreed that the Tibetan government would provide protection to the king's family and the king would in turn safeguard his territory under the authority of the Tibetan government. The king took an oath to comply with the government's order.

In the same year, Lachag Khenchung Khenrab Phuntsok, with assistants, was sent to investigate the dispute between Nyarong and Chakla. Dapon Sonam Topyal, with a force, was sent from Chamdo to assist him. From Lhasa, Tsedron Lobsang Trinle and representatives of the Three Monastic Seats were sent to Peking by sea from India to lodge a complaint that the Sichuan governor was meddling in the governance of Nyarong and disturbing the peace in the area. As a result, Dranagshogsum, Dampa Rangdol Monastery and Chakla, along with their peoples, properties and livestock, were returned to the Tibetan government. The Chinese army officer Tangli and his troops were immediately withdrawn from Tibet and were punished for illegally entering Tibet. All those who were involved in the Nyarong violence stirred up by the chief of Chakla were punished severely.

The military leader Dapon Dzasak Horkhang of the U army was appointed the new governor of Nyarong, and staff and troops were assigned to him.

Chapter Ten

Anglo-Tibetan Conflicts

—◆◆—

Causes of the conflicts

In the 19th century, Britain conquered many Asian countries, taking advantage of their weakness, through peaceful or forceful means. After colonizing India, the British started their colonial campaign towards China, resulting in the Anglo-Chinese Wars, popularly called the Opium Wars[1]. The British Empire in those times had spanned across the globe, so it was said, "The sun never sets on the British Empire."[2]

The British in India were greatly concerned over Tibet and other Himalayan states, and designed various policies regarding them. They amalgamated Ladakh into Kashmir and incorporated Spiti and Lahore or the Garsha regions of Ladakh into another Indian state. Nepal's area Almorah was made their colony, and Bhutan and Sikkim their protectorate states. They planned to construct trade routes into Tibet. The Tibetan government came to know about this, but remained silent and suspicious, instead of trying to find out the reasons for the construction of roads into Tibet. At the instigation of the Manchus, some pro-Manchu Tibetan lamas and government officials spread rumours that if the British were allowed to enter Tibet they would destroy the Buddhist religion and gradually seize the whole country, just as "A drop of oil spreads on a paper". The Tibetan government neither investigated the matter, nor tried to communicate with the British.

The British learnt that China had no authority over Tibet, but they suspected that Tibet and Russia were establishing relations. The fact however is that there were no foreign powers in Tibet. Moreover, Tibet's policy was to remain an independent

---

1   The Opium Wars, also known as the Anglo-Chinese Wars, were the climax of trade disputes and diplomatic difficulties between China under the Qing Dynasty and the British Empire after China sought to restrict illegal British opium trafficking. It consisted of the First Opium War from 1839 to 1842and the Second Opium War from 1856 to 1860.

2   This was a saying referring to the fact that Britain had colonies all around the world. So as the earth rotated the sun continually shone on British territory. In the 19th century, especially during the Victorian era, the phrase resurged, when it became popular to apply it to the British Empire at a time when British world maps showed the empire in red or pink to vividly highlight British imperial power spanning the globe. The British Empire is the largest ever Empire in the history of humanity. It spanned 13,000,000 square miles.

nation and to oppose any interference into its political affairs by any foreign countries, including China, Britain, Russia and Japan. Not knowing this fact, the British worried unnecessarily about Tibet. Tibet was strategically important for the British Empire, as it served as a buffer state on the Himalayan range to prevent any external danger to India. They therefore maintained a flexible policy towards Tibet, changing their words and actions vis-à-vis Tibet from time to time. This proved disastrous later on both to India and Tibet, creating major political complications and border issues.

The Manchu government, as mentioned above, with evil intent, using its lackeys and spies, spread a rumour that if foreigners were allowed to come into Tibet, they would destroy the Tibetan religion. Some senior officials of the Tibetan government as well as lamas, *trulkus* (reincarnated lamas) and monks blindly believed the rumour and complicated the situation.

In 1782, the British government of India sent a mission[3] to Tibet to establish contact with the Panchen Rinpoche (sixth Panchen Lama).[4] In 1826, Britain incorporated Assam into India as their colony. In 1842, the British defeated the Chinese forces and made direct contact with the Manchu Emperor. In 1817 and 1861, the British and Manchu governments signed separate treaties, making Sikkim a protectorate state of Britain. In 1863, the British handed a 23-point proposal to Sikkim, stating that if the proposal was accepted, they would return the four districts of Sikkim previously seized by them, and they would pay rent for Darjeeling. The proposal also stated that Sikkim's king, who had fled to Tibet for asylum, should return, and that Tibet was not allowed to interfere in Sikkim's governance. In 1865, the British invaded Bhutan and forced it to sign an agreement. In these ways, Britain expanded its empire and established military bases in the southern and western border areas of Tibet. The Tibetans feared that Britain would extend its powers into Tibet eventually, by any means, peaceful or military.

In 1858 and 1876, Britain and China signed treaties at Tianjin and Chefoo, whereby China was given some powers over Tibet. Hearing this, the Tibetan government and the Tibetan National Assembly made a strong protest against them. In 1879, the British government of India sent a Bengali man named Sir Chandra Das, in the disguise of a Buddhist scholar, to Tibet to see whether China and Russia had any influence in Tibet. He first stayed in Tsang and then went to U,

---

3   In all other sources, including Shakabpa's history, the mission was sent in 1774. The mission, which was led by George Bogle, consisted of an army surgeon named Alexander Hamilton and Purangir Gosain (an agent of the Third Panchen Lama, the effective ruler of Tibet), as well as a retinue of servants. Returning to India Bogle fulfilled the Lama's request to establish a temple on the banks of the Ganges, not far from the East India Company headquarters, where Buddhist monks could return to their spiritual roots in India.
http://en.wikipedia.org/wiki/George_Bogle_(diplomat)

4   Lobsang Palden Yeshe (1738–1780), the Sixth Panchen Lama of Tashilhunpo Monastery in Tibet, was the elder stepbrother of the 10th Shamarpa, Mipam Chödrup Gyamtso (1742-1793).

and with the help of Shigatse Sengchen Trulku and Dapon Phala's wife, he managed to secretly compile a report about Tibet's security. When the Tibetan government came to know about his activities, an order was sent for his arrest. He however got a tipoff and managed to flee before being arrested. Sengchen Trulku and Dapon Phala were severely punished for giving hospitality to a foreigner without knowing the background of the person.

In 1885, the British government of India sent the Colman Macaulay Mission to Tibet on a visa given by the Manchu government. The Tibetan government did not accept the visa and stopped the mission from entering Tibet. At the same time, it posted sentries at the borders to prevent such infiltration of foreigners into Tibet in future. The reality of the Manchus having no authority over Tibet became clear, and the Manchu Emperor felt embarrassed. In 1886, Britain and China signed a treaty relating to trade in Tibet and Burma, and in 1890 they again signed a treaty about the Tibet-Sikkim border, trade, and pastureland and establishing a trade mart at Dromo, without consulting the Tibetan government. Tibet protested strongly against these treaties. The Tibetans destroyed the border marking-stones and walls erected by the British, and posted a garrison at Gegong on the Tibetan southern border.

In 1890, the year of the Iron-Tiger, a new mint was set up in Kongpo Shoka and new currency coins were struck. The coins were distributed as offerings during the Great Monlam Festivalin 1892, the Water-Dragon year, and then issued throughout the country, with an edict, for circulation.

Regarding the political status of Tibet in those times, the Political Officer in Sikkim, (JC) Claude Whitesaid clearly in his report on his mission to Tibet in 1894 that the Manchu government had no authority and right over Tibet. Regarding the continuous efforts by the British to establish trade relations with Tibet, Edmund Candler (1874–1926)[5] wrote that amidst rivalry and suspicion between Russia, Britain and China, Britain was pursuing its policy of expansionism, just like "A blind man runs on the ground." This is true. Sir Charles Bell wrote:

> Manchu officials reluctantly admitted "The Dalai Lama's position among the Tibetans is such that no Chinese [i.e., Manchu] authority in Tibet, however eminent, can oppose him on equal terms. Indeed the young dynamic ruler steered Tibet on an independent course, refusing to recognize any Manchu authority in Tibet.[6]

---

5   Edmund Candler (1874-1926) was a Daily Mail correspondent accompanying the expeditionary force led by Sir Francis Younghusband into Tibet in 1903-4. His experiences in Tibet, including witnessing the storming of the Gyantse Fortress, later provided material for his travelogue *The Mantle of the East* and the short story "At Galdang-Tso". His account of the expedition, for which he is today principally known, was published in 1905 as *The Unveiling of Lhasa*.

6   Namgyal Wangdu does not mention the name of the reference source from where he has taken this passage. I have copied this from Michael C. van Walt van Praag's *The Status of Tibet - History, Rights, and Prospects in International Law*, p. 31.

Asian countries, especially Tibet, a vast highland that lies at the heart of Asia, were strategically important internationally, both politically and militarily. With the decline of China's power as a result of invasion by British and Japanese forces at different times, the Dalai Lama, taking a lesson from the past, strengthened border security and restricted relations with the Manchus, because the Manchus had been conspiring with the British against Tibet and because they maintained an unreliable policy on Tibet, instead of helping it on the grounds of the priest-patron relationship. He thought it was more advantageous to make friends with Russia. Many people from Mongolia, Kalmyk (Dzungar), Buryat and others used to visit Tibet every year either to have an audience with the Dalai Lama, to visit sacred places in Tibet or to do religious study.

In 1898, the Bruno Mission arrived in Lhasa. Likewise, a Buryat monk scholar named Ngawang Lobsang Dorjeiff, who had studied at Drepung Monastery for many years before, came to Tibet to pay his respects to the monasteries and to present an invitation to the Dalai Lama to the Great Monlam Festival. He afterwards became an attendant of the Dalai Lama. After that, a Japanese man named [Ekai] Kawaguji[7], who knew the Tibetan language, arrived in Tibet in the guise of a Ladakhi. He joined Sera Je College and stayed in Pethub Section of the college. He collected and sent many reports, both true and false,to the British government in India, further intensifying the British suspicions about Tibet. In those days, many foreigners were very eager to visit Tibet, secretly or openly. The Manchu Emperor used to pretend to have authority over Tibet, although he did not have. This prompted Tibet to follow a difficult policy towards both Britain and China.

In 1900, in order to establish relations with the Czar of Russia, the Dalai Lama sent a mission led by his attendant Dorjieff aka Ngawang Lobsang to Russia. The delegation was received warmly at the royal palace by Czar Nicholar II. A few years later, the second Tibetan mission again headed by Dorjieff was sent to Russia, and the mission was treated with great hospitality by the Czar. The news appeared in various Russian newspapers. This further perturbed the British government of India. Though Britain and Russia reportedly clarified the matter to each other through correspondence, the British in India were not fully relieved of their doubts. On the grounds of Dorjieff's mission to Russia and Kawaguji's report that Tibet was receiving weapons from Russia, they believed that Tibet was embarking on political relations with the Russian Czar. Further, they became convinced that China had no power over Tibet.

For these reasons, Lord Curzon, the British Viceroy in India, sent a proposal to London that a military expedition should be sent to Tibet as soon as possible

---

7   According to some other sources, he came in the guise of a pilgrim. Ekai Kawaguchi (1866–1945) was a Japanese Buddhist monk who visited Tibet twice (1900-1902 and 1913–1915), being the first recorded Japanese citizen to travel in both countries.

to prevent Russian and Chinese influence extending into Tibet. London gave the go-ahead to his proposal. Accordingly, he sent a military mission led by Colonel Younghusband to Tibet for the purpose of making direct contact with the Lhasa government, to establish trade marts in Lhasa and other important places in Tibet, to setup a Trade Agent at Gyantse and to discourage Tibet from establishing political relations with other countries, including Russia. However, as explained below, Britain's aim was not to colonize Tibet and destroy its independent status.

The Anglo-Tibetan battle of 1900

In 1876, the kings of Sikkim and Bhutan sent letters to the Tibetan government advising it to hold a peaceful negotiation with the British to prevent the impending British military expedition into Tibet. The Tibetan government did not pay heed to their advice. It fortified the country's borders and issued edicts to all districts and estates to stop any doubtful foreign mountaineers, tourists and others from entering Tibet.

The British sent a proposal to the Tibetan government, stating that they wanted to construct vehicle roads through Tibet's borders and to send tourists and traders to Tibet. The Regent and the Kashag convened a Full National Assembly[8] to discuss the matter. The Assembly, which was normally dominated by the representatives of the Three Monastic Seats, unanimously passed a resolution and took a vow that they must not allow any foreigners to come in Tibet at any cost, and every effort should be made to prevent them from entering the country. According to the resolution of the National Assembly, the Kashag mobilized soldiers from U, Tsang, Lhoka, Dakpo, Kongpo, Powo, Kham and northern Tibet, and collected local militias from these areas. Weapons were procured. The weapons included mainly locally made wooden-wheel muskets, locally made firearms, gunpowder, bullets, gunpowder-lighters, swords, spears and slings. Grain was collected on a large scale to feed the soldiers. Monasteries performed rituals for the success of the Tibetan forces. The Nechung, Gadong and Lamo Tsangpa oracles were consulted, and the records of their advice were sealed and submitted to the Dalai Lama. The Tibetan government received frequent reports on British activities at the borders.

---

8   The Full National Assembly of Tibet *(bod ljong tshong 'du rgyas pa)* included the ex-throne holder of Ganden, the ex-abbot of the Ganden, the junior and senior tutors of the Dalai Lama, Shartse Choeje, Jangtse Choeje, all the reincarnated *trulkus* above the rank of Tsogchen Trulku, the abbots of the Three Monastic Seats, the abbots of the upper and lower tantric colleges, the manager of Drepung Phodrang, the manager of Sera Simkhang, all the cabinet ministers, the Chief Abbot Official, other officials who were entitled to seats during official ceremonies, the four *tsipons*, the four *khendrung*, all the lay, ecclesiastic and military officials present in Lhasa, the stewards of Lingshi, and the local rulers of Tashilhunpo, Mardzosangsum, Derge, Chabdrag. The total membership came around 500-600 in all.

The government decided to construct fortifications and check posts at the borders, and to deploy strong forces to staff them.

The British in India requested the Tibetan government to allow them to build a guesthouse at Kalimpong, but the request was not granted. To check the situation, the Tibetan government sent Khenche Drugyal and Dapon Tsarong Wangchuk Gyalpo of the U army, with representatives from Tashilhunpo Monastery and the Three Monastic Seats, to Lungtur. After examining the situation there, they sent a report to the Kashag. As a result of the report, the government sent a team led by Dapon Sarjung to Lungtur in 1887. They constructed a check-post with a fortification. They decided to place the instruments of the Pehar Gyalpo deity and an effigy of the Nechung deity inside the fortification, facing toward the enemy. The image and articles were prepared in Lhasa and brought to the Potala Palace, and the Nechung Oracle was invited to consecrate them. The Oracle appeared uneasy and frightened, saying, "What shall be done if these attack us instead of destroying the enemy?" Nevertheless, the image and articles were taken to Lungtur and arranged inside the fortification. Tsipon Changlochen Dorje Tsering as the leader, with staff, a ritual performer, a cook and one platoon as guards, were posted there. Horkhangpa, with a force under the command of Dapon Demon Drudul Dorje of the Dingri regiment, was dispatched to Lhodrak, Tsona and Mon to organize the defense of these areas.

The British complained that Tibet had constructed a military fortification at Lungtur despite Lungtur being an area of Sikkim, and they expedited their preparations for a military campaign to Tibet.

In the same year, the Tibetan government dispatched Kagung Lhalu Yeshi Norbu Wangchuk as the chief military leader, with Dapon Ngabo and Dapon Surkhang, and a force of about 1,000 troops, to Lungtur to counter the British mission. Sikkim's king and prince tried hard to bring reconciliation between the British and the Tibetans, to prevent any violence between them. The Tibetans always claimed and proved Lungtur as an area of Tibet, while the British, without understanding this, threatened to demolish the Tibetan outpost constructed at Lungtur if the Tibetan troops posted at it were not withdrawn.

With evil intentions, China propagandized everywhere that they had authority over Tibet. The Manchu Amban Wenshi in Lhasa also acted a similar manner, so he became an object of hatred to both the Tibetan government and the public. He therefore could not stay in Tibet long and returned to China in the same year.

In 1888, the Earth-Rat year, the Tibetan government dispatched a team led by Kalon Rampa Tashi Dhargye, Dapon Ngabo Se of the U army, Dapon Kharnawa of the Tsang army and Dapon Kyito Se, with many troops, to reinforce the Tibetan garrison at Lungtur. Many monk and lay officials were sent to different parts of the country to collect as many local militias as possible. Weapons and grain were procured on a large scale and were sent to the Tibetan army at Lungtur by way of Dromo. The king and prince of Sikkim mediated and made great efforts to bring reconciliation between the Tibetans and the British, but in vain. However, their efforts at least postponed the conflict. The king and the prince as well as the people of Sikkim stood firm in their loyalty to the Tibetans on the grounds that their faith and race were the same as that of the Tibetans. Instead of siding with the British, they several times sent information to Tibet about the British military preparations.

The British were quite confident about their weapons and military strategy, but they felt that they would not be able to defeat the Tibetan army in hand-to-hand fighting. They therefore brought with them four cannons, machine guns and long-range rifles, so that they could attack from a distance. The Tibetan troops remained on alert and cautious all the time. They organized themselves into many small groups and patrolled the nearby hills and valleys during the daytime. When they returned to their camp at night, they conducted a roll call to ensure that no one was missing.

The Anglo-Tibetan battles, as detailed below, were fought first at Lungtur, then at Nagthang, Chumig Shongko, Dzatrang, Gyantse, Nenying, Tsechen and Khola in succession.

The Anglo-Tibetan battle at Lungtur

The British brought more than 1,000 Gurkha troops from Kalimpong and arrived at Rongling Chukhaat the feet of the Lungtur pass. Next day, they were reinforced by more than 2,000 troops. Climbing up from Rongling, they first attacked the Tibetan position at the Lungtur pass on the 2nd day of the 7th month of 1888. The Tibetan army put up a stiff resistance, killing or wounding a few British troops. The British force retreated to some distance away. The next day the British troops attacked with cannons and machine-guns, and under the cover of the artillery fire, many of their troops converged on the Tibetan post. The Tibetan troops defended courageously. Rupon Ngoshiwa of the Drapchi regiment and Gyapon Ngodup Tsering of the Dingri regiment rushed out of the fortification, shouting "ki hi hi"[9]. They charged fearlessly at the British soldiers, using whatever weapons they had in their hands, killing or wounding more than 100 British officers and soldiers. The Tibetan side lost 20 officers and soldiers, including the officer Ngodup Tsering.

Another Anglo-Tibetan battle was also fought at Lungtur. The Tibetans confronted the British, using Tibetan traditional weapons such as firearms, swords, spears, axes and slings. When their ammunition was exhausted, the British took

---

9 War cry: screaming "ki hi hi" was believed to bring courage to the troops.

their opportunity and fired extensively on the Tibetan position. Under the cover of firing, a large number of their troops rushed toward the Tibetan post. The Tibetans defended their outpost courageously, and the enemy was amazed at the bravery and determination of the Tibetan soldiers. For the first time the Tibetan army faced the British army, who were armed with different kinds of modern weapons. The Tibetan troops had never seen modern weapons, let alone used them. The Tibetan army was no match for the British army, considering the quality of their weapons, military organization and training.

When the Tibetan troops were about to lose their Lungtur outpost, their leader Kagung Lhalu, leading his troops, fearlessly charged at the enemy. He nearly fell into the enemy's hands, but at the request of his soldiers, he retreated. Kagung and his force left their Lungtur outpost and headed to Nagthang, where they camped and reviewed the battle. Dapon Surkhang had fled to Phari by way of Bhutan. Tsipon Changlochen fled straight to Phari. The news about their defeat reached Lhasa. The people of Lhasa sang the following satirical songs:

> Lhalu has returned
> After losing the *seril*
> The outpost built over a lifetime
> Was destroyed in one morning.
>
> Ngabo was feigning courage.
> Surkhang ran away secretly.
> Changchen, being so clever,
> Rode off on his brown horse faster than a bird.[10]

The above songs mean that the two Tibetan cannons called *seril* taken to Lungtur outpost were lost to the British force, and Tsipon Changlochen fled from the battlefield on his brown horse.

The second Anglo-Tibetan battle at Nagthang

In the hope that they could push back the British, the Tibetan army constructed fortifications at different locations along the Nagthang plain and Narto-la pass, collected military supplies and remained there ready to attack the British troops. The British fired cannons and guns from a distance on the Tibetan outpost at Nagthang, but there were no casualties since all the Tibetan troops were hiding

---

10 Lha klu log nas phebs 'dug// se ril bskyal nas phebs 'dug// tshe gang brgyab pa'I dgra rdzong// zhogs gang gcig la bskyal song//

Nga phod ngar mdog gnang is// Zur khang zur nas thad song//lcang can spyang rang drags nas//zags pa bya alas mgyogs ka/ /

in the forest or inside their embankments. Following this, a British detachment arrived near Nagthang. A Tibetan force, comprising of a detachment of the Drapchi regiment and local militia of Shotarlhosum, attacked the British army camp at Nagthang under cover of night, killing or wounding many British soldiers. After suffering heavy losses, the British retreated. A few days later, the British brought their remaining troops from Lungtur and attacked the Tibetan army camp at Nagthang. There were no casualties on the Tibetan side, but the British seized Nagthang and camped there. They then attacked using cannons and machineguns, forcing the Tibetan troops to retreat to Chumbi in Dromo.

After losing Lungtur and Nagthangto the enemy, Kagung Lhalu consulted the Lhasa government about the future course of action. The government convened a National Assembly and held a series of meetings to discuss the matter. Finally, the Nechung Oracle was invited and consulted. The oracle spoke,

> Whatever work was initiated,
> It is important to complete it.

Accordingly, the government resolved to continue with their efforts to resist the British armed mission. Dapon Phunraba Wangdu Dorje and Tsedron Jampa Tenzin, with four monk and lay cadres, were sent to organize the defense at the border. They mobilized 2,800 local recruits—1,200 from Kongpo Gyamda, Jomodzong, Tsegang and Shogadzong, and 1,600 from Lhoka regions such as Nedong, Chongye, On, Olga, Lhodrak Dodzong, Darma, Lhakhang and Senge Dzong. In addition, Lhading Se and Tsedron Sonam Gyaltsen were sent to Dakpo and Kongpo, while Tsedrung Gomang Tenzin Dhondup and Shodrung Lhalu Surchiwa to Markham, Tsawarong, Dzogang, Drakyab and Gojo to collect more local militias. An order was sent to the district officers of Mardzotsasum (Markham, Dzogang and Tsawarong), the Gojo leader and the Drakyab treasurer to assist the above officials. The officials sent to collect militias were also instructed to choose leaders of different ranks from among the militias in accordance with their needs, and to dispatch the militias to the battlefields as soon as possible. The additional local troops collected from U and Tsang were dispatched to Phari and Dromo.

From Sikkim, the British mission sent Phodong Lama and Dronyer Khangsar to Tibet to deliver a message that read, "We resorted to force since Tibet had rejected our previous proposal to build trade roadsin Tibet. Now we are willing to hold negotiations, so a prompt reply is expected from the Tibetan government." The Gurkha king also sent a letter to the Tibetan government, expressing his desire to mediate in the ongoing Anglo-Tibetan problems to help the two sides reconcile peacefully, without further fighting. By that time, the British had already demolished the Tibetan military outposts and walls at Dzaleb-la pass and others, and had camped there. Further, a huge British detachment, comprising several thousand British troops and a large number of Gurkha troops provided by the Gurkha prince, carrying along with them food and other military supplies, arrived at Dromo in the beginning of August of the same year. They started attacking the Tibetan outpost with cannon and machineguns. The Tibetans tried hard to defend their posts, but they failed, as their inferior weapons were no match for the modern weapons of the British forces. They had to pull back to their camps at Gupo and Dungchu. The British forces advanced further by way of the Dzaleb-la pass and Namra, arriving at Dromo Rinchen Gang on 20 August.

The Tibetan government called on many lamas and monks and conducted extensive rituals to defeat the British. People evoked deities and *nagas*. The government mobilized more than 10,000 local militiamen and deployed them at upper Dromo, Phari and Duna for defense purpose. The government also sent an order to all the districts to send monk volunteers and local militias to fight the British as and when they were needed. The Manchu Amban Wenhai arrived at Dromo from Lhasa and pretended to have come to intervene in the Anglo-Tibetan conflicts. The Tibetan government announced that until and unless the British troops who had entered Tibet left the country without returning, Tibetans would never tolerate them, and would resist them until the end. Orders were also issued to the Tibetan forces stationed at Dromo, Phari and other outposts to defend their positions with the utmost courage and dedication for the sake of their country.

Around that time, Tibet and Russia were renewing their relations. Knowing this, the British hurriedly invaded Sikkim and then entered Tibet to make direct contact with Lhasa. At the instigation of the representatives of Sikkim and Bhutan, as well as the Manchu Amban in Lhasa, Tibet sent Kalon Rampa from the battlefield and Deputy Kalon Lama Bumthang Yeshi Phuljung, with assistant staff from Lhasa, with the resolution passed by the National Assembly, to Dromo to talk with the British mission and settle the issue through negotiation. At that time, the government heard that the Manchu Amban had gone to Calcutta from Dromo and signed an agreement with the British, claiming that he was doing so at the instruction of the Manchu government. Therefore, the Tibetans could not hold negotiations with the British.

In 1892, the Tibetan government again sent a delegation, led by Chief Abbot Official Darhan Jigme Chojor, including Dapon Surkhang Se of the U regiment, Tsedrung official Bumthang Jampa Tharjin, cabinet steward Kadron Chijag, with assistant staff, to Dromo to conduct negotiations with the British. Kalon Lama was already at Dromo at that time. In the meantime, the Manchu Amban had signed an eight-point trade treaty with the British in Calcutta, shocking the Tibetan government. Tibet protested strongly against the Manchu Amban's action. In the same year, the Amban returned from Calcutta and died shortly afterwards from an illness. Otherwise, he would have suffered death at the hands of Tibetans who had been greatly angered by his drastic action.

In 1893, the Manchu and the British governments signed a nine-point agreement on trade in Tibet, without the knowledge of the Tibetan government. In such ways the Manchu government made every effort to show that it had authority over Tibet, even though this was not so. Britain did not want to lose the privileges it was enjoying in China, so it allied itself with China. The Tibetan government and the Tibetan National Assembly rejected and protested strongly against the Sino-British agreement, and only then did Britain realize that China had no political role in Tibet. This also prodded the British to expedite their military expedition into Tibet to establish direct contact with Lhasa, to prevent Russia's influence into Tibet.

The Anglo-Tibetan war of 1904

Russia and Britain had different political perspectives on Tibet. From Russia's point of view, British extension of its power into Tibet was a danger to its borders, while the British saw Russia's relations with Tibet as a threat to the Indian borders. They were therefore in a race to establish friendly relations with Tibet. However, in contrast to China, their aim was not to conquer Tibet for territorial expansion. As mentioned above, the Thirteenth Dalai Lama, the Tibetan government and the Tibetan National Assembly were always striving for Tibet's independence, as had existed during the Tibetan imperial period. Meanwhile Britain secretly signed treaties with China at different times, carried out incursions into the Himalayan regions several times and invaded the countries neighbouring Tibet. This led the Tibetan government to regard Britain as a threat and think it was best to seek friendly relations with Russia and Japan.

The British Viceroy in India Lord Curzon (1859-1925) decided to send a military expedition led by Colonel Younghusband to Tibet to make direct contact with the Lhasa government. In the first sixth months of 1903, news reached Lhasa from Sikkim that a British military mission was heading to Gampa Dzong to discuss trade matters relating to Tibet and Sikkim. Following this, the British mission sent a letter dated 13 March 1903 stating that the Tibetan government should immediately send a fully authorized representative there to discuss the border issues. Lhasa sent the Khendrung monk official Lobsang Trinle and Dapon Tsarong Wangchuk Gyalpo of the U regiment, with the Tsedrung official Gendun Chodar and army officer Gyapon Gyurme as assistant staff, to Dromo. When they arrived at Dromo the delegation prepared to meet the leader of the British mission and Sikkim's chief minister, but the Kashag received a letter from the British mission, stating that the meeting would be held at Gampa, bordering Sikkim. The Kashag immediately sent instructions to the Tibetan delegates to proceed quickly to Gampa Dzong to meet the British leaders.

The Kashag received a report from Sikkim that the British mission, consisting of 5 officers and about 700 troops, had left Gangtok on June 19, 1903by way of the Lachen pass in Sikkim. By that time, the Tibetan negotiation team had also arrived at Dromo. A few days later, Captain William O'Connor, who spoke Tibetan, with about 200 troops, arrived at Dromo. The Gampa district officer asked him not to enter Tibetan territory, saying that they could conduct talks there (Dromo) because the Tibetan delegation would be arriving there soon. The officer replied that they had already decided to hold the talks at Gampa Dzong and they were leaving for Gampa the next morning. He further said that their fully authorized officials and the fully empowered Tibetan delegates would meet there for talks. On their way, the officer and his troops met the Tibetan delegation, who urged them to hold the discussions right there if there was anything to discuss. However, the officer did not listen and the British delegation headed straight to Gampa Dzong, where theycamped and stayed.

After the British force arrived at Gampa, the Tibetan delegation received an order from the Tibetan National Assembly in Lhasa that they must not allow even a single British soldier to enter Tibet and that the government would dispatch backup troops immediately to help them. The government summoned all the government's troops of Shigatse, Gyantse and Dingri, and ordered them to be ready to leave for Dromo to resist the British forces. Soon after that, Colonel Younghusband, leading about 400 soldiers, arrived at Gampa. At that time, three delegates from the Three Monastic Seats also arrived there to participate in the negotiations. A Chinese officer named Ho Kaungsi who was living in Shigatse also arrived, saying that he had come to take part in the negotiations as the representative of the Manchu Amban in Lhasa. The Tibetan delegation objected and did not allow him to attend the meetings. Ho returned to Shigatse, stating that the weather and environment of the place did not suit his health.

The Tibetan delegates told the British that unless all the British troops were withdrawn from Gampa, it was not possible to hold talks. The leader of the British mission replied that the negotiation would be possible only when a fully empowered Tibetan delegate came and the Manchu Amban acted as the witness. The Tibetans replied that they would ask their government to send a plenipotentiary provided the meeting was held at Dromo,but there was no need for the Manchu Amban's participation in the negotiations. The two sides reiterated their conditions for negotiation. Since Gampa was under the jurisdiction of Tashilhunpo, the Panchen Rinpoche sent the abbot [of the Tantric College] and a fourth-ranking official, with assistants, to witness the negotiations. Three months passed without any concrete talks, during which the British toured and surveyed the places around Gampa.

In Lhasa, as per the great resolution passed by the National Assembly, the government decided to fight the British, whatever the consequences might be, good or bad. It continued to mobilize militias from various areas of the country to reinforce the Tibetan defense force at Dromo. Additional troops were summoned from Shotarlhosum, Mardzosangsum and Richabpasum. Local militias were collected from 18 districts and estates—Gyatsa, Kunam, Kyemtong, Gyada, Jomo and Tsegang districts and Nangshi and Shoga estates in Dakpo and Kongpo; Taktse, Lhudup and Chushul districts and Neu estate in U; and Nedong, Gongkar, Samye and Chongye districts and the estates of Drapchi, Dranang, Dol, Senge Dzong, Do Dzong, Lhakhangestate, Darma estate, Jayul Dzong, Jora estate, Drigu estate, Sangri estate, Olga estate, On estate and Ling estate.

Local militias were also collected from northern Tibet based on the old recruit system created by the Tibetan government during the 18th century when the Dzungars invaded Tibet. Northern Tibet comprised upper and lower Drongpa, upper and lower Chogchu, six divisions of Nagtsang[11], four states of Nagchu, eight states of Amdo, five states of Barta, six states of Sangshung, six states of Lhoma, six states of Jangma and six states of Mema. The recruits were kept ready for deployment. Since Nagtsang was near Lhasa, about 1,800 militias from Nagtsang were instructed to wait at Shang Lhabu, Gyatso and Namlingin accordance with the orders. About 4,800 *khal* measures of grain were procured from different districts of Tibet and sent to Shigatse, Panam, Juding and Gyantse to be transported to Phari as rations for the Tibetan border troops. The situation was tense and both the Tibetan government and people were facing an exorbitant burden because of the war preparations.

The Tibetan delegates at Gampa were still unable to hold negotiations with the British, but they kept in constant touch with the British mission. They sent a mounted courier, with instructions to gallop day and night, to Lhasa to ask whether they should inconspicuously deploy the troops from Shigatse, Gyantse and Dingri around Gampa fortress, since the British were quite likely to bring more troops to Gampa. In the meantime, whether they were unable to bear the extreme cold weather of winter, their plan failed, or for other reasons, the British troops left Gampa, saying that they had received orders from their government to return to India. Led by the infantry and followed by the cavalry, all the British troops gradually left by way of the border area of Topo on the 17th day of the 9th Tibetan month of the same year.

In that year, unfortunately, there was a disagreement between the Kashag and the Tibetan National Assembly. Kalon Shadra was accused of taking bribes from the British when he was in Darjeeling. The Nechung oracles aid that there was someone in the Kashag who was siding with the enemy. Kalon Shadra, Sholkhang,

---

11 Ponshung, Tatrokarsum, Sangchusersum, Laponomasum, Gomnag and Dropal. These can be 11 also, as Pontso, Shungme, Tatro, Kartso, Sangser Chugso, Mato, Poto, Gompo, Gomnag and Dropal.

Changkhim and Kagung Lhalu's successor Dzasak Horkhang were removed from their office and put in custody at Norbulingka. A committee was set up to investigate them. Being timid, Horkhang committed suicide, fearing that he would have to undergo a harsh trial. Shadra submitted a petition to the Assembly to clarify his innocence. He managed to prove his innocence before the Anglo-Tibet crisis was solved. At that time, the Thirteen Dalai Lama was on the eve of his trip to Mongolia. He sent the ministers to their own home estates.

The Tibetans surmised that the British army had entered Tibet through Gampa not to invade Tibet, but to examine the situation, reasoning that if their aim was to invade Tibet, they would have come through Dromo and Phari. The Tibetans deployed their garrisons and remained prepared. In the hope of solving the issue through negotiation, Rupon Kyipugpa of the Gyantse army was posted at Dromo for that purpose. He met the British officers several times, but it did not prove fruitful. Not long after that, on 16 December 1903 Colonel Younghusband, Political Officer Claude White, Captain O'Connor and Brigadier-General James McDonald, with several thousand Sikh and Gurkha troops armed with artillery, machineguns and rifles, as well as doctors, supply officers, reporters, 4,000 porters and a few thousand horses and mules, plus several thousand yaks that had been provided by the Gurkha king, arrived at Phari by way of Dromo, behind the Dzaleb-la pass.

The Phari district officer Shodrung Bumthangpa, Denja Tsangpa, Rupon Kyipukpa, leaders and representatives of upper and lower Dromo communities urged the British leaders not to move further into Tibet, saying that the Tibetan negotiating team would arrive there soon. The British did not listen. The Tibetans at Phari immediately sent a mounted messenger to Lhasa, with instructions to gallop day and night, to report the matter. The Tibetan government had mobilized troops collected on taxation system and local militias which were dispatched to resist the British army. In addition, it sent 11 representatives of the National Assembly and the Three Monastic Seats with instructions to travel day and night until they reached Phari, to negotiate with the British leaders.

Upon their arrival at Phari, the delegates immediately contacted the British leaders several times and urged them to discuss the issues. However, the British, as preplanned, stationed one group of their troops at Phari and sent the remaining troops to Dune, by way of Khambu. The Tibetan negotiating team, expecting that the negotiations would be successful, kept a few troops at the outposts at Dromo and Phari, and sent the rest to Gyantse. They requested the British leaders not to cross the Tibetan border, arguing that their military action toward Tibet was not approved by any other nation, that it would cause unnecessary hostility and disputes among Tibet's neighbours and bring suffering to the people. They further asked that British troops should not move further into Tibet from Phari, as the fully empowered Tibetan delegation would be arriving soon to conduct negotiations.

They did their best to win the goodwill of the British officers. The British explained that they had had several discussions on the borders but without result, so they must meet the real ruler of Tibet and discuss with him personally in accordance with their orders which had arrived from London. They further said that it was impossible to go back. On the 6th day of the 11th Tibetan month, two divisions of British troops joined forces at Dune and camped there.

The third Anglo-Tibetan battle at Chumig Shongko

The Tibetan government resolved to block the British mission militarily. The Tibetan troops posted in Gyantse were deployed along the strategic roads between Phari and Gyantse, along Kala, Chalu, Sam and Chumig Shongko to defend them. At the same time, deities were invoked and rituals were performed. The Nechung oracle was consulted. The oracle advised that it was best to pursue peaceful negotiations to resolve the crisis. The government sent another group of delegates and representatives from Tashilhunpo to Dune to conduct negotiations.

Previously, when the British forces had proceeded from Sikkim to Tibet, the people in Kalimpong, Darjeeling and Gangtok, who were loyal to the Tibetans, had sent information to the Tibetan government reporting that the British had sent its advance unit to Tibet and that they were also mobilizing more troops and collecting weapons, food, horses, mules, pack animals and porters in Kalimpong. They also said that Tibet would not be able to match the British forces in terms of weapons and military supplies. Similarly, Trongsa Pon and Kazi Ogyan Dorje of Bhutan also sent letters to Lhasa advising the Tibetan government to try to negotiate with the British and expressing their willingness to mediate in the British and Tibetan negotiations. They also came to Phari with the British forces. Likewise, Sikkim's king and queen, out of consideration for their closeness to him, told Dapon Lhading that it would be best to reconcile with the British since the Tibetans would not be able to resist the British militarily. They told him in detail about the British preparations for war. The Nepalese minister Tin Sarkar Chandra Shamsher, through Nyasho Drelpo, sent a letter to the Tibetan government, suggesting that Tibet would be better to compromise with the British and that he would send representatives to witness the negotiations.

Keeping in mind the answers given by the deities and the advice it had received from many concerned people, the Tibetan government realized the impossibility of defeating the British force, but it decided to uphold the great resolution passed with an oath by the Tibetan National Assembly, that not a single foreign enemy should be allowed to enter Tibet. The government also resolved that if the negotiations with this mission failed, it would resort to armed conflict, and made military preparations.

Dapon Lhading and Namse Lingpa were assigned 1,500 national troops and 5,000 local militia troops collected from U, Tsang, Lhoka, Dakpo, Kongpo and Kham, and posted them at the battle site as the vanguard force. The two army leaders, with the Tibetan negotiating team, consisting of Ta Lama Lobsang Trinle and representatives from Tashilhunpo and the Three Monastic Seats, went to a village called Guru located at a distance of two-*gyangdrag* from Chumig Shongko, close to the British army camp at Dune. There they camped, constructed temporary stone fortifications and trenches on the hills, and waited. Dapon Monlingpa and Dapon Rampa of Tsang army, with their forces, had camped at the upper and lower ends of Sam, southeast of Chumig Shongka. Dapon Trelingpa of Dingri and his troops had been deployed at Kala, Chalu and Dochen. All of them had the indestructible and unmatched determination and courage to fight the enemy at the cost of their lives for the sake of their country. However, only their leaders had machine guns and most of the fighting men were equipped with only swords, spears, axes, slings, locally made guns, etc. The British however suspected that the Tibetans had Russian weapons, and dared not advance to Gyantse directly by the main road. They bribed two Tibetan porters and sent them to Kala in the guise of shepherds to spy on the Tibetan military conditions. One porter was caught by the Tibetan troops at Chalu. The other escaped and informed the British leaders about the about the weapons and Tibetan military preparations at Chumig Shongko, Dochen, Chalu and Kala. The British immediately changed their plans; they dropped their strategy of tricking the Tibetan army. On the morning of the 15th day of the first Tibetan month of 1904, from Dungne they sent a letter to the Tibetan force, stating to the effect that:

> Since no fully empowered Tibetan delegates have come so far, no proper negotiations have taken place. If you wish to hold talks at this place, the Tibetan government must send its plenipotentiary here immediately.

The next day the British mission leaders' cavalry, followed by foot soldiers, pack animals and porters, marched in the direction of Chumig Shongko. The Tibetan negotiation team and forces were on their way down to meet them. On the road, they received reports from their spies about the arrival of the British mission. Dapon Lhading Se, Namlingpa and Rupon Kyipugpa, Khangshar, representatives of Tashilhunpo and the Three Monastic Seats discussed among themselves what they should do. They decided that they should first try to hold talks with the British as the British had mentioned in their letter, and if that did not work, they should resort to armed force. They first sent a proposal to the British officers for talks, and the British agreed. The Tibetan negotiating team sent Lhading Se and Namlingpa, with others, to talk with the British mission. They met the British officers and they together went to a stone fortification near Chumig Shongko to conduct the meeting. They introduced themselves with their names and official ranks. The British proposed that both sides should lay down their weapons and unload their guns. The Tibetan officers therefore ordered their troops to extinguish the matchlocks of their guns. All the Tibetans troops remained relaxed, believing that the negotiations would go peacefully. However, in the meantime the British troops secretly surrounded the Tibetan positions from behind. The Tibetans saw that they had brought oil tins filled with bullets and were loading their guns. About 20 minutes after the negotiation meeting began, a British officer took out a pistol and fired at the two Tibetan army officers and other Tibetans who were present. When the sounds of the shots were heard, Lhading's servant who was guarding the horses shouted, "Our officers have been killed!" Immediately all other servants took out their swords and charged on the British officers, brandishing their swords blindly, killing or wounding around 10 British officers and troops, including a colonel, two captains and one lieutenant. Their own lives were bravely lost in the fight for the sake of their country.

One Tibetan army officer, angered by these developments, resolved to fight and die rather than to run away. Taking a sword, he rushed out from the stone fortification into the British troops. Other Tibetan troops followed him to fight the British troops. A British officer blew a loud whistle and the British troops hiding on the nearby hills fired upon the Tibetans with hails of bullets, killing or wounding most of the Tibetan officers and troops. Among those killed were Surkhang Nubpa, a representative of Tashilhunpo, one member of the representatives of the Three Monastic Seats, and Rupon Khangsar Jama. Those among injured included Rupon Kyibugpa, who had been injured in the legs; he hid among the corpses. The Tibetans suffered a heavy defeat.

After the firing stopped, in the evening, some British troops came to the battlefield and checked each dead body, and left. British porters came and took all the rings, earrings and other valuable things from the bodies. Some Tibetan troops, who had pretended to be dead and had hidden among the dead bodies, returned to their camps in the night. Those who received minor injuries ran away with others' help. Rupon Kyibugpa was taken by his servant on his back. Rupon Tengpa of the Shigatse regiment was also wounded and he was carried to his camp by his soldiers. All the seriously injured were then taken to Rupon Kyibugpa's estate at Chalu, where they were given medical treatment and food. Rupon Kyibugpa sent a report to Lhasa, giving details about the incident. He also sent letters to different army camps telling them how to tackle the British. Thereafter, he and two other wounded soldiers went to Gyantse for medical treatment.

Dingpon Chushar Tseten Wangchuk, a commander of the 25 soldiers, who hid among the dead bodies and escaped from the battlefield at Chumig Shongko, recounts the following eyewitness account in his report:

> While our *dapon* officers and British leaders were having the meeting, we were instructed to put out the fires in our matchlocks, and we did so. After a while,

suddenly, hails of bullets came upon us from different sides on the hills. We did not have time to draw our swords. The firing continued for as long as it would take to drink five or six cups of tea. Thereafter, many soldiers with guns with bayonets came to examine the dead bodies. They pricked me with a bayonet; I kept quite still by holding my breath. It made a wound on my back. Just near me was lying my relative Dhondup, who had been injured in the legs. They took him away, along with other wounded soldiers. Although, because I was afraid, I was not able to look around a lot, I saw Drakpa-la, whom I recognized from his plaited hair, and Singma Khangchung Agula lying dead close to me. As soon as the dusk arrived, I ran away to Dochen via Guru. My relative Dhondup, who had been treated by the British, returned with other 50 wounded soldiers. He told me that they were questioned by the British about whether the Tibetan government was receiving military help from Russia and other countries. The British had also said to them, "Our army is such that if we lose 100 soldiers, we can replace them with 1,000 soldiers. We have binoculars through which we can see behind mountains. Poor people, you are villagers; go back to your homes. If you come back, we will kill you." Each of them had been given Indian Rs. 5 and a packet of cigarettes, and they were given food and medical treatment.

According to the Tibetan government's record of this battle, 523 Tibetans, including Dapon Lhading Se, Dapon Namlingpa, Rupon Changkyimpa, Khangsar Jangma, along with the representatives of Ganden Monastery and Tashilhunpo were killed and more than 300 troops were wounded. Many weapons were seized.

A British officer wired a summary report to the British government in India about the battle as follows:

> Our casualties are—Major Wallace Dunlop slightly wounded, Candler, Daily Mail reporter, severely wounded; seven soldiers (*sepoys*) were wounded. About 500 soldiers of the enemy were killed or wounded, and about 200 prisoners. All of their camps and baggage, 60 yaks, 30 mules, 2 Tibetan gingalis, a large number of matchlocks and swords and several machineguns, two of which were of Russian make. Among the Tibetans killed were Lhasa Dapon and the representative of Ganden, ShigatseDapon. Phari Dapon was captured, seriously injured.

There is a slight discrepancy between the Tibetan and British records on the battle; further research is required.

The battle of Chumig Shongko was a disaster for the Tibetans. Many of their troops were killed or wounded and many outposts were lost to the British, as well as weapons, cattle and horses. The main reason was that the British had better weapons, training and military supplies, and they played a trick on the Tibetan army. The tragedy of the incident at Chumig Shongko is still remembered with great sadness. However, the Tibetan troops amazed the enemy by their courage to fight for the sake of their country. The British dared not confront them face to face; they preferred to attack from a distance, using cannons and machineguns.

The Fourth Anglo-Tibetan battle at Dzatrang

The Tibetan soldiers who escaped from the battlefield and those who had been injured arrived at upper and lower Sam, Chalu and Kala. They and the officers discussed the incident and sent a report to Lhasa. Only 400 Tibetan troops had survived the war. Finding it impossible to resist the British forces, they pulled back to Khangmar in good order and reinforced their numbers by summoning all the soldiers stationed at nearby outposts. Their numbers rose to 3,000. Dapon Trelingpa and Dapon Rampa, with their soldiers, were assigned to defend Khangmar. The rest of the troops were sent to defend Dzatrang. The British troops continued to advance, sacking and looting Jangling and Kumbum monasteries and burning other monasteries as they went. When they arrived at Sholam Monastery, behind the mountain to the southwest of Khangmar, the Tibetan forces defending Khangar made a surprise attack on the British army camps under the cover of night, killing or wounding around 60 British troops and seizing several guns. The Tibetan troops then moved to Dzatrang, a narrow defile not far from Khangmar, on the way to Gyantse. To the south of Dzatrang were steep cliffs and to the north a river flowed from east to west in the direction of Gyantse. They drew a plan to corner the British troops on the defile. They decided to gather atDode, a place to the west of Dzatrang, that night.

There, the Tibetan defense force had mobilized several thousand fighting men. They included 1,500 monk volunteers from U and Tsang, and 1,300 troops collected on military service from Dakpo and Kongpo, national troops under the command of Dapon Trelingpa, Dapon Monkyipa, Dapon Ngonlungpa, Dapon Rampa andDapon Chagdrakpa, and a group of militia under the command of Tsedrung Hardong Lobsang Tenzin of Tashilhunpo and Dobdob Aga and Dobdob Kundur of Sera Monastery. There was also a group of monk volunteers led by Dresam Lho Tenam, Hardong Lobsang of Sera Je, Ganden Jangtse Loga and Rato Jampa Phuntsok. The above groups camped separately, and prepared food and weapons, such as swords, bows & arrows, and spears. Different groups were assigned different areas for defense. The troops who were to occupy the mountaintops and the areas between the foot of the northern mountain and the slope of the southern mountain through which the main road passed, hid in embankments, with two wooden wheeled Tibetan muskets. One division of troops was placed on the slopes of the northern mountain, and they dug trenches and hid in them with many rocks and logs to roll down on the enemy. They planned to lie in wait there and let the enemy pass through, whether they came during the daytime or at night, and as soon as they reached the western end of the road, they would attack them from their respective positions from all sides. With this plan, they all remained silent in their embankments without letting the enemy suspect that they were there.

Dapon Trelingpa, Rupon Lhagyal of Dingri, Hardong Loten of Tashilhunpo and Dobdo Aga of Sera, with 150 Dingri troops, hid in their trenches on the slopes of the mountain to the southern side of Dzatrang. Dapon Chagdrak, Rupon Sonam Dradul and Lobsang of Sera, with 50 soldiers, positioned themselves in their embankments on the slopes of the mountain at the middle of Dzatrang. Dapon Monkyi Lingpa, Dapon Rampa of Gyantse and some leaders of monk volunteers, supported by 1,200 troops, were deployed on the northern side of Dzatrang to support the vanguard force. Rato Jampa Phuntok, Dresam Lho Tenam and some leaders of the monk volunteers, with monks of Drepung Gomang and Loseling colleges, volunteered to support the vanguard force led by the Dapon Trelingpa. In this way, the Tibetan forces remained fully prepared.

On the morning of the 28th of the 2nd Tibetan month, two Tibetan spies came and reported that the enemy was approaching. Immediately, the Tibetans were on the alert, as they had prepared. They remained silent. At around midday, about 50 British advance cavalry troops arrived, followed by a large number of infantry soldiers, marching in line. The cavalry soldiers scanned the nearby mountains through binoculars as they moved. They did not see the Tibetan troops, as they were hiding inside the trenches. Unfortunately, when they reached the middle of the Dzatrang pass, they saw a Tibetan soldier rolling a stone down the hill, so they knew that Tibetan soldiers were hiding on the mountain. They immediately took precautions and fired their cannons and machineguns. Due to the tough terrain and strong embankments, the Tibetans did not suffer any casualties. The Tibetans fired back, and rolled down rocks and logs. The Tibetan vanguard force led by Dapon Trelingpa fired Tibetan cannons and guns continuously. The result was that except for a few, most of the British troops entrapped in the defile were killed, and the remaining British troops retreated.

The British sounded a bugle call and all their troops pulled back. After a while, they reinforced themselves by calling all their troops from different positions, and planned to seize the mountaintop from the northern and southern sides under the cover of artillery fire. The next day, they attacked the Tibetan positions on the mountaintop with artillery fire. The Tibetans retaliated with full force, but were overwhelmed by the artillery attacks of the enemy. Moreover, their ammunition was exhausted, so they had to leave the mountaintop. Many British cavalry and infantry troops again advanced through the Dzatrang path. The Tibetan forces tried their best to block them, but had to retreat eventually since the mountaintop was lost to the British. The battle at the Dzatrang path lasted for more than three days and nights, leaving more than 230 enemy troops killed or wounded. The casualties on the Tibetan side were 80, including Rupon Lhagyal, a leader of the vanguard division; the monk leaders Drasam Lho Tenam and Rato Jampa Phuntosk; Shigatse Gyapon Phuntsok Dorje; and a few leaders of the monk and *donmag* troops.

The Fifth Anglo-Tibetan battle at Gyantse

The leaders of the Tibetan defense forces discussed their future course of action, and decided to gather all their troops stationed at and around Dzatrang at Gyantse to make another attempt to resist the British forces. A team led by U Dapon Chagdrak was sent to Gyantse to make advance preparations as well as to send a report on the outcome of the Khangmar and Dzatrang battles to Lhasa and to receive advice on a future course of action. The chief army leader Dapon Trelingpa went from Sapugang to Gyantse to oversee the preparations. They called the local leaders and officials of the local monasteries, briefed them about the incidents at Khangmar and Dzatrang and requested them to provide volunteer troops and military supplies to fight together against the enemy. The local leaders and monk officials promised to send volunteer troops and other services as and when they were demanded by the government. Drongtse under Phala's estate and two estates of Gashi Kharkha volunteered to send 50 militiamen each. Riding, Gurpa and Serkhang monasteries in Palcho promised to send 30 monks each. The total militiamen became 500, including those who were already on the battlefield. They were named the Vanguard Force and given an emblem. The volunteers from Shigatse, Gyantse and Dingri who had been posted to different locations were summoned and organized, ready for deployment. A mounted messenger was sent to Lhasa with an instruction to gallop day and night to request the government for permission to take grain from the government's grain store at Gyantse to be used for the new group of militias. The Tibetan defense force made urgent preparations to confront the British. At that time, it was found after an investigation that Dapon Rampa had disappeared from the Dzatrang battlefield and arrived at Lhasa. He was demoted. The news boosted the morale of the other soldiers.

Soon after that, the British forces were advancing to Gyantse by way of Sapugang, and they were at a distance of one-day's march from Gyantse. A contingent of the British army had arrived and camped at Drakhu, near Gyantse Fortress. They announced that the district officers, people and monasteries should surrender to them. However, instead of surrendering, everyone, monks and lay people, gave full support to the Tibetan forces. The British cavalry troops toured around Gyantse Chode and other nearby areas to examine the areas. The monasteries distributed swords, guns, spears, and any other weapons they had to their monks.

A large British force, including cavalry and infantry, arrived from Phari at Changlo, near Changlo Bridge, to the south of Drakhu. However, they did not camp there due to fear of the Tibetan troops stationed in nearby villages and other areas. Based on their experiences from the previous battles, the Tibetans made careful preparations, such as making ditches and embankments and sending out a reconnaissance mission. The next day, the British troops at Drakhu suddenly charged at the Tibetan position, but retreated when the Tibetans reacted strongly. The British troops then fired cannons, machineguns and other weapons from Drakhu and Chang, and under the cover of the artillery fire they converged on the Tibetan position. The Tibetan forces fearlessly resorted to hand to hand fighting, killing around 30 British troops. The majority of the British troops pulled back to Changlo. This marked the beginning of Anglo-Tibetan battle of Gyantse.

That night, the Tibetan Army Headquarters summoned all the Tibetan troops from Shigatse and Dingri posted at Tsechen Monastery, and deployed them at Palcho Monastery, Latse and Gyalkhar for defense. The vanguard unit was placed at the front of the Fortress and behind the Wall Fence. The experienced gunmen from the *donmag* troops and local militias were given the responsibility of supporting the defenders of the Fortress. The Fortress was considered as the main battle site and all the troops at Drakhu village were grouped at Palcho Monastery.

There was a British artillery detachment on Gangdruk Mountain, behind the Gyalkhar village, near and to the northeast of the Gyantse Fortress. The Tibetans felt that they must destroy it since it was of great danger to them. They discussed how to destroy it, but there was no consensus among them. One day, the British at Changlo and Gangdruk jointly poured heavy artillery and machinegun fire onto the Tibetan position (at Gyantse Fortress). The Tibetans put up stiff resistance and were reinforced by troops arriving from Gyalkhar village. There was no decisive victory on either side. At that time, Dapon Ngonlungpa, gathering all his courage, went out of the Fortress to confront the enemy, despite his soldiers begging him not to go. Just after he arrived near the main gate of the Fortress, he was blown up by artillery shot from the enemy. He lost his life for the sake of his country and religion. The Tibetan forces fought very bravely, but due to the poor quality and quantity of their weapons and military supplies, they suffered high casualties. The British set Phala's estate at Gyalkhar on fire. The Tibetan troops fled from Gyalkhar to Latse village, located at the foot of a mountain to the north of the Gyantse Fortress.

After this, the British placed new cannons at Gyalkhar. From Gyalkhar village and Changlo, they shelled the Fortress every day, with cannons and machineguns, irrespective of the firing range. From the Fortress, the Tibetans retaliated with mortars and Tibetan guns. However, due to the long distance between them, neither side was able to cause any casualties, even after several days. Their shells and bullets fell on the fields in between their positions.

The chief army leaders and volunteers from Shigatse, Gyantse and Dingri armies, as well as the leaders of the local militias and monk troops convened a special meeting at the Fortress to draw up new battle strategies. Some of the army leaders considered that it would be useless to fire from a distance because of their poor weapons, and that they must crush the enemy by resorting to hand-to-hand combat in night attacks and guerrilla warfare, after making good plans and preparations. Otherwise the enemy would destroy the Fortress. All of them agreed. The vanguard force volunteered to go first. About 100 troops from Shigatse, Gyantse and Dignri, with 60 monks and the local militia, volunteered to back up the vanguard force, and they were instructed to remain ready. Fortifications were constructed from the Fortress to Latse village, and then around the wall-fence of the fortress, Palcho and Chagtsaldong to enable safe passage between them. Guards patrolled the areas day and night. Sacks were brought from wool traders in the village to be used to construct embankments. In this way, they made the best defensive preparations that they could.

Then one night the vanguard scouts, carrying swords, axes and other weapons, followed by troops carrying Tibetan guns, embarked upon their mission to attack the British army camp at Changlo under cover of darkness. When they got near the British army camp they were not seen, but when they touched the barbed wires surrounding the camp it woke the guards. The guards whistled loudly and instantly the enemy opened fire. The Tibetans fired back but had to flee, so their night mission did not bring any result.

After that, the British intensified their artillery fire on the Gyantse Fortress, continuing for days. To support the Tibetan force defending the Fortress, a cavalry from the six nomadic regions of Nagtsang and 1,000 local militiamen from Markya, Nyemo and Rinpung, through Rongyung-la pass, had arrived at Rinang, to the northeast and close to Gyantse Fortress. Dobdob Aga, with several cavalry troops, went from the Fortress to receive them. However, since the British forces had occupied the area surrounding the Fortress, they did not find a clear road to pass through, so they returned. The Commander-in-Chief Trelingpa asked Tsang Dapon Monkyi, who was on defense duty at Nyenying, to keep a number of local militia from among those who had arrived at Rinang under his command and deploy the rest at Goshi and Ralung for the time being, according to the situation. Trelingpa instructed him to send his men to do this. Accordingly, Monkyi selected 150 militiamen from Nagtshang and 150 from Makyang, Nyemo and Ringpung, and brought them to Nenning. The remaining 400 men from Nagtsang, led by Lhadar, the representative of Shentsa Dzong, were dispatched to Rinang, and the remaining 300, cavalry or infantry, under the command of secretary Lode, the deputy district officer of Rinpung, were sent to Ralung and Nakartse.

Subsequent developments will be discussed in the next section, which concerns the battle of Nenying Monastery.

The Sixth Anglo-Tibetan battle site: Nenying Monastery

Nenying Monastery was located to the southeast at a distance of about a half day's walk from Gyantse, and it was an important route for the British for transportation and travelling between Gyantse and Phari. Therefore, on the instructions of the Commander-in-Chief, 500 local militia, comprising 300 local militia from Shotarlhosum, who were under the command of Tsang Dapon Monlingpa and Dumra, and 150 militia and 50 monk troops selected from the militias and monk troops from Kongpo Dzomo Dzong, Tsegang Dzong and Sho-kha, who had been stationed in Lhasa, Gongkar and Chushur, were stationed at Nenying Monastery. Embankments and secret holes were made on the boundary walls of the monastery. One detachment was placed on the mountaintop to the east of the monastery to block the passage of the enemy through the monastery. Another group of soldiers was stationed on the western mountain to guard the monastery. Another group was kept at the foot of the monastery to destroy the enemy's troops when they arrived.

As the Tibetans repeatedly caused casualties among the British troops and blocked the roads, the British officers regarded Nenying as strategically important for them and decided to besiege the monastery and mountaintop from both the northern and southern sides. However, due to a large concentration of Tibetan troops in Gyantse, the British faced difficulty in taking action immediately.

British troops from Phari, carrying large quantities of cannons, different types of machineguns and ammunition, arrived at Dode and Saphu Gang in the fourth month. They were reinforced by several hundred troops who had come from Gyantse Changlo. Under the cover of cannon and machinegun fire, many of their cavalry and foot soldiers converged on the monastery in a concerted attack. The boundary walls of the monastery were very thick and high, and there were many secret holes on the walls from which to watch the enemy. There were strong guards at both the main and the internal gates, and a few troops with machineguns as well as several troops who were experts with Tibetan guns had been placed inside concealed locations on the roof of the monastery. With this preparation, the Tibetans put up a stiff resistance with great courage, causing high casualties on the British side. The British therefore retreated for the time being.

Tsang Dapon Monlingpa and Dapon Dumra secretly went to Gyantse to consult with the Commander-in-Chief about their future course of action. During that time, Shortarlhosum militia's leaders Dorje Topgyal and Lhawang Yulgyal, and militia leader Jomo Dzong Adar Nyima Drakpa and his younger brother, Jomo Dzong Adar Samphel and Dumrawa's aide-de-camp Adruk Shokha Dotop and Shoka Samdup and Tsegang Adar Gonpo Lhadar met and discussed their future war plans and strategies. All of them voiced the same thing:"They had left their homes with the pledge that they would fight the enemy at the cost of their lives, and they did not want to bring humiliation to their people, so they must stand fast with their pledge."Twenty-five men led by Adar Nyima Drakpa and Adar Dotop and 30 militiamen from Shotarlhosum volunteered to confront the British forces, and remained fully prepared.

The next day, the British attacked the Tibetan positions from a distance, as they dared not approach too close. That night, the British changed their strategy. They bribed one of their porters named Phuntsok, who was from Dode, to guide them. Travelling through the upper end of Jangpephu, the birthplace of Nangsa Obum[12], to the west of Nenying Monastery, and climbing the Rili mountain range, they reached the Nenying mountaintop. They then started attacking the monastery. The Tibetan force fought back. Fourteen militiamen from Nagtsang volunteered to attack the enemy, killing or wounding about ten enemy soldiers with swords. They bravely lost their lives in the fight. After more than seven hours of skirmishing, the Tibetan forces who were occupying the mountaintop lost ground, due to the overwhelming size of the British force.

Soon after they had taken the mountaintop, the British army's bugle calls could be heard. Under the cover of firing from the mountaintop, the British vanguard troops converged at the boundary walls of the monastery and destroyed a portion of the wall with explosives. (The damaged wall is still there). They entered the monastery, and after struggling for several hours, they pushed the Tibetans back to the Assembly hall of the monastery. The Tibetan leaders immediately decided that they must charge the enemy en masse and resort to hand-to-hand fighting, or else they would all be killed. The British shouted, "You must surrender if you want to save your lives!" Further angered, the Tibetan troops rushed out to fight, saying, "It is better to fight and die rather than to surrender. We must avenge our soldiers who have sacrificed their lives. We will never retreat!"

Adrug Dotop, Adar of Kongpo and his brother, with their men, charged at the British troops and fought with them face-to-face, killing many of the British soldiers. While this was happening, a British army officer called Dunlop Sahib, holding a pistol, was giving commands to his soldiers. Dotop threw a sword at him, slashing one of his shoulders and killing him on the spot. The two sides engaged in fierce hand-to-hand fighting which lasted several hours. The British casualties were more than 100 officers and troops killed or wounded. Their blood flowed down the staircases of the monastery. The remaining British soldiers fled to Saphugang, and the battle ebbed temporarily. The Tibetans removed the dead bodies of the Tibetan martyrs and gave medical treatment to the wounded soldiers. Dumarawa's group member Atruk Dotop had been seriously injured and medical treatment did not help him. He succumbed to his injuries. To his last breath, he encouraged his compatriots to keep fighting. The Anglo-Tibetan battle at Nenying Monastery is still popular in the oral tradition of the Tibetans. The people sang this song in praise of those Tibetan martyrs:

> Kongpo soldier Adar arrived;
> He vanquished the British troops on the battlefield.

---

12 Nangsa Obum's story was mixed with fiction. Her tale is performed in opera.

The staircases of the Nenying Monastery
Were drenched with red blood.

Even these days, people still praise and talk about the bravery and dedication of Adar Nyima Drakpa and his brother, as well as Dumrawa's troop Adrug Dotop and the other brave Tibetan fighters who volunteered to fight the enemy for their country. Among them, Yonten Gyatso, a monk fighter from Pal Chokhor Monastery, was physically robust and extremely brave. When he started from his monastery for war, the monk officials and lamas of the monastery offered him scarves and sang the song:

Sera monk Yonten Gyatso
Is going to fight a battle;
Boys and girls of Gyantse,
Please make way for him.

During the battle at Nenying Monastery, he brandished his sword and charged at the enemy, yelling:

Destroy the enemy of the doctrine
of Atisha and Lobsang Drakpa!

Tsechen Monastery and the mountaintop were lost to the enemy, and only a small number of Tibetan soldiers remained. They moved to Gyantse, where they regrouped and decided to fight again. At Nenying Monastery, the British soldiers carried the dead body of Commander Dunlop on their shoulders and performed military tributes at his graveside. In vengeance, they damaged the monastery and took all its religious articles, and burned the rest.

After the battle of Nenying, the British stationed only a few solders on the road and sent the rest to help their detachments at Gyadrong and Changlo to the south of the Nyangchu River and Gangdruk range in the north. They again attacked the Tibetan positions at Nenying, Palcho and others, with cannons and machineguns.

The Seventh Anglo-Tibetan Battle at Tsechen Monastery

On the 30th day of the 3rd Tibetan month, about 500 British cavalry soldiers arrived at Tsechen Monastery from Gyadrong to inspect the situation. At that time, the monastery was guarded by around 300 Tibetan troops and 30 monk troops, who were commanded by Ngawang Jampal. The British troops returned to Gyadrong. After that, British cavalry in groups frequently patrolled the south and northern banks of the Nyangchu River. On the 15th day of the 5th Tibetan month, a large British contingent, consisting of cavalry and infantry, crossed the Nyangchu River from the northern side opposite Tsechen and arrived at Gashi Latsel. Another British contingent, by way of the upper end of Panyul and Kharag, climbed and occupied the mountaintop behind Tsechen Monastery. Confronting them were about 400 local militiamen from Kongpo and Dakpo, as well as troops sent to Tsechen from Gyantse to reinforce the Tibetan defense force. From Gashi, the British force fired at the monastery continuously, damaging some portions of Dolma Lhakang temple and boundary walls of the monastery. They also fired machineguns at the monastery from the mountaintop. The Tibetans made counterattacks with great force and courage, making the British difficult to seize the monastery. The British intensified their attacks, using all kinds of weapons. Due to the overwhelming strength and superior weapons of the British army, the Tibetan force suffered a defeat, losing both the monastery and their garrison below the monastery. The casualties on the Tibetan side were 58 monks of Tsechen Monastery and 15 local militiamen either killed or wounded. The British took away all the property and drove away a large number of horses and cattle belonging to the monastery. They also raped women and fired ruthlessly on the local people. The people of Gyantse thus sang this sad song:

> Gyantse, a narrow turquoise valley,
> has been filled with foreign soldiers;
> Alas! When we see them
> The wealth we have amassed is useless.

My noble father, Gyapon Kharsam Gyalpo, captain of the Gyantse Regiment, told me the following story about the arrival of the British in Tibet when he was a child:

> I was at that time around nine years old. War was going on in Gyantse. One day, British troops arrived at Tsechen, by way of Gashi. (My father's village was called Kharsam, and it was located near and to the north of Tsechen Bridge.) At that time, all the people, including children, carrying their possessions, fled and hid in the forests. One day, my parents left our maidservant and me alone at home to guard them. From Tsechen Bridge, about 100 cavalry came straight and stopped near our house, and lined up. I went up to the roof of our house, watched them through the beams and listened to their conversation. One soldier said something aloud and all other soldiers fired many shots at the monastery. After that, they headed to Gyantse. I went to the spot from where they fired, and collected the used bullets and took them to home (We made a good tub welded with those bullets).
>
> Another day, about 10 cavalry solders suddenly entered our house. They forcibly took about 100 goats and sheep from our courtyard and drove them to Gyantse Changlo. I cried and prostrated, and tried hard to win their sympathy, but they did not listen. I could do nothing. With the hope of getting some money from them, I followed them, crying. They took them straight to Gyantse and put them into a fenced yard. I cried louder and stayed there. A solder slapped me hard and told me to go home. I stood at their door. After a length of time in which two

cups of tea might cool, a solder came and gave me a piece of raw sugar, as big as a palm. With a gesture of his hand, he told me to go away—dif I did not, he would kill me. So I lost hope and returned home. Unlike children of these days, I was very clever.

One day, my parents told me to go to the front compound of the Dzong to inquire about my uncle Majang-la, who was a captain of the Gyantse army. Taking some food, I traveled through the fields to the water-mill of Dromnyer. There was no one. I looked into the water-tunnel of the mill and saw many dead bodies. I was told that a few days ago when the British came many people out of fear rushed and hid inside it, and the British fired at them and killed them. I was quite frightened. Then I headed towards the front of the Fortress in search of my uncle. A man told me that my uncle was in the Fortress. I returned home happily and told my parents that he was in the Fortress. Soon after that, the battle of Gyantse ended, with the siege of the Fortress by the enemy. We heard that the British had massacred around 200 of the best Tibetan troops on the field of Shogdup near Changlo. Among them was my uncle, who had been badly injured. We brought him home, but he succumbed to his injuries after a few days.

After seizing Tsechen Monastery, the British intensified their attacks on the Gyanste Fortress. The Fortress was the main base of the Tibetan defense force, and it was guarded by about 2,000 troops from Gyantse, Shigatse and Dingri. All of them had a very strong determination and courage to defend it, even at the cost of their lives for the sake of their country. Retaining 450 selected soldiers at the Fortress, the rest were deployed uniformly at Palcho Monastery, behind the wall fence of the monastery, in front of the Fortress and Chagtseldong, together with the local militias.

General Kalon Yuthog of Tsang arrived from Lhasa and stayed at Yagde Khangsar. The leaders of the Tibetan defense forces reported to him about the general war situation, the loss of Nenying and Tsechen to the enemy and the danger of losing even Gyantse Fortress. They told him that in spite of the bad situation the Tibetan forces were defending with great courage and determination. They suggested that since Rongyul and Nyemo were near, the Tibetan forces posted at them should be sent to Nyangto Lungmar and Goshi, in accordance with the situation, and requested him to report this information to the Kashag.

The Kashag decided to postpone further British attacks through diplomatic means, as long as the Tibetans were not able to mobilize a strong force enough to defend against the British, regardless of whether the ongoing battles at Gyantse Fortress brought victory or loss. The Dalai Lama sent a written order to Deputy Kalon Lama, his assistant and Deputy Kalon Yuthog to make their best efforts to bring the British to the negotiating table.

Before the Dalai Lama's order was received, at dawn of the 7th day of the fifth month, from the Gangdruk Mountaintop and Changlo, the British started pounding Palcho Monastery and the Gyantse Fortress, with machineguns, cannons and guns. In retaliation, the Tibetans fired locally made mortars and guns rapidly. The Tibetan troops guarding the Wall Fence and posted at the village opposite the Fortress fired on the British force at Changlo. There was no decisive victory on either side, and the firing ceased as dusk approached. On the 28th day, the British again attacked the Palcho Monastery and the Fortress from the same directions, and about 60 British troops attempted to storm the Fortress through the main gate under the cover of artillery fire. The Tibetan vanguard force of about 150 troops countered them with Tibetan guns. The British kept advancing. The Tibetan troops rushed out and charged at them, using swords in face-to-face combat. About 40 British soldiers were killed or injured, and the rest ran away. On the Tibetan side, about 8 brave soldiers were killed or wounded. Hearing this, the Tibetan Generals at Gyantse Fortress immediately granted praise and rewards to their soldiers, and advised them to keep on fighting.

Gyantse Fortress was constructed during the time of Chogyal Kunsang Rabten Phag of Gyantse and his son. The fortress is high, broad and strong. It was bombarded by the British cannons and the damage is still visible.

The British decided to destroy the Tibetan force at the foot of the Fortress in order to storm it. The Tibetan General moved his headquarters to Palcho Monastery from the Fortress.

In the early morning of the 30th day of the same month, the British forces from Latse village and Changlo bombarded the Fortress from the front, and under cover of the cannon attacks, many of their troops equipped with machine guns and handguns rushed to the Fortress. The Tibetans defended heroically. Unfortunately, whether it was due to bad luck or for some other reason, the house where they had kept the ammunition caught fire and a thick cloud of smoke billowed up into the sky. There were two different explanations about how the ammunition house caught fire: some say that when some Tibetan soldiers went to fetch ammunition, they accidentally dropped an ember into the room, while others say that British bribed a Tibetan woman who had been employed to fetched water for the Tibetan army, to start the fire. When the British saw this, they shouted with joy, thinking that they got a good opportunity. They intensified their attack on the Fortress. They sent additional troops to the Fortress, the hilltop and behind the wall fence. The Tibetan defenders remained determined to fight back and did not retreat, even a step. There was no decisive victory on either side.

From Latse village, about 50 British troops in each detachment began arriving and climbing up to the Fortress. The Tibetans at the Fortress rolled down boulders and logs, and threw sling shots, preventing them from seizing the Fortress. The next day, however, the British troops from Latse again climbed up the hill to the Fortress. They tried to break into the Fortress through its northern door. The Tibetan defenders rolled down boulders, killing or wounding many of the enemy's soldiers.

Many British troops continued to climb the hill. When they were about to get into the gate, some tough Tibetan soldiers went outside and fought the British soldiers in hand-to-hand combat, killing or wounding many enemy soldiers. However, the British troops were so numerous that they overwhelmed the Tibetans and gained control of the Fortress, where they installed a British flag.

Due to the loss of Latse, the ground in front of the Fortress as well as the Fortressitself to the enemy one after another, the defenders at Palcho Monastery, Wall Fence and Chagtseldong lost their courage to fight. In the above incidents, besides those who were captured by the British, the rest returned to Trokhul to the south of the Nyangchu River and other places. The British executed about 200 of the best soldiers among those captured on a field near Shogdub. They cruelly pillaged and robbed the local monasteries and villages. There was no peace and happiness in the area. There were many such stories, but I have not written all of them here.

Captain O'Connor went with his troops to Shigatse, where he met the Sengchen Lama and other important lamas and local leaders, pretending that the meetings were friendly. Then he returned to Gyantse. They made a medical camp and treated the wounded Tibetan soldiers, and sent some captured troops home with money. They bought grain, peas, firewood and hay from the local people at high prices. They fooled the people through their false behavior, which prompted some Tibetan troops to say that British troops were kind.

After the end of the battle of Gyantse, the remaining Tibetan troops from Shigatse, Gyantse and Dingri returned to their homes. The militia troops and monk volunteers who had been scattered could not regroup. The army chief Yuthog stayed at Nyemo and did not display any leadership qualities toward his troops. During the battle of Gyantse, there were no Tibetan forces to attack the British forces from behind. Moreover, the Tibetan fighting force was small and their weapons were primitive. Because of these reasons, the Tibetans lost the battles and their positions.

The eighth Anglo-Tibetan battle at Kharo-la pass

Local militias collected from Rinpung, Lingkar, Markyang and Nyemo were about 1,400 in number. As their leaders, Nyemo Treshongpa, Oyuk Rabkar Trinley Dradul, Darteng Sonam Dargye and Tagtse Dolingpa Phuntsok Dradulwere appointed as *dapon, rupon* or any other ranks as suitable. They were sent to defend Nakartse. Tsedrung Ngawang Trinley and Shodrung Nyemo Dokharwa were sent to collect militias from Shigatse, Namling, Lhabu and Gyatso. The army chief Yuthogpa, with a small elite force, went to Nakartse. Upon arrival at Yarsig, he summoned the district and village leaders of Gongkar, Paldi, Chushur and others, and gave them detailed instructions on how to obstruct the British troops, by making strong barricades at strategic and important locations, such as narrow passes and rivers. At Nakartse, he immediately selected 250 of his best troops and stationed them at Kharo-la pass, and gave detailed instructions to their leaders Nyemo Treshong, Langthong, Darteng Sonam Dargye and Oyug Rabkar Trinley Dradul on how to defend their position. At that time he received an order from Lhasa that he should return to Lhasa immediately for discussions. Instructing the Nakartse district officer Shodrung Dodrongpa, Norgyepa, Oyuk Taktse Dolingpa Phuntsok Dradul and Lingshi Shodrung Palhun to take joint responsibility, he returned to Lhasa.

When the militias arrived at Kharo-la pass, they were divided into different groups and assigned to occupy different locations on the mountainsides. They built embankments on the mountainsides (the remains of which still exist). Two different secret watchtowers were constructed at the northern side of the mountain and lookouts were posted there on a rotation basis day and night to keep a continuous watch for the enemy. The Kharo-la is on the southern range of the snowy mountain called Nojin Gangwa Sangpo, between Ralung and Nangkartse, to the northeast of Gyantse at a distance of one and half's days walk. On the 2nd day of the 6th Tibetan month, from the direction of Ralung, a contingent of British cavalry, followed by a large number of foot soldiers, arrived at Nangkartse. The Tibetan defense forces were informed about the arrival of British troops by their lookouts. They quickly hid in their embankments and lay in wait. As soon as the British troops arrived near the Tibetan position, Oyuk Darteng fired, and immediately other Tibetan troops started firing from all sides. They killed almost all the British soldiers, cavalry and infantry, who had been trapped on the narrow path. All the other British troops who had not reached the narrow path quickly retreated and camped at the western foot of the Kharo-la pass. As a result, Lieutenant-Colonel Brander, with a number of troops, came from Gyantse to find other roads to cross the Kharo-la pass. He bribed some herders from Nyingro and Ralung to guide them to the mountaintop. With the help of the herders, they reached the mountaintop and descended and attacked the Tibetan positions with cannons. Two groups of British infantry came from the eastern and western ends of the mountain and repeatedly fired Maxim guns and rifles at the Tibetans garrisons. The Tibetan forces retaliated with great courage and force. However, due to their inferior weapons, the Tibetans suffered high casualties. Losing hope of defending their position, the remaining Tibetan soldiers retreated.

At that time, although the war was at its peak and the situation was very grave, the Lhasa government suddenly called back the Tibetan army chief Kalon Yuthog from the battlefield to Lhasa. This made a very bad impression and disturbed the fighting spirit of the Tibetan warriors. After that, the British forces moved further from Nakartse and easily reached Lhasa, facing only minor resistance from the Tibetan defense forces. On 25 July, crossing the Gampa-la pass, the British mission reached the Chaksam ferry crossing.

Fearing that if the British mission came to Lhasa, serious problems would erupt since Lhasa had large crowds of people and many monks at the three Monastic Seats, the Dalai Lama sent the Chief Abbot Official Barshi Ngawang Ngodup, with a few assistant staff, with a letter embossed with his seal, to negotiate with the British. He also issued two letters on the 5th and 8th day of the sixth Tibetan month respectively to the Bhutanese representative Trongsapon, stating, "In your recent letter, you have said that the British are coming to Lhasa to meet me for a final decision and, you have attached a separate document containing nine points for easy negotiation. However, since it is a border issue of great importance, I need to discuss them with the Kashag and the National Assembly, and I will send you a reply as soon as possible. It is of no use for the British officers and troops to come to Lhasa. You should do your level best to stall their advance to Lhasa."

The Thirteenth Dalai Lama's flight to China and Mongolia

The Chief Official Abbot, the main member of the Tibetan negotiation team, met Younghusband, the British mission leader, to whom he gave the Dalai Lama's letter and tried his best to persuade him[to conduct negotiations where they were. Younghusband however insisted that since was already close to Lhasa, he must go to Lhasa for the negotiations. He further promised that unless the Tibetans obstructed his mission, he would not harm any villages or monasteries on the road. He headed to Lhasa from the Chaksam ferry crossing. The Chief Abbot Official quickly returned to Lhasa and reported to the Dalai Lama what he had been told by the British officer and what he had observed about the weaponry and military strength of the British. A meeting was convened immediately for the Kashag and the National Assembly. As agreed at the meeting, they appealed to the Dalai Lama to go to somewhere else for the time being for the sake of the country's political and religious affairs in general and the Dalai Lama's own life in particular. At that time, the Dalai Lama was in meditation on Vajrabhairava. Rising from the meditation on the 13th day of the 6th Tibetan month of 1904, he summoned the Ganden Tripa Lamoshar Lobsang Gyaltsen to his residence, the Sunlight Chamber, at the Potala Palace and said,

> Though our government made continuous efforts to conduct peaceful negotiations with the British military mission, they did not listen, so we had to resort to armed force to obstruct them and fought several battles. We requested the Manchu Emperor for military help, saying that the British force was invading us, just as "a

big insect eats a small one", but there was no response. Moreover, the Manchus in Tibet also criticized our war of resistance. All our garrisons at the Fortresses and defense forces posted at other important places beyond Nakartse to block the British have been defeated. Now the British leaders and troops are approaching Lhasa. If I do not do anything, there are likely to be unforeseen consequences to the political and religious affairs of Tibet, at present and in the future. Therefore, I shall temporarily go to China and Mongolia. I will meet the Chinese Empress and the prince, and try my best to protect the Tibet's independence. You are the most suitable person to hold the responsibility of the government during my absence. At this critical juncture, you have to run the government courageously.

Saying so, the Dalai Lama granted him the Regent's seal. He told his elder brother Yabshi Langdun Gung Dhondup Dorje, cabinet ministers, *drungtsi* officials, lay and monk secretaries, abbots of the Three Monastic Seats and representatives of the National Assembly that he had appointed Lamo Shar to take the overall responsibility of the government. He instructed all the officials to perform their duties with dedication and work jointly for the sake of the country's political and religious affairs. He further told them that his trip must be kept secret from the Amban. He also said that he had pardoned Kalon Shadra, Shokhang and Changkyim and they should be sent to their own estates, and instructed his secretariat to issue the order regarding this through the chief steward office at the Potala Palace.

At dawn on the 15th day of the 6th Tibetan month, the Dalai Lama, accompanied by a small retinue composed of monk and lay officials, and 30 Buryat monks studying at Sera, Drepung and Ganden monasteries, left the Potala Palace, by way of Reting and Nagchu, towards Tsongon.

The arrival of the British military mission in Lhasa and the signing of the Anglo-Tibetan treaty

The Tibetan government had decided to keep the British troops outside Lhasa. Once the British forces had come close to Lhasa by way of Chushur, the Tibetan government told the British mission to use Lhalu Gatsel as the residence for the British officers and the Tsesum ground for the troops. On the 22nd day of the sixth month (19th day of the sixth month, August 3, 1904), the British mission arrived in Lhasa and camped at Kyangthang Gang and Lhalu's premises. Lhasa Amban Yutai went to meet Younghusband, carrying food, to please him. The next day, the Gurkha ambassador and Lhasa's Muslim Community leader went to meet the British. Before the National Assembly and the Kashag could take steps, the Gurkha and Bhutan representatives had paid several visits to the British camp in an effort to bring the Tibetans and British officers to the negotiating table.

After this, the Regent, with a small retinue, went to the British camp and met with Younghusband. The foundations of the negotiations were laid. The Regent returned and told the Kashag, "I went and met with the British officers. They are ordinary people who listen and speak; they are not the type of people who kill or capture others unexpectedly. You ministers, instead of remaining in fear, should go and talk with them." The ministers were embarrassed. Carrying many gifts, the ministers went and met with the British officers, and had free and frank discussions with them.

A few days later, two monks burst into the tent of the British and wounded Captain T. Kelly and doctor Cookyoung. The two monks were arrested and harshly questioned, and finally executed. To avoid such incidents in the future, some Tibetan officials and representatives from the Three Monastic Seats were kept at the British army camp.

The British drafted a treaty, including points regarding future trade between Tibet and India, setting up trade marts in Tibet, Tibet and Sikkim's border issues, war indemnity to be paid to the British and the release of prisoners captured during the war by both sides. Though the terms of the treaty were not satisfactory to the Tibetans, the Regent, the Kashag and the Tibetan National Assembly decided to accept the treaty rather than bargaining. Their reasons were that the Dalai Lama was not in Lhasa. Tibet was militarily and economically weak; the Walung and Kyidrong border crises were still not solved. The Chinese often harassed the Tibetans at border areas such as Nyarong, Lithag, Ba and Chatreng in the Kham region, and the Tibetans' repeated request to the Manchu Emperor in Peking was fruitless, like "throwing a stone into a sea." As we have the sayings, "If you have two enemies, it is better to befriend one of them," and "A strong poison may turn into an effective medicine," it was better to accept the British terms of negotiation and make friends with them.

Finally, on the 17th day of the 7th month of the Wood-Dragon year, corresponding to 7 September 1904, the British officers and the Tibetan representatives met at the Sishi Phuntsok Hall in the Potala Palace. The Tibetan side was represented by the Regent Ganden Tri Rinpoche, the four cabinet ministers, *drungtsi* officials as representatives of the National Assembly and representatives of the Three Monastic Seats. The British side was represented by seven officers led by Colonel Younghusband and Claude White. Amban Yutai in Lhasa, Nepal's ambassador in Tibet Captain Jit Bahdur and Drongtsapon Wangchuk of Bhutan, among others, acted as witnesses to the treaty. Since the full content of the treaty is found in many books, I have not copied it here to avoid taking up too much space.

The British troops did not do harm to any villages and monasteries along the road, except during the course of the war. They moreover paid good prices for whatever they purchased or hired from the people, such as transportation, hay, meat, vegetables, etc. Therefore, the following street song became popular in Lhasa:

First, they were called enemies of the Dharma.
Then they were called foreigners.
When they gave Indian rupees,
They were called Mr. Sahib.

Younghusband once asked Manchu Amban Yutai in Lhasa, "You have no any official functions, how do you pass your time?" He must have said this after knowing that Manchu officials had no role in Tibetan politics.

As the winter approached near, Younghusband and his troops began their journey back to India. They left Lhasa on 23 September 1904 for India by way of Gyantse and Phari. Captain O'Connor again went to Shigatse to meet the Panchen Rinpoche and reminded him about their earlier discussions. In the same year, the Panchen Rinpoche went to Calcutta to meet the Prince of Wales and Lord Minto, and exchanged gifts with them. This caused a political misunderstanding between him and the Tibetan government.

The British military mission brought to Tibet a total of about 18,600 people, including troops and officers. The Tibetan government spent about 320,000 *khal* measures of grain for the war. At that time, one *khal* of grain cost 5 *srang* of Tibetan money. The mission caused many deaths among people living in villages along the road. They burned monasteries and villages and stole many valuable religious articles from the monasteries. They transported in total 460 loads of goods by way of Phari, without transportation charges. They looted treasures belonging to private families, the government and monasteries. The exact value of property looted by them is found in the report of damage prepared by the joint committee of monk and lay officials. The British troops grazed their horses and mules on the fields of villages along the road, destroying the crops. According to the records maintained by district headquarters, the government gave compensation and donated large quantities of grain to the owners. I will not write all of them here to avoid too much detail.

The Anglo-Tibetan war was a war of resistance fought by the Tibetan government and people jointly against the British military expedition for the protection of their country, and their religious and political status. According to the Tibetan government's record, the war caused 1,400 Tibetan casualties, including those killed or injured. Following is a list of Tibetan war heroes who performed excellently in the Anglo-Tibetan war:

1.   Dapon Trelingpa of the Dingri Regiment
2.   Dapon Monlingpa of the Shigatse Regiment
3.   Deputy Dapon Chagdrapa of the U Regiment
4.   Lhoka militia leader Dumrawa
5.   Yarto Tsetre of the U Regiment

6. Rupon Kyibugpa of the Shigatse Regiment
7. Tenpa Tsering, servant of Rupon Trelingpa of the Shigatse Regiment
8. Rupon Gyashar Nyigyal of the Shigatse Regiment
9. Hardong Loden, a leader of the Tashilhunpo's local militia
10. Rupon Kyem Lho Pema Dradul of the Dingri Regiment

In total, 442 Tibetan war heroes were granted rewards by the government, by way of promotion or gifts, in accordance with the value of their performance. They included 233 Tibetan national troops; 188 war heroes from among local militias from U-Tsang, the four northern regions of Tibet, Lhoka, Dakpo, Kongpo and Shortarlhosum, leaders of the volunteer monks and ordinary soldiers; and 22 war heroes, including Druklha Pema Lhagyal and Tengkar Sodar, who survived the battle of Nenying, during which some local militia from Kongpo, including Jomo Dorje Topgyal and Shoka Adar Nyma Drakpa, lost their lives.

From among the soldiers who lost their lives at different battle sites, U Dapon Lhading Se and Namselingpa, who were killed in the battle of Chumig Shongko, were rewarded by giving 250 *tamkar* money each to their families every year from the Namsey treasure at the Potala Palace. The eldest son of Lhading Se was made 4th-ranking army payroll officer under special consideration. The Panchen Rinpoche granted the Surnub Shika estate in the Jepe area to the Master Chamberlain of Tashilhunpo's western chamber with permanent ownership over it for his marvelous performance in the war. Shagtsang Geshon was appointed special private chamberlain to the Panchen Lama. Army officers in the rank of colonel (*rupon*) and captain (*gyapon*), and leaders of local militias and monk volunteers were granted 333 *khal* measures of grain and the officers in the rank of lieutenant (*dingpon*) were granted each 83 *khal* measures of grain. Others local soldiers who risked their lives in the wars were granted each 25 *khal* measures of grain from their respective regions. The Tibetan army chief Treling and others requested the Panchen Rinpoche to consider rewards to Hardong Lobsang Tenzin, the leader of monk volunteers from Tashilhunpo, and Tengpa Rupon Tserab for their brave performance in the wars. He appointed Hardong a monastic official and granted 150 silver coins from the army salary office for his lifetime. Tengpa was granted the life-long right to collect revenue from the Lhatse district for his personal use. The details are found in the government's records.

There are many documents relating to the Anglo-Tibetan conflict of 1904, but I will not copy all of them here to avoid too much detail. These documents include the Thirteenth Dalai Lama's edicts given to the Tibetan Commander-in-Chief Deputy Kalon Lama and Deputy Kalon Yuthog at different times, two letters sent to the Bhutan government's representative Trongsapon and one letter given to the Gurkha king; and a proposal sent to the council of deputy ministers by army leader Langthongpa; documents recording the rewards given to the Tibetan war heroes; a petition forwarded by the people of Gyantse regarding the damage to crops and the destruction of their houses and properties during the Anglo-Tibetan wars; two separate reports on free transportation provided by people of Tsang to the bodyguards of the British Trade Agent at Gyantse Changlo; and the ten-point Anglo-Tibetan Treaty signed at Lhasa.

The Thirteenth Dalai Lama returns to Lhasa after his sojourns in Mongolia and China

Travelling by way of Tsongon, the Dalai Lama arrived at Dakhuree in Outer Mongolia on the 20 October of the same year (1904). There he was greeted with great honor by Chinese and Mongol civil and military officials as well as monks and lay people. He was also given a warm official reception and accorded guards of honor and a retinue. Helha Jetsun Dampa and his wife, regional rulers, high-ranking Chinese and Mongol officials arrived there to meet him, officially or privately. From Peking, the Manchu Emperor Guangxu and his mother Taihu (Empress Dowager Cixi) sent the Chintran Amban, with assistants, to offer their first greetings to the Dalai Lama.

Following this, the Russian consul in Peking, Pokoti, with his staff, arrived. He presented the Dalai Lama with a letter and rich gifts sent by the Russian emperor Czar Nicholas II. The Czar had four daughters, but no sons. Therefore, through Dorjieff, the Czar requested the Dalai Lama to bless him with a son. The Dalai Lama performed a divination and promised to bless him with a son, and sent a protective cord and blessing articles to both the Czar and the Czarina. In 1904, the Czarina gave birth to a son, who was named Alex. After this, the Tibetan government sent many religious texts and articles to Russia as gifts, which gave birth to the present Tibetan library in Leningrad. The Dalai Lama reportedly appealed to the Czar to support Tibet's political struggle. British protested. Russia in those times was in a period of great turmoil, caused by the revolutionary movement within the country and its ongoing war with Japanese on its borders.

In 1906, the Dalai Lama, with his retinue, visited the monasteries and places in Da Khuree[13] and Buryat. He visited and stayed at Ganden Phelgyeling[14] in Khuree.

---

13 Ulan Bator has had numerous names in its history. From 1639–1706, it was known as Orgoo (also spelled Urga), and from 1706–1911 as Ikh Khuree, Da Khüree or simply Khuree/Huree. Upon independence in 1911, with both the secular government and the Bogd Khan's palace present, the city's name changed to Niislel Khuree. It is called Bogdiin Khuree (camp/monastery of the Bogd) in the folk song Praise of Bogdiin Khuree. When the city became the capital of the new Mongolian People's Republic in 1924, its name was changed to Ulaanbaatar (literally "red hero"), in honor of Mongolia's national hero Damdin Sukhbaatar, whose warriors, shoulder-to-shoulder with the Soviet Red Army, liberated Mongolia from Ungern von Sternberg's troops and Chinese occupation. His statue still adorns Ulan Bator's central square.

14 The Gandantegchinlen Monastery is a Tibetan-style monastery in the Mongolian capital of Ulaanbaatar that

From Peking, the Chinese Emperor and the Dowager Empress sent gifts to him through ministers Koutsuo and Bitshyi. In return, the Dalai Lama sent Abbot Jamyang Tenpa to deliver gifts to the Emperor and Empress. In the eighth Tibetan month, the Dalai Lama and his party visited Ulaanbaatar. A delegation from Lhasa arrived there to invite the Dalai Lama back to Lhasa. In the first week of the ninth Tibetan month, the Dalai Lama went to Husosamli, where he was greeted by the abbot, officials, lamas and *trulkus* of Kumbum Jampaling Monastery, and the local leader of Landru and Sining Amban. At their request, he headed to Sining, where he was received with great honour and festivity, including a military parade. He then visited Kumbum, the birthplace of the great Je Tsongkhapa. There, the Dalai Lama received a petition (from the local people), describing the extensive criminal activities of Zhao Erfeng, who led military incursion into Doto, killing people and sacking villages and monasteries. He received several invitations from the Empress Dowager and prince, requesting him and his retinue to visit Peking. From Lhasa, delegations arrived one after another to invite him back to Lhasa. As he was already in Doto, he found it important to make a short visit to Peking, so that he could appeal to the Empress and the Prince (Kwang Hsu) to withdraw Lu Chun's army from Kham. He sent Payroll Officer Khenchung Tencho and Chibche Kyisurwa, with a letter to the Regent, the Kashag and the National Assembly of Tibet, giving details about the situation.

Duringhis stay at Kumbum, the Dalai Lama spent his time mostly in religious and political activities. He met a Japanese secret agent Termato, who introduced to him the Japanese priest residing at Riwo Tsenga and the Japanese ambassador to China. From Lhasa, another Tibetan delegation arrived to request the Dalai Lama to return. Chatreng Sampheling's representatives, the secretaries of Lithang, the staff of Ba Chodey and the father of the Chamdo chieftain approached the Dalai Lama and reported on the situation in Doto.

In the same year, on the 27th day of the 11th month, the Dalai Lama left Kumbum for Riwo Tsenga. He travelled in a special palanquin arranged by the Tibetan government, accompanied by his retinue. The Sining government provided

---

has been restored and revitalized since 1990. The Tibetan name translates to the "Great Place of Complete Joy." It currently has over 150 monks in residence. It features a 26.5-meter-high statue of Migjid Janraisig, a Buddhist bodhisattva also known as Avalokitesvara. It came under state protection in 1994.

The monastery was established in 1835 by the Fifth Jebtsundamba, then Mongolia's highest reincarnated lama. It became the principal center of Buddhist learning in Mongolia.

In the 1930s, the Communist government of Mongolia, under the leadership of Khorloogiin Choibalsan and under the influence of Joseph Stalin, destroyed all but a few monasteries and killed more than 15.000 lamas. Gandantegchinlen Khiid monastery, having escaped this mass destruction, was closed in 1938, but then reopened in 1944 and allowed to continue as the only functioning Buddhist monastery, under a skeleton staff, as a token homage to traditional Mongolian culture and religion. With the end of communism in Mongolia in 1990, restrictions on worship were lifted.

an army retinue, bodyguards and palanquin bearers. On the 5th day of the 12th month, the party arrived at X'ianfu, which was called Chang'an during the period of the Tang Dynasty. Xian was once seized by the Tibetan army during the reign of King Trisong Detsen of Tibet, and the Tibetan troops removed the emperor (Daizong) and enthroned Gaowang, a nephew of Kimshing Kongju, and gave him the Tibetan name Tashi Gyalpo, or the "Auspicious King."

As will be told below, in that year a Manchu official named Chang Yingtang arrived in Calcutta to participate in the Anglo-Tibetan trade negotiations. After that, he went to Lhasa, via Darjeeling. In Bhutan, the people, ordained and lay, unanimously appointed Ogyan Wangchuk Gyalpo (51st *desi* of Bhutan) as the first hereditary king of Bhutan. He had sincerely mediated during the Anglo-Tibetan conflicts. Therefore, the Tibetan government sent the Phari district officer to offer congratulations and ceremonial gifts to him.

In 1908, the Dalai Lama celebrated the Tibetan New Year at Wutai Shan (Riwo Tsenga), the holy place of Manjushri, where he spent several months, visiting sacred places, performing prayers and meditation and giving religious sermons. Thousands of Chinese and Mongol devotees and dignitaries came and received his visual blessing. From Lhasa, a Tibetan delegation, including Khenche Drakpa Loden and Tsipon Rampa Se, arrived there to invite the Dalai Lama back to Lhasa. The German ambassador residing in Tanchin and Sonyu Otani, younger brother of Japanese scholar Kazui Otani, arrived to have an audience with the Dalai Lama. The Japanese consular Lieutenant-General Yasuma Fakuji, among others, also came to meet him. The Dalai Lama then proceeded to Riwo Dangsil, where he was met by William [Woodville] Rockhill (1854-1914), the American Minister in Peking, and his interpreter. This marked the first official contact between a Tibetan and an American. Rockhill has written a book in which he describes Tibet and China as two distinct nations[15].

On 27th day of the 7th month, the Dalai Lama and his party left Riwo Dangsil, seen off by a large retinue composed of Tibetans, Chinese and Mongols, and headed to Peking on a special yellow train arranged by Empress Dowager. At Pauring railway station, to the south of Peking's wall, the Emperor's special envoy Chunji Darin received the Dalai Lama and served tea to all the members present there. Manchu officials also arrived there to meet the Dalai Lama. The local government served lunch to the Dalai Lama and all the members of his retinue. On the 27th day of the 9th month, at Chanmin railway station, to the south of the Peking Wall, the emperor's Prime Minister Ta Trunthang and Chinese and Mongol ministers, including Likang Puntang, Hutuktu with his retinue and priests of Peking

---

15 Namgyal Wangdu might be referring to *The Land of the Lamas: Notes of a Journey through China, Mongolia and Tibet* by WW Rockhill.

monasteries arrived to greet the Dalai Lama. Then, accompanied by a large retinue, including Chinese, Tibetans and Mongolians, preceded by a military parade and a procession of lamas and in front of a large crowd of hundreds of thousands of the faithful who cheered for him in an expression of devotion, the Dalai Lama proceeded to the Yellow Palace. The palace was built by the first Manchu emperor Shunzhi[16] for the Fifth Dalai Lama,when the later was invited to Peking, and was later renovated and prepared for the Thirteenth Dalai Lama for his residence. At the Palace, the Manchu government received him with a banquet and bodyguards were assigned to him. Tangkan Darin and Chang Darin were assigned as his regular attendants. The Manchu government told him that it would provide any assistance that he needed at any time.

Although the meeting with the Emperor was scheduled for the 6th day of the 8th month, the meeting could not take place as planned due to a disagreement between the Tibetans and the Manchu officials over the protocols of the meeting. After a few days, they agreed to arrange the meeting on the 20th day. All the preparations were made at the palace before the meeting. On the day of meeting, Empress Dowager and the prince greeted the Dalai Lama at the palace with scarves. Thereafter, through interpreters, they asked after each other's health, and settled on their respective thrones. A banquet in the Chinese traditional style was hosted for the Dalai Lama. After the day's meeting was over, the Dalai Lama returned to his residence.

Following this, Empress Dowager and Emperor Kwang Hsu[17] came to meet the Dalai Lama at his residence. During their meeting, the Dalai Lama raised Tibetan issues, told them the details about the arrival of the British military expedition in Tibet, and requested them to withdraw all the troops of Lu Chun from Tibet. The Empress and the prince promised that they would try their best to fulfill his wishes. They presented him with a letter, stating that he should stabilize and continue the old age Sino-Tibetan relations, and a gold plate with an inscription, "Buddha of the western land of Avalokitesvara," written in Manchu, Chinese and Tibetan scripts. They also presented him with rich gifts. In return, the Dalai Lama presented a large quantity of valuable Tibetan articles, including an image, texts and a stupa—representations

16 The Shunzhi Emperor (1638-1661) was the second emperor of the Qing dynasty, and officially the first Qing emperor to rule over China from 1644 to 1661. He ascended to the throne at the age of five in 1643 upon the death of his father Hong Taiji, but actual power during the early part of his reign lay in the hands of the appointed regents, Princes Dorgon (posthumously titled Emperor Chengzong) and Jirgalang. With the Qing pacification of the former Ming provinces almost complete, he died still a young man, in circumstances that have lent themselves to rumour and speculation. He was succeeded by his son Xuanye, who reigned as the Kangxi emperor.

17 The Guangxu Emperor (1871–1908), born Zaitian, was the tenth emperor of the Qing Dynasty, and the ninth Qing emperor to rule over China proper. His reign lasted from 1875 to 1908, but in practice he ruled under Empress Dowager Cixi's influence, only from 1889 to 1898. He initiated the Hundred Days' Reform, but was abruptly stopped when Cixi launched a coup in 1898, after which he was put under house arrest until his death. His reign name means "The Glorious Succession".

of the Buddha's body, speech and mind—and a prayer and praise written with gold ink on a dark blue paper. Their meeting was on a footing of equality. However, there were no definite agreement and promise from the Manchu government in support of Tibet, since the Dalai Lama's stand on Tibet and the Manchu government's foreign policy did not coincide, and the Manchus pressed the Dalai Lama not to publicize the private discussions that took place between them.

Soon after that, Emperor Kwang Hsu died on 12 November 1908. As requested, the Dalai Lamapresided over the funeral ceremony and performed prayers for the king. Two days after Kwang Hxu's death, Empress Dowager crowned Xuantong (Puyi)[18], a two-year old child, who became the tenth or the last Manchu emperor. The Dalai Lama was invited to the investiture ceremony. He offered auspicious verses and congratulations to the new emperor. A few days later, on 20 November, the Dowager Empress died, after consuming poison. The Empress was alleged to be very selfish and autocratic.

While in Peking, the Dalai Lama visited local Buddhist monasteries and gave religious discourses to a large assembly of Chinese and Mongol Buddhists. The Manchu government did not extend full support to him on political issues. However, he considered it very important to establish relations with foreign countries in order to maintain Tibet's independence. To achieve this, he sent a mission to Russia, with an edict. He sent envoys to meet the official representatives of the USA, Britain, France, Japan and Germany in Peking. In return, the British consul Sir John Jordon came to meet the Dalai Lama. The Japanese ambassador Sukiashi and an army officer named Nasa Noni also met with the Dalai Lama, and they had a free and frank conversation on political matters. He requested the Japanese to give Japanese military training to the Tibetan army. Accordingly, Yajjima, a retired Japanese army officer, came to Lhasa, and he gave a Japanese style of military training to one regiment of the Tibetan army. Through Rockhill, the Dalai Lama sent details of the Tibetan political situation to the US president.

In summary, during his tour in China and Mongolia, lasting for more than four years, the Dalai Lama publicized the political and religious status of Tibet as widely as he could[19]. He had farsighted plans to resolve the Tibetan political

---

18 Aisin-Gioro Puyi (1906-1967) was the last Emperor of China. He ruled in two periods between 1908 and 1917, firstly as the Xuantong Emperor from 1908 to 1912, and nominally as a non-ruling puppet emperor for twelve days in 1917. He was the twelfth and final member of the Qing Dynasty to rule over China proper. Later, between 1934 and 1945, he was the Kangde Emperor of Manchukuo. In the People's Republic of China, he was a member of the Chinese People's Political Consultative Conference from 1964 until his death in 1967. His abdication was a symbol of the end of a long era in China, and he is widely known as The Last Emperor. However, Yuan Shikai, the first President of the Republic of China later claimed the title of "Emperor of China."

19 In Peking, the Dalai Lama also met Gustaf Mannerheim, a Russian army colonel (who later became the president of independent Finland); a German doctor from the Peking Legation; an English explorer named

crisis, reestablish Tibet's independence and introduce reforms in Tibet. However, due to obstruction from monastic sections, he could not put his noble plans into practice.

Christopher Irving; R.F. Johnson, a British diplomat from the Colonial Service; and Henri D'Ollone, the French army major and viscount. Mannerheim even gave the Dalai Lama a Browning revolver and showed him how to reload the weapon, out of great concern about the Dalai Lama's safety.

List of correct spelling of Tibetan names

❖

Phonetic	Correct Tibetan spelling in Wylie
Baga	ba ga
Barag	rba rag
Be Phoser Lekong	was pho sher legs kong
Chidey	spyi sde
Chinglung	'phying lung
Chitsang	ci gtsang
Chogla	cog la
Chompa	com pa
Chugtsam	phyugs mtshams
Dakpo	dwags po
Lhaje	dwags po lha rje
Debkar Khenpo	deb dkar mkhan po
Detsam	sde mtshams
Donden	don ldan
Dorde	dor sde
Drampa	
Drangtsam	'brang mtsams
Dring	bring
Dritsam	'bri mtshams
Drom Tonpo Gyalwai Jungne	brom ston pa rgyal ba'i 'byung gnas
Drompa	grom pa
Gangtrom	
Gotsang	rgod tshang
Guge	gu ge
Gungthang Lama Shang	gung thang bla ma zhang
Jetsun Milarepa	rje btsun mi la ras pa
Jongmey	'jong smad
Jongto	'jong stod

Kechog Lingje Gyesar Norbu Dradul 'dul	skyes mchog gling rje ge sar nor bu dgra
Khangsar	khang gsar
Kharo	kha ro
Khasang	kha zangs
Khon Konchok Gyalpo	'khon dkon mchog rghyal po
Kusung Jangchokpa	sku srung byang phyogs pa
Kusung Lhochokpa	sku srung pho phyogs pa
Kusung Nubchokpa	sku srung nub phyogs pa
Kusung Sharchokpa	sku srung shar phyogs pa
Kyimey	skyi smad
Kyito	skyi stod
Kyitrom	skyi khrom
Lachen Gongpa Rabsel	bla chen gong pa rab gsal
Langmi	lang mi
Latse	la rtse
Lha Lama Jangchup Wo	lha bla ma byang chub 'od
Lhodrag	lho brag
Loro	lo ro
Mangkhar	mang khar
Manglor Silu	mang lor zi lu
Mangma	mang ma
Marpa Lotsawa	mar pa lo tswa ba
Nagsho	nags shod
Nema	
Ngadag Tride	mnga' bdag khri lde
Nyagyi	
Nyal	gnyal
Nyangro	myang ro
Nyankar	nyen dkar
Nyanyi	nya gnyi
Nyema	gnye ma
Nyenkar	
Ocho	'o co
Pang Gesin	spang ge zin
Phokar	phod dkar

Phothon	pho mthon
Porab	spo rab
Ra Lotsawa Dorje Drak	ra lo tswa ba rdo rje grags
Rag	rag
Remey	ra smad
Reto	re stod
Rulag To	ru lag stod
Shang Phosher	zhang pho sher
Shang Pipi	zhang pi pi
Shangchen	shangs chen
Shangshung	zhang zhung
Songde	gzong sde
Songtsen Gampo	srong btsan sgam po
Sumpa	sum pa
Tong	stongs
Tongchen	stong chen
Tradruk	khra 'brug
Tripom	
Trithang	
Trithey	khri 'thad
Tsamo	tsa mo
Tsethon	rtse mthon
Tsongo	
U-ru Me	dbu ru smad
U-ru To	dbu ru stod
Yarlung	yar lung
Yartsam	yar mtshams
Yartsang	yar gtsang
Yerab	yel rab
Yeru	g.yas ru
Yonru	g.yon ru
Yoru Me	g.yo ru smad
Yoru To	g.yo ru stod
Yubang	g.yu 'bangs
Yumten	yum rten

Medals granted by the thirteenth Dalai Lama to Tibetans soldiers in the Fire-Dragon year of the 15th *Rabjung*

The emblem of the
Tibetan army

a) Rank insignia of Chupon (squad leader)
b) Rank insignia of Instructor

a) Rank insignia of Senor Instructor
b) Rank insignia of Dingtsab (Deputy Lieutenant)

232

a) Rank insignias of Dingpon (Lieutenant)
b) Rank insignia of Gyapon (Captain)

a) Rank insignia of Rupon (Colonel)
b) Rank insignia of Dapon (Regimental Commander)

a) Rank insignia of Commander-in-Chief
b) Rank insignia of Senior Commander-in-Chief

Military flag
A sample of regimental flag

A British official flanked by Tibetan army officers

Soldiers doing Bren gun practice on the ground in front of the Palri hill in Lhasa

During a ceremonial parade on the ground of the Bodyguard Regiment
at Norbulingka

A. T. Steele. 1944

Military parade in Lhasa: Band Party, followed by flag bearers and troops

Band Party member Lobsang Tashi of the Bodyguard Regiment and Colonel Tungtsing

Drabchi Dapon Kunsang Tse in British army officer's uniform before he was appointed Tsipon

Dzasag Kheme Sonam Wangdu who served as Commander-in-Chief from 1947 to 1952

Dapon Muja of the Shigatse Regiment in British army uniform

Tibetans soldiers practising machine guns

Dapon Phala and other officers of the Bodyguard Regiment who accompanied His
Holiness to Dromo in 1951

238

Commander-in-Chief Tsarong with Kalons and army officers

Back standing from right to left: unknown, Dapon Ragshar Phuntsok Rabgye, unknown,
Dapon Doring Dorje Gyaltsen, Dapon Kyipug Sonam Wangyal, Dapon Kyipug Wangdu
Norbu, Dapon Nornang Sonam Dorje, Rupon Penpa Tsering
Seated: Dapon Shasur, Dapon Drumpa, Dapon Trethong Gyurme Gyatso, Legden-la
Front rows: Rupon Pema Chentra, Dapon Sonam Gonpo
Photo taken in 1920 in Lhasa

Soldiers on parade near the Norbulingka Palace

Military parade by Tibetan soldiers posted on border duty in Dokham

Troops of the regiments based in Lhasa in British military uniform

Drongdrak Regiment's Dapon Yuthog and
Dapon Taring

Bodyguard Regiment's Dapon Takla
Phuntsok Tashi (seated) with three officers
(standing)

Senior Commander-in-Chief Tsarong, who
defeated and expelled the Chinese
Lu-chun's troops from Lhasa

Commander-in-Chief Jampa Tendar, who
ejected all the Chinese troops from Eastern
Tibet between 1914 and 1918

Drapchi Dapon Tashi Palrab and Drapchi Dapon
Sampho Tenzin

Matt Gruninger (the sponsor of this translation project) with the committee members of the Tibetan Ex-Army Welfare Association
From left to right: Ngodup Dorje (treasurer), Mr. Matt Gruninger, Lobsang Tenzin (assistant to treasurer), Dawa Tsering (President of the Tibetan Ex-Army Welfare Association)